The Chicago Black Renaissance and
Women's Activism

The Chicago Black Renaissance and Women's Activism

ANNE MEIS KNUPFER

UNIVERSITY OF ILLINOIS PRESS

Urbana and Chicago

1 2 3 4 5 C P 5 4 3 2 1

Library of Congress Cataloging-in-Publication Data
Knupfer, Anne Meis, 1951–
The Chicago Black renaissance and women's activism /
Anne Meis Knupfer.
p.   cm.
Includes bibliographical references and index.
ISBN-13: 978-0-252-03047-5 (cloth : alk. paper)
ISBN-10: 0-252-03047-8 (cloth : alk. paper)
ISBN-13: 978-0-252-07293-2 (paper : alk. paper)
ISBN-10: 0-252-07293-6 (paper : alk. paper)
1. African Americans—Illinois—Chicago—Intellectual life—20th
century. 2. African Americans—Illinois—Chicago—Social
conditions—20th century. 3. African Americans—Illinois—Chicago—
Politics and government—20th century. 4. African American
women—Illinois—Chicago—Political activity—History—20th
century. 5. African American women political activists—Illinois—
Chicago—History—20th century. 6. African American women—
Illinois—Chicago—Societies and clubs. 7. Community life—Illinois—
Chicago—History—20th century. 8. Chicago (Ill.)—Intellectual
life—20th century. 9. Chicago (Ill.)—Social conditions—20th
century. I. Title.
F548.9.N4K57   2006
977.3'1100496073—dc22   2005012420

To my son, Franz Paul Knupfer, and
his father, W. R. Knupfer
and to Robert Cary

Contents

Acknowledgments

THERE WERE MANY people who contributed to the writing of this book. First and foremost, I must thank Darlene Clark Hine for inviting me to write an essay about black women's participation in the Chicago Black Renaissance. When Darlene asked me in the late spring of 1998, I remember telling her, "I know nothing about the Chicago Black Renaissance." In fact, the only Chicago Renaissance I had heard about was associated with the founding of *Poetry* magazine in 1912. So I politely said no. Several hours later, I realized my foolishness. Here was an opportunity to work with a marvelous scholar and to learn, once more, about another incredible chapter of black Chicago history.

During the summer of 1998, I spent time at the Vivian G. Harsh Research Collection of Afro-American History and Literature. I owe thanks to its archivist, Michael Flug. Michael probably knows more about the Chicago Black Renaissance than anyone. When I told him about the project, Michael forewarned me that this would require an interdisciplinary approach and lots of background reading. He asked me, for example, what I knew about black literature and music. With Michael's generous assistance, I learned a great deal about the movement, and subsequently I sent an essay to Darlene that fall.

I thought I was through with the project until Darlene returned the essay with comments. One comment I remember well. In the margin next to the section on black women's clubs, she wrote, "This begs for a book-length manuscript." She was right. By then, I was so excited by the material that I continued archival work on the topic while finishing my second book, *Reform and Resistance: Gender, Delinquency, and America's First Juvenile Court.*

There are many others who gave me intellectual, financial, and editorial assistance to complete the book. I thank the Spencer Foundation for a one-year grant, and I am also grateful for grants from Purdue University's Humanities and Social Sciences Library and the Purdue Research Foundation. Numerous scholars gave me valuable feedback and encouragement, and asked me important questions. I thank John Bauman, Adam Green, John Rury, William Winders, Christopher Reed, John McCluskey, and my colleague and friend Jill May. I also thank Victor Margolin for asking me to write a conference review of the Chicago Black Renaissance's graphic artists; I learned much from this project. I am also grateful to the three anonymous reviewers who carefully read the manuscript and gave thoughtful comments. And lastly, I thank Joan Catapano, editor in chief of the University of Illinois Press, with whom I have enjoyed working, as well as editors Angela Burton and Karen Kodner.

To the many librarians and archivists who assisted in locating materials, thank you as well. They include the late Archie Motley and others at the Chicago Historical Society, as well as archivists at the Municipal Collections of the Harold Washington Public Library in Chicago, Northwestern University's Archives and Special Collections, Southern Illinois University's Special Collections, the University of Illinois at Chicago's Special Collections, the University of Chicago's Special Collections at the Regenstein Library, and the Louise Noun Women's Archives at the University of Iowa Library.

On a personal note, some chapters were written in the late summer of 2002 when one of my dear relatives was critically ill. The writing was a blessing in that it kept me from thinking constantly of his sorrow and pain. I am glad that he is doing better and hope he will enjoy this book. And to Bobby Cary, how do I thank you for all of your support? We have explored so much of Chicago together. And to my son, Franz, thank you so much for your love and understanding. May you continue to grow in heart and spirit.

The Chicago Black Renaissance and Women's Activism

Introduction

ALTHOUGH MANY READERS know of the Harlem Renaissance, few have heard of the Chicago Black Renaissance that followed from 1930 to 1960. Like its predecessor, the Chicago Black Renaissance was a revitalization of the black expressive arts, especially music, art, literature, theater, and dance. It was also a period when Chicago black artists, scholars, teachers, and activists drew from the cultural politics of a pan-African identity, thereby expanding their social protests to include the worldwide exploitation of people of African descent. Put differently, activists during the Chicago Black Renaissance did not view lynchings in the South, restrictive covenants in the North, the segregation of black soldiers during World War II, or the Italian invasion of Ethiopia as isolated events but rather saw them as linked by colonial, racist practices.

If the Chicago Black Renaissance was such an important movement, why have so few people heard of it? First, the movement has been studied by mostly literary scholars, although only recently. In 1986, Robert Bone wrote a seminal article in *Callaloo* about how the Sociology School at the University of Chicago influenced novelist Richard Wright. Other scholars, too, focused on Richard Wright's life and his protest novels, including Michel Fabre and Margaret Walker.[1] But there were many other authors associated with the movement besides Wright, including Margaret Walker, Gwendolyn Brooks, Fenton Johnson, Langston Hughes, Arna Bontemps, Charlemae Rollins, Richard Durham. Shirley Graham (later Graham Du Bois), Alice Browning, Willard Motley, Frank Marshall Davis, and Era Bell Thompson. Fortunately, recent publications by scholars Craig Werner, B. J. Bolden, and Bill Mullen have enlarged the literary study of the Chicago Black Renaissance to include some of these authors.[2]

However, the Chicago Black Renaissance was more than a literary movement. Perhaps the second reason that the movement is not well known is because scholars have not focused on linking the remarkable creativity of artists in so many disciplines. To illustrate, besides the writers listed above, the movement encompassed artists Margaret Goss Burroughs, Rex Gorleigh, and Charles White; dancer Katherine Dunham; playwright Lorraine Hansberry; theater directors Helen Spaulding and Bertha Moseley Lewis; jazz and gospel performers Mahalia Jackson, Earl "Fatha" Hines, and Duke Ellington; composers Margaret Allison Bonds and Thomas Dorsey; and journalist Thyra Edwards.

And yet, even if someone were to write about all of the artistic accomplishments of this remarkable movement, the Chicago Black Renaissance would still not be completely examined. That is because the expressive arts represent only one meaning of the term "culture." Culture also refers to how people make meaning from their lives and create identities for themselves and future generations. During the Chicago Black Renaissance, there were many community institutions that cultivated the arts, nurtured a pan-African identity, and taught children about their venerable ancestors. These institutions included the South Side Community Art Center (SSCAC), the first black art museum in the United States; the Parkway Community House (PCH), a premier social settlement; the George Cleveland Hall Library, which I consider to be one of the intellectual centers of Bronzeville; and various theaters, newspapers, and literary magazines. Further, those affiliated with these institutions "defended" their culture by protesting the enormous inequities and discrimination that they and other community members faced in Chicago and society at large.

Yet the reader may wonder about the title of this work, *The Chicago Black Renaissance and Women's Activism*. Why a focus on women's activism? This is the third aspect of the movement that needs to be examined, because many of the artists, writers, theater directors, and musicians involved were women. Furthermore, as schoolteachers, clubwomen, founders and administrators of community institutions, activists, volunteers, and caretakers, black women were largely involved in promoting the expressive arts, sustaining community institutions, and fostering black solidarity through social protests. As Appendix A demonstrates, at least 250 black women were active in such endeavors, although I suspect the involvement of many more.

Why did the movement occur in Chicago? To be sure, Chicago was the crossroads of northern urbanity. African retentions were continuously nurtured through successive migrations. Migrants perpetuated their traditions of syncretized religion, dialectal speech, and the music genres of blues, jazz, and spirituals. Darlene Clark Hine's observation that migrants were both northern Southerners and southern Northerners reflected the cultural revitalization that took place in Chicago.[3] Although some social and cultural institutions in Chicago's Black Belt closed during the 1920s, many others endured and even thrived, most notably women's clubs, black churches, and social settlements. Alongside these organizations, another set of "institutions" flourished and reinvigorated Chicago's southside: storefront churches, dance halls, theaters, and jazz clubs. Every night couples flocked to the Savoy and the Rhumboogie Cafe to dance to big band and scat music. When the Regal Theatre opened in 1928, southside residents could sit under a domed ceiling awash with painted stars and listen to Duke Ellington, "Fatha" Hines, Fats Waller, and King Oliver. Sundays also offered cultural edification, including the gospel music of Mahalia Jackson and her chorus at the Ebenezer Church. In other words, the migration "Africanized" the southside black communities of Chicago. To this sensibility were added two other layers of Africanism: a pan-African intellectuality, which was nurtured through the study of black history, sociology, art, and politics; and social protests, which connected racism in Chicago to the diaspora.

Despite the promotion of cultural solidarity, there were class and occupational differences among Chicago blacks. By 1930, the city's "Black Belt," as it was commonly called by sociologists, had become almost completely segregated, with dilapidated tenements, high rentals, and crowded flats divided into kitchenettes. Those blacks fortunate enough to buy homes found their choices limited by restrictive covenants, redlining tactics, and virulent protests in white neighborhoods. Further, the Depression had exacerbated these conditions, as competition increased for jobs, decent housing, and social and health services.

Despite the gravity of these problems, blacks took great pride in their southside communities and institutions. In 1930, the black newspaper, the *Chicago Sunday Bee*, held a contest to elect a mayor of Bronzeville. The renaming of their community as "Bronzeville" held deep political and social significance for the residents. It was no longer known as "the Black Belt," a term used by sociologists and vice commissions to highlight increased rates of delinquency, dependency, and crime.[4] Instead, Bronzeville, then the largest black community in the country, signified a collective spirit, with its own legendary mayoral elections. As such, Bronzeville became one of the centers, if not *the* center, of black Chicago culture.

International conditions, as well as national and Chicago politics, also influenced the pan-African ideology of the Chicago movement. The *Chicago Defender,* a local black newspaper with a national black readership, kept blacks informed about political events in Jamaica, Haiti, Morocco, and Ethiopia. As early as 1930, the newspaper had published an article about Africa as the origin of civilization.[5] Alongside this coverage were reports on incidents of discrimination in the South and attendant court cases. The Italian invasion of Ethiopia in 1935 received front-page coverage, as did the U.S. Supreme Court's reverse decision in the *Scottsboro* case, which ordered southern courts to select blacks for jury service. When the *Defender* publicized lynchings and white mob violence in the South during World War II, blacks had to ask themselves whether the war they were fighting was overseas or in their own country. Their concerns were fueled by the editorial columns of Mary McCleod Bethune, Langston Hughes, W. E. B. Du Bois, Carter G. Woodson, Walter White, and Enoc Waters. Persistent acts of racism fueled black Americans' quest for the "double V": victory at home and abroad.

But black Chicagoans did not simply read the news. They made the news. In 1941, A. Philip Randolph, founder of the National Negro Congress and president of the Brotherhood of Sleeping Car Porters, threatened President Roosevelt with a mass march in Washington, D.C., to protest discrimination in wartime employment. In response, Roosevelt established the national Fair Employment Practice Committee (FEPC). This agency investigated discrimination in defense-related employment and training. Black women, too, contributed to civil rights nationally and internationally. Among them was prominent activist Irene McCoy Gaines, who in 1932 became a member of the Committee on Negro Housing as part of Hoover's Conference on Home Building and Home Ownership. During the late 1940s, as a spokesperson for the Congress of American Women before the United Nations, she expressed concern about the "subjugation" and "exploitation" of black women both by colonial powers and in the United States. She would be joined by black lawyer Edith Sampson, whom President Truman appointed as delegate to the United Nations General Assembly.[6]

In essence, then, black Chicago activists conjoined local, national, and international issues, largely through a pan-African ideology fostered through historical and anthropological scholarship. One such scholar was black historian Carter G. Woodson, who, in founding the Association for the Study of Negro Literature and History (ASNLH), promoted research about the "African triangle," that is, Africa, the Caribbean, and the United States. Through local chapters, journal publications, and the inauguration of Negro History Week (designated for the second week of February to include the birthdays of Frederick Douglass and President Lincoln), the ASNLH disseminated this knowledge to black communities. As such, Woodson sought to reeducate the "miseducated Negro" and to emphasize black Americans' venerable and intellectual African past. Anthropologists, too, most notably Melville Herskovits of Northwestern University, refuted the long-held idea that black Americans lacked a culture or an African past. Rather, Herskovits noted the African retentions that he and others found in black church rituals, music, and dancing. Even his study of Chicago's black radio programs showed that jazz, blues, spirituals, boogie-woogie rhythms, and shouting styles drew from West African traditions.[7]

Chicago black activists, especially women, acted upon this transnational perspective through community institutions. For example, the mostly female staff of PCH organized outreach programs for children and youth in the black creative arts. Under the directorship of black sociologist Horace Cayton, the women directed a People's Forum, where residents discussed local and international politics. Similarly, a group of black women founded the SSCAC, which not only showcased African and black art but also sponsored art and writing classes and workshops. There was also a flourishing black literary movement in activities of libraries, the press, and theater and literary groups. In the early 1930s, Chicago philanthropist Julius Rosenwald built the first black library in Bronzeville. As the first director of the George Cleveland Hall Library, Vivian Gordon Harsh was determined to build its repositories, and she traveled throughout the South each summer to search in small towns for older books by and about blacks. Along with a children's librarian, Charlemae Rollins, Harsh organized a formidable collection. She also initiated a number of community programs, including storytelling sessions, book and drama clubs, a Negro history club, and a series of "appreciation hours" that underscored black contributions to literature and the arts.

Harsh and Rollins were joined by the all-female staff of the *Chicago Sunday Bee,* a black newspaper founded in 1928. Under the editorship of Olive Diggs, the staff recorded, among other events, contributions to the war effort by both black men and women. This coverage included full-page photographic spreads of black soldiers, pilots, nurses, and women on the front in Europe and at home. Like the *Bee*'s preceding editor, Ida B. Wells, Diggs conceived of the newspaper as an agency of change. As such, there was a steadfast focus on the connections among literature, art, history, and politics. For example, columns such as "Labor News" and "Art Notes" were published side by side. Subscribers could read weekly installments of Wright's *Native Son* or order the book directly from the newspaper's book department. A corresponding literary undertaking was the founding of *Negro Story Magazine.* Like the *Bee,* the journal was staffed mostly by women. Although short-lived, publishing only from 1944 to 1946, it too exemplified black women's sponsorship of black literature and the arts, publishing works by Gwendolyn Brooks, Margaret Goss Burroughs, Elie Mills Holden, Margaret Cunningham, and Margaret Walker.

Black theater, influenced by the community theater movement and the Federal Theatre Project (FTP), also burgeoned on Chicago's black southside. Under the capable directorship of writer and musician Shirley Graham Du Bois, the FTP theaters in Chicago produced a number of politically contentious plays by and about blacks. Katherine Dunham, a prominent black dancer who had studied African and Caribbean dance, frequently performed in Graham's productions. As part of the FTP's outreach programs, children's plays by black writers Arna Bontemps and Langston Hughes were performed in local churches, schools, and parks. Black women assisted with these efforts, working on costume and stage design, publicity, and stage direction.

Black women's clubs, affiliated with the National Association of Colored Women (NACW), likewise sponsored music recitals, theater performances, and lectures that promoted black history and the arts. Although scholars have argued that the activism of NACW clubs generally subsided during the 1920s and 1930s, this was not true in Chicago. If anything, my intention in this book is to show that there was a singular renaissance in the Chicago black women's club movement. This was largely due to the leadership of the Chicago and Northern District Association of Colored Women's Clubs (CNDA), and most notably the efforts of its president Irene McCoy Gaines. Gaines's visibility at the state and national levels of the club movement gave the Chicago clubs further incentive to become involved in international and national events.

As with most community studies, this book documents the ways in which social class, gender, nativity, educational attainment, and professional affiliations influenced Chicago black women's commitment to social activism. In particular, this work examines the critical roles of mostly middle-class black women in the development and sustenance of community institutions on Chicago's southside. As a point of contrast, it also examines the overlooked activism of working-class and poor women in two public housing projects: the Ida B. Wells Homes, which was in the Bronzeville neighborhood, and the Altgeld Gardens Homes, located in the far south of Chicago, near wartime industries. Not surprisingly, differences in ideologies and leadership styles arose when public housing tenants worked with their middle-class counterparts. However, I argue that these cross-class alliances demonstrated the complexity of black women's activism, as did coalitions with interracial organizations.

Overview of Chapters

Chapter 1 examines three types of activism used by Chicago black women from the 1930s through the 1950s: a pan-African intellectuality, the expressive arts, and social protest. These three types of activism were not mutually exclusive but functioned synergistically to create the momentum necessary for the Chicago Black Renaissance. Black historians, sociologists, and anthropologists promoted a pan-African ideology, as did teachers, artists, and journalists. Likewise, artists, teachers, librarians, and journalists helped to found and sustain community institutions that fostered the arts. The second section of chapter 1 looks at three types of organizations that black women joined to protest issues of segregated schools, substandard housing, and discriminatory practices in employment: (1) organizations in which black women were members only; (2) black community organizations, joined by both men and women (some of which were headed by black women); and (3) interracial organizations. I argue that black women carefully chose their memberships in these organizations based upon the issue(s) at hand and the degree to which the organizations could wield influence.

Chapter 2 provides a portrait of one of the more innovative black social settlements in the country during this period, the Parkway Community House (PCH). The breadth of its programs was remarkable, encompassing a nursery; an after-school program for "latchkey" children; classes for children, youth, and adults; a theater group; a People's Forum; and a dormitory that housed female wartime workers who also volunteered for social projects. The PCH was largely successful, at least through the mid-1940s, because of federal and philanthropic support. Monies from the WPA, the Lanham Act, and leading city foundations gave its director, Horace Cayton, the opportunity to enact group work that he hoped would ultimately lead to critical citizenship. Following the war, however, Bronzeville became poorer and more congested, and the PCH's resources became overtaxed. Cayton, humiliated by the pressures of white philanthropists, left the PCH, which subsequently fell even further into debt and relocated to a farther southside neighborhood of Chicago.

Chapter 3 discusses those community institutions that sponsored black literature, theater, and the arts. As noted, there were newspapers, literary magazines, and theater and writing groups that published black literature and book reviews and sponsored forums, lectures, workshops, and essay and writing contests. Once again, black women were largely responsible for establishing programs and staffing these events, either professionally or through volunteerism. As with many endeavors, community institutions worked together, cosponsoring, for example, a children's play or an essay contest. Indeed, many of the writers of the Chicago Black Renaissance—Arna Bontemps, Langston Hughes, Shirley Graham, Charlemae Rollins, and Margaret Burroughs—wrote for children and youth. Many writers also wrote for the larger community, hoping to spur black residents to activism and whites to a better understanding of their problems.

The SSCAC was another formidable institution for which black women took the lead, not only in founding the museum but also in fund-raising, staffing, and volunteering. The museum exhibited the paintings of Chicago black artists along with African sculptures and artifacts. It also sponsored programs and classes for children and youth to cultivate their artistic talents and cultural identity. The museum still thrives today in its original location, testimony to the strong activism of its women founders.

Schools as sites of activism are the focus of chapter 4. Southside black schools were so overcrowded that most black children attended school only for half-days. Segregation was kept intact by drawing district boundaries, transferring students and teachers to other schools, or setting up branch schools or temporary structures. Black and white teachers, parents, and interested citizens established the Citizens Schools Committee (CSC) in 1933, documenting schooling inequalities and protesting at school board meetings. Their efforts met with varied success; more often than not, direct protests were sometimes most effective. For example, when the black residents of Lilydale asked that a new school be built in the early 1930s, the Chicago school board ignored them. However, when there was a fire (possibly arson) and residents decided to picket and boycott, the school board took notice and built a new school.

Another successful reform was the institution of a multicultural curriculum used by the entire Chicago public school system from 1942 through 1945. This curriculum was unique in emphasizing the contributions of black Americans and their African heritage. So impressive was this curriculum that Woodson gave it his approval. In addition, black teachers and female activists worked together to remove negative stereotypes and depictions of blacks in textbooks. This was accomplished in part through the adoption of Woodson's teaching materials, along with black teachers' extensive involvement in and promotion of community institutions that educated children in black history, the arts, and literature.

Chapter 5 explores the activism of black women's clubs in Chicago and to some extent nationally. Although the later Chicago clubs were perhaps as class conscious as those at the turn of the century, their activism during the Depression, the war years, and the decade of the Great Migration deserves recognition. During the 1930s, much of their work focused on relief, especially assisting dependent and orphaned children, poor mothers, and the unemployed. Yet at the same time, they advocated for an anti-lynching bill, protested the *Scottsboro* case, and participated in other national issues. During the 1940s, they rallied for more employment for black women and cited cases of discrimination. In the late 1940s and 1950s, Chicago clubwomen moved to the forefront as their club sister, Gaines, became president of the NACW. Although Gaines was successful in internationalizing the NACW's agenda to some extent, internal dissension and personal ambitions within the organization thwarted her attempts and left her with a sense of defeat.

Chapter 6 investigates women's activism in two public housing projects in Chicago: the Ida B. Wells Homes and the Altgeld Gardens Homes. When originally constructed in the early 1940s, the Chicago Housing Authority (CHA) and the black community praised both sites as ideal places to raise families. Indeed, many blacks wanted to live in public housing, which offered ample space, modern kitchens, plumbing and bathing facilities, gardens and flower beds, community centers, and nearby parks. The CHA promoted tenants' social activism through establishing women's and mother's clubs and tenant groups. Many black female residents took up the challenge, organizing nurseries, kindergartens, fund-raisers, and family events. To some extent, their activities paralleled the NACW-affiliated clubs, especially their attention to child welfare issues and wholesome recreation for youth. However, during the 1950s, the CHA changed its eligibility requirements, lowering the incomes of public housing residents. This diminished the working-class presence in public housing and also encouraged outside groups, such as the South Parkway YWCA (SPY), to intervene and institute programs. Differences in ideology, leadership style, social class, and marital status between the SPY staff and the women in public housing created conflicts and ultimately led to a decline in community participation by both groups of women.

Chapter 7 focuses on the activities of several Chicago YWCA branches: the West Side Y (WSY) and the SPY. The WSY was one of the first branches to desegregate its swimming facilities, clubs, and residence in Chicago, largely in response to the protests of its white and black members. The SPY, one of two black Y branches in Chicago, took another turn, focusing instead on the promotion of black politics and arts. Given its Bronzeville location, this was not surprising. However, as the SPY's membership and funding decreased during the late 1940s, it was forced to relocate to the Ida B. Wells Homes' community center and to work directly with its tenants. This presented challenges to the SPY's staff, both in terms of how they conceptualized "community" and their outreach mission and how they attempted to impose a middle-class model of leadership within the Wells Homes.

The book concludes with two appendices. Appendix A is a list of black female community activists, artists, and professionals in Chicago from 1930 to 1960. I use the term "community activists" to include those women who improved the lives of other community residents in some way. As such, the list includes teachers, clubwomen, tenant leaders, labor union activists, professional women, and ministers. I have also tried to be as inclusive as possible so that readers can gain a better understanding of the complexity of black female activism. All too often, scholars privilege only those individuals whose contributions were more visible, while leaving out those who contributed to the chain of events that made possible those gains and progress. Appendix B contains several lists to assist the reader in better understanding Chicago's black social, economic, and political life. The lists of names and addresses of black southside community organizations, again ranging from 1930 to 1960, include churches, social institutions, newspapers and presses, businesses, private and public housing sites, jazz clubs and nightclubs, schools, and men's and women's clubs. These lists are not necessarily complete, although they are fairly representative.

Clearly, many black women in Chicago contributed to the sponsorship of black arts, literature, drama, music, and history during the Chicago Black Renaissance. Their involvement with the PCH, the SSCAC, the George Cleveland Hall Library, the *Chicago Sunday Bee,* and black theaters and literary magazines attests to their far-reaching influences. Building in part upon the veritable practices of the preceding generation of clubwomen, the women of the Chicago Black Renaissance grafted black literature, arts, and history onto the larger map of pan-Africanism. Crossing geopolitical, social, and cultural boundaries, Chicago's black women linked black art, literature, music, history, and community outreach to greater transnational struggles. This was accomplished largely by the prodigious activism and steadfast leadership of Chicago's black women, who exemplified, in Paul Robeson's words, the "brilliant generalship in our people's struggle."[8]

1

Models of Black Activism
in Chicago

Introduction

The fact that the Chicago Black Renaissance thrived for three decades is nothing short of astonishing. Even more astonishing is that the movement flourished through the tumultuous years of the Depression, World War II, and the Great Migration of the 1950s. What conditions led to the Chicago Black Renaissance's enduring legacy? In this chapter, I examine three strands of activism that prevailed during the movement: pan-African intellectuality; promotion of the expressive arts, including literature, drama, dance, and art; and social protest. I want to emphasize at the onset that these aspects were not separate or unrelated. Rather, they were all interwoven and together provided the momentum necessary for continuation of the movement. For purposes of analysis, however, I examine each strand separately, showing their interrelationships. Subsequent chapters will examine particular institutions, organizations, and women's activism in more depth.

To illustrate this interconnected activism, we can begin with an examination of the activities of Chicago's black teachers. Many were deeply influenced by Carter G. Woodson's promotion of a black- and African-centered curriculum through an organization he founded, the Association for the Study of Negro Life and History (ASNLH). Many teachers joined history clubs, where they read and discussed the association's publications.[1] Based upon these readings and their own research, the teachers created a meaningful black curriculum for their students. Clearly, these teachers engaged in a pan-African intellectuality. Additionally, many were involved in the promotion of black arts. For example, some teachers coordinated their curricula with writing activities for children sponsored by the George Cleveland Hall Library or the black newspaper, the *Chicago Sunday Bee*. Some teachers also volunteered to assist with the productions of children's plays by Langston Hughes and Claude McKay.[2] Lastly, many female teachers engaged in social protests. As members of the black women's clubs, the Chicago Council of Negro Organizations (CCNO), and the Citizens Schools Committee (CSC), they protested inequalities in the black schools, such as overcrowded classrooms that resulted in half-day sessions.[3] They understood that, despite the implementation of a black-centered curriculum, black children were not receiving their full share of education. Accordingly, black female teachers did not separate their activism into intellectual, artistic, and political realms. Rather, they centered their activities on devising ways to best educate children in their communities.

There are further examples of how these three strands of activism synergistically worked. For instance, Parkway Community House (PCH), administered by a largely female staff, was one of the leading intellectual centers of Bronzeville. It sponsored weekly forums with presentations by eminent scholars, such as W. E. B. Du Bois and University of Chicago anthropologist Robert Redfield. Spirited discussions usually followed.[4] At the same time, PCH did not neglect the arts. Langston Hughes, Richard Wright, and Arna Bontemps gave readings there. Parkway Community House also had its own theater troupe, directed by Helen Spaulding, which produced experimental plays.[5] Lastly, PCH did not neglect the pressing needs of the community. For example, young female wartime workers who resided in its dormitories engaged in volunteer work throughout the community. Similarly, PCH established after-school programs for children and youth, staffed by female professionals.[6]

The following sections focus on each strand of activism in depth. The last section highlights three models of social protest organizations, with particular reference to community issues and to black women's participation.

The Activism of Pan-African Intellectuality

Woodson was not the only scholar to promote a pan-African intellectuality during the Chicago Black Renaissance. Contributions were also made by Du Bois, Horace Cayton, Paul Robeson, Allison Davis, St. Clair Drake, and Melville Herskovits. In their studies of anthropology, sociology, and history, these

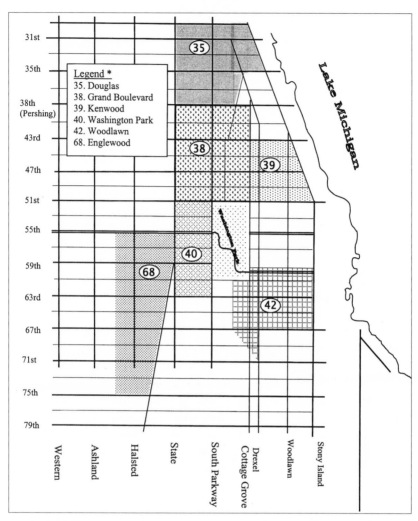

Southside black neighborhoods, circa 1950s. Map created by Robert Cary and Anne Meis Knupfer.

scholars emphasized African retentions, as well as the structural inequalities faced by Africans and black Americans. In turn, their ideas fueled a creative outpouring of art, literature, theater, and dance that celebrated African expressions of form and representation. Their ideas also set in motion a series of protests in which Chicago activists linked racism against black Americans to a worldwide oppression of people of African descent.

Woodson's affiliation with Chicago began as early as 1915, when he attended the Exposition of Negro Progress and subsequently founded the ASNLH. Through the association and other intellectual endeavors, Woodson sought to reeducate the "miseducated Negro" by documenting the venerable and intellectual traditions of Africa and black America.[7] Woodson's intellectual presence in Chicago, especially through the association, was an enduring one. For example, the Chicago ASNLH chapter was remarkably active, especially in the black schools' celebration of Negro History Week, an event that was inaugurated by the association (held during the second week of February to include the birthdays of both Frederick Douglass and President Abraham Lincoln). Many of the Chicago chapter's members were teachers who utilized ASNLH publications to create black curricula. For example, Madeline Morgan, an elementary schoolteacher, spent eighteen months at Chicago libraries conducting research about African and black American history. Based upon her research, she created social studies curricula for grades one through eight that was used in all of the Chicago public schools from 1942 to 1945.[8] Woodson himself critiqued Morgan's lesson plans and called them "a creditable piece of work."[9]

But schoolteachers weren't the only ones influenced by Woodson's encouragement to study history. As will be discussed more fully in chapter 5, black clubwomen studied black history and literature not only for their own education but also so that they could be better informed about what to recommend for schoolchildren. One outgrowth of their study during the 1930s was the formation of a history department in the Chicago and Northern District Association of Colored Women's Clubs (CNDA) to promote black-centered curricula in the schools.[10] Similarly, librarians Vivian Harsh and Charlemae Rollins of the George Cleveland Hall Library took up Woodson's call for the study of black history. Each summer, Harsh traveled throughout the South to collect books about black America. She brought the books back to the library, which became a reputable repository of black history and literature. As will be examined more fully in chapter 3, Harsh also organized black history clubs, literary study clubs, a literature forum where the likes of Zora Neale Hurston and Gwendolyn Brooks read their works, and black art exhibits.[11] Rollins was a children's librarian who promoted readings of biographies of famous black Americans, and she wrote these works as well. Similarly, she continuously advocated for respectful representations of black characters in children's literature.[12] Through such activities, these librarians also participated in conjoining all three strands of activism.

Another organization that reflected Woodson's pan-African approach was the National DuSaible [*sic*] Memorial Society, started in 1929 by teacher and businesswoman Annie Oliver. During the 1933 Chicago World's Fair she was asked to conduct research on the first black settler to Chicago, Jean Baptiste Pointe DuSable, which awakened her interest in Chicago black history. Although the original purpose of the National DuSaible Memorial Society was to erect a memorial to DuSable, its later mission became "disseminat[ing] facts about the role of the Negro in the development of civilization especially in the United States."[13] At the 1934 Century of Progress Exposition, for example, the society recognized DuSable during National DuSable Day. The Chicago Colored Women's Band, directed by Irene Howard Harrison, and the National DuSaible Memorial Society chorus, directed by Antoinette Tompkins, provided music. The society would later be instrumental in renaming a new black high school after DuSable.[14]

Like Woodson, Du Bois and Robeson did not separately consider the economic and political futures of black Americans and Africans. They, too, envisioned intellectual reciprocity and kinship. In adopting socialism, both Du Bois and Robeson linked black America to African countries' struggles for independence from European colonialists.[15] For this reason, when Robeson articulated that the black American was a "tragic creature, a man without a nationality," the hope he expressed was one of transnationality, an identity that would embrace pan-Africanism.[16] He further argued that by absolving themselves of allegiances to nation-states and devoting themselves to freedom in multiple contexts, black Americans would achieve a truer, indigenous identity.[17] Robeson himself engaged in these multiple contexts. For example, he joined the working-class struggles in the Spanish Civil War. Accordingly, he enlarged his vision of black freedom to include the struggles of common people against fascism and Nazism. Likewise, he vehemently disagreed with the U.S. government's World War II policies, comparing them to Hitler's. He pointedly questioned why black Americans should fight for the freedom of those who had oppressed them for hundreds of years.[18]

Robeson, however, was not the only one to express such wartime sentiments. Horace Cayton also questioned who the "real" enemy was. Not only was he skeptical of the war but also of postwar promises made to black soldiers.[19] The *Chicago Defender,* too, remained skeptical about black progress during and after the war. The editors published frequent accounts of racism in the South, including incidents of lynching, unequal conditions in black public schools and higher education, black teachers' lower salaries, and poll taxes. In fact, the *Defender*'s editors declared, there seemed to be more of a war in the South than there was in Europe.[20] To be sure, black Americans in segregated armed forces understood the contradictions of fighting for freedom overseas, while they suffered the indignities of separate blood banks, threats of lynching, and discrimination in housing. As such, the symbol of their resolution became the "double V," representing victory both at home and abroad.

Robeson refused to accept the promises of gradualism, which he considered simply another form of racism. Instead, he emphasized "coordinated action" among black Americans of all social classes and organizations. Leadership, he argued, should be representative among "all sections of Negro life," including the working class, the poor, and women.[21] Perhaps the Chicago black organization that most exemplified this approach was the Chicago Council of Negro Organizations (CCNO). In the late 1930s, the CCNO had organized a mass protest at which nearly a hundred black organizations—including churches, lodges, women's clubs, and civic groups—demanded "more and better jobs." As one of the protest's speakers pointed out, in an area of less than six miles, at least 200,000 blacks lived in crowded conditions. Yet 85 percent of the retail merchants and 95 percent of the real estate owners and operators lived outside of the neighborhood. Those outside merchants, who received $40 million from the black community, contributed no more than $2,000 to its community agencies. Protesters also signed petitions to demand laws to strike down restrictive covenants, to appoint a black to the board of education, to stop the discrimination in assignments of Chicago public schoolteachers, and to support low-cost housing projects.[22]

Finally, Robeson's ideas regarding transnationality and the caste-like status of black Americans and Africans were similar to those found in writings of Chicago anthropologists and sociologists. During the 1930s and 1940s, anthropological studies had nurtured a transnational ideology through, for example, the study of African retentions in the New World. Perhaps in one of the most cited publications, *The Myth of the Negro Past,* Melville Herskovits refuted the long-held notion that black Americans lacked a culture or an African past. Rather, he emphasized the African retentions that he found, for example, in poorer black American church sermons that featured handclapping, dancing, and shouting. Herskovits even claimed that musical styles such as jazz, blues, spirituals, boogie-woogie rhythms, and shouting featured in Chicago's black radio programs originated from West African traditions.[23]

Herskovits was not alone in his study of the African diaspora. During the 1940s and 1950s, William Bascom conducted field studies of Afro-Cuba, African languages, and West African art; Hortense Powdermaker studied the

Deep South; and Michael G. Smith studied Nigeria. A cadre of well-qualified black anthropologists joined in this research. Fisk University faculty member Lorenzo Turner studied Gullah speech; Allison Davis, a faculty member at the University of Chicago, turned his attention to caste relations in the Deep South, as well as social-class biases found in IQ tests. Chicago anthropologist St. Clair Drake examined Chicago's black churches and associations, and he coauthored *Black Metropolis* with Horace Cayton. Katherine Dunham, one of Herskovits's protégées, studied dance forms in Haiti and Jamaica and incorporated folk elements into her choreography.[24]

Sociological studies of caste offered a more complex analysis than the earlier theories about black marginality. For example, University of Chicago sociologist Robert Park differentiated between prejudice and racism, postulating that northern whites exhibited prejudice, whereas southern whites practiced racism. But one of Park's students, William Oscar Brown, himself the son of a black Texas migrant farmer, disagreed. He thought that both northern and southern whites practiced racism, saying that the only distinction was that the northern version was more indirect and nuanced. Likewise, he questioned other theories of the Chicago School, poignantly asking how blacks could accommodate to white society when blacks were segregated and relegated to a caste-like status.[25]

Cayton would enlarge these ideas of caste. In collaboration with University of Chicago professor Lloyd Warner, Cayton underscored the idea that blacks and their institutions could not be understood without considering the dire effects of discrimination and caste-like status. Together they argued that, overall, black and white social-class structures in both southern and northern churches, families, and community associations were separate.[26] But Cayton would extend the concept of caste to disenfranchised people worldwide, not only black Americans. At one PCH forum, for example, he gave a presentation on his groundbreaking copublication, *Black Metropolis*, which gave community members a sociological framework for understanding local issues. Later the concepts of democracy and freedom were debated at the forum by those who also emphasized the larger politics of the "colored races of the world."[27]

Clearly, a pan-African intellectual activism framed the perspectives and activities of Chicago's black teachers, librarians, clubwomen, and social protest groups. The creative arts also drew upon a pan-African identity. At the same time, the arts were a powerful form of social protest against the discriminatory social and economic conditions that besieged the black southside communities.

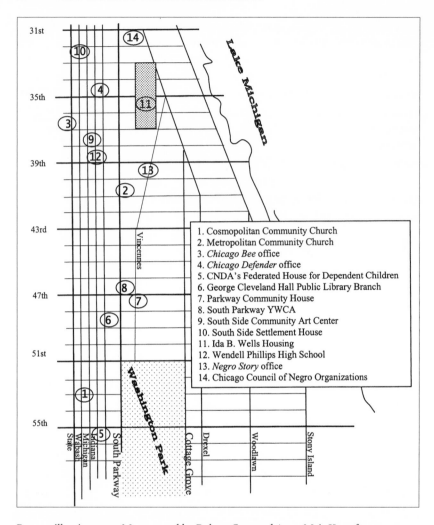

Bronzeville, circa 1945. Map created by Robert Cary and Anne Meis Knupfer.

The Expressive Arts

Many of the subsequent chapters discuss more fully the renowned cultural institutions and organizations of the Chicago Black Renaissance. These institutions and organizations included the South Side Community Art Center (SSCAC), the George Cleveland Hall Library, the Federal Theatre Project (FTP), and PCH. Further, a number of prominent writers and artists represented the movement, including Richard Wright, Gwendolyn Brooks, Margaret Walker, Katherine Dunham, Richard Durham, and Margaret Burroughs. This section, as the preceding one, demonstrates the linkages between the expressive arts, social protest, and a pan-African intellectuality.

The establishment of the first black art museum in the country speaks especially to how Chicago's black women artists and activists were in the vanguard. As discussed more fully in chapter 3, five black women initially met to discuss the idea of a black museum. These women would become the foundation of the SSCAC, serving as fund-raisers, administrators, board members, and teachers. Their vision of the museum was multidimensional; that is, it was to be a place to showcase the talents of African and black American artists, as well as a community facility where activist groups and writers would meet. Further, it would be a "school" that offered art classes to children and youth.[28]

Margaret Burroughs, one of many black women who made the SSCAC so successful, drew from a pan-African intellectual philosophy similar to Alain Locke's. Locke, a philosophy professor at Howard University, conceived of black art as an indigenous art form, one that was built on the "racial idiom" of Africa. Dispelling the idea of racial inferiority, he argued that much of modernist European art had actually been inspired by African sculpture. Accordingly, he encouraged black artists to build upon their traditional forms, while also experimenting with various mediums. African-centered art, he believed, should be a source of pride and celebration for black artists and their people.[29] Burroughs echoed these ideas, arguing that "racial solidarity" could only be achieved through black pride. She extended this idea especially to children, emphasizing that they needed to learn black history and art, not "white history, white invention, white art."[30] Consequently, the museum offered art classes to children, showcased children's artworks at exhibits, and collaborated with other black community institutions to promote children's creative talents.

Similarly, other black cultural institutions sponsored children's theater, dance, and writing, not only as a means of cultural expression but also as a means to foster black pride and knowledge. Prominent black artists and writers played a large part in these endeavors. For example, Shirley Graham (later Graham Du Bois) produced children's plays while she was director of the Federal Theatre Project (FTP) in Chicago during the Depression years. Katherine Dunham, who studied dance forms in the Caribbean, assisted in these productions, and she also taught African dance lessons to children. And, as noted, librarian Charlemae Rollins encouraged black children's pride in their heritage through her biographies of famous black Americans.[31]

But black pride was only one side of the coin. The expressive arts were also used as a powerful means of social protest. To illustrate, when Graham became director of the black unit of the FTP in Chicago, she did not want to produce entertaining plays but ones with a political message. Her first production was Theodore Ward's *The Big White Fog,* whose plot revolved around a black Chicago student who had to drop out of college because he was too poor. Members of the white audience objected to the play because they thought it would exacerbate already-tense race relations in Chicago. But Graham refused to back down and continued to advocate for change through her selection of protest plays.[32]

However, Graham was not the only playwright to push the message of inequality before Chicago theatergoers. Perhaps one of the best-known plays from the Chicago Black Renaissance is Lorraine Hansberry's *Raisin in the Sun.* Centered on the theme of black pride, expressed both in home ownership and a daughter's pan-African lifestyle, the play was based on the Hansberry family's experiences when the father purchased a house in the covenanted Washington Park area (directly west of Hyde Park and the University of Chicago) in the late 1930s. When the court ruled in his favor in 1940, other blacks took up the challenge and moved to the area.[33] Despite Hansberry's victory, however, white restrictive covenant associations did not give up but continued to prevent blacks from buying homes in other white neighborhoods.

Hansberry's play spoke directly to many black Chicagoans because restrictive covenant associations had successfully hemmed them in, thereby creating black enclaves. Many white associations had claimed that the value of their homes would depreciate if blacks moved into their neighborhoods. But several sociologists disputed this idea. One sociologist argued that blacks did not depress property values; instead, property in poor black areas brought the highest return rate of any city property, at least in Chicago. Another study countered that before blacks moved into a neighborhood, housing values had already started to decline. In fact, the study contended, blacks could not have purchased homes unless they had depreciated due to their limited incomes.[34]

Writer Richard Durham, in his radio plays for "Destination Freedom," also spoke out against restrictive covenants, substandard housing, and discrimination in public housing for blacks. In one of his 1949 radio plays, two European men visiting the United States remarked how the black neighborhoods reminded them of "Nazi ghettoes."[35] In another 1949 radio play, Durham portrayed "Slums" as a character, pursued by black politician Archibald Carey. Durham was referring to Carey's ordinance to outlaw discrimination in public housing, which did not pass.[36]

Durham also used his craft as a journalist to continue his protest of restrictive covenant associations. He especially targeted one of the most virulent ones, the Oakland-Kenwood Property Owners' Association. In one editorial in the *Chicago Defender,* Durham called the association one of the "wealthiest and most active anti-Negro organizations above the Mason-Dixon line."[37] The association countered that the *Chicago Defender* should devote more of its space to criticizing black residents' "backward" behavior. As they further advised, "Try Bathing and not Bellyaching."[38] Turning the tables, the association blamed blacks for their segregated and crowded neighborhoods: "The Negro has shown neither disposition or ability to maintain a decent American Community. The College Graduate will live next door to the pickpocket. In fact he will rent a room to a prostitute, etc. because of this insistence upon indiscriminate mixing, his community, school, churches are all contaminated with vice and crime to which the normal white American objects."[39] But as Cayton had sadly noted: "The Negro's only mobility [wa]s within the boundaries of the 'concentration.'"[40]

To be expected, restrictive covenants and subsequent overcrowding had resulted in further deterioration of once-grand neighborhoods. During the 1920s, black leader Charles Bentley, doctor Daniel Williams, and lawyer Laing Williams lived in Grand Boulevard. A neighborhood where only a few privileged blacks had once resided, it was 48 percent black by 1938. The Douglas neighborhood, later known as Bronzeville and the Black Metropolis, was one of the oldest southside Chicago neighborhoods, with many Victorian mansions.[41] During the late 1930s, many of these homes were converted into kitchenettes or demolished for the first all-black public housing project, the Ida B. Wells Homes. Journalists and novelists wrote of the tragic effects of such living conditions. Richard Wright's novel, *Native Son,* was a poignant social protest regarding the kitchenettes and the psychological effects upon their dwellers. As the novel's main character, Bigger, described his neighborhood: "That was the way most houses on the South Side were, ornate, old, stinking; homes once of rich white people, now inhabited by Negroes or standing dark and empty with yawning black windows."[42]

Wright's description was not an exaggeration. The conditions of many older homes were classified by the city as substandard, that is, they had no toilets, baths, or even, in some cases, running water. According to one 1940 Chicago Housing Authority survey, some 9,000 black families still used outdoor toilet facilities and 65,000 families shared toilet facilities. Even as late as 1948, one building had seventy-four black persons who lived on the top floor; forty children lived on another floor. There was no bath in the building, and all of the families used coal stoves, which were dangerous in terms of fire hazards and smoke inhalation. Some activists argued that it would be safer for the residents to be evicted and live in the streets than to stay in such places.[43] Tragically, Bigger was unable to escape from his caste-like status in the North, just as he could not in the South.[44]

Because of restrictive covenant associations, many Chicago black writers and artists lived in these segregated southside neighborhoods. As such, they lived with the poor and the working class, with the "old settlers" and incoming migrants. They saw firsthand the effects of racism: crowded kitchenettes and laid-off workers. They used their art as a weapon to expose the wounds and injuries of discrimination. But they also brandished it to bestow upon their black readers and audiences a deep ancestral pride.

Social Protest Organizations

There were many social protest organizations beyond those described above. Most not only joined in battles against restrictive covenants and substandard housing but also directed their attention to discrimination in employment, health facilities, and the schools. However, social protest did not necessarily result in immediate change. To assist those in need, black women's organizations also continued to engage in social uplift, especially during the Depression. This section examines the social protests of various black organizations, with particular reference again to women's roles.

During the Chicago Black Renaissance, black women activists participated in three types of social protest organizations: those in which black women were members only; black community organizations comprising both men and women; and interracial organizations. However, it is important to mention that there were black and interracial organizations in which black women were largely excluded. For example, in 1937, black businessmen had formed the Negro Business Men's Association to "encourage better living conditions in this area."[45] Not unlike other black community organizations, the association organized efforts to clean alleys, mow lawns, and propose legislation against restrictive covenants. As one researcher concluded, however, their agenda was so broad that the organization's effectiveness was questionable. Nonetheless, in working with other black organizations, the association did accomplish a number of its goals. The association distributed a petition to help employ blacks on Chicago's streetcar lines; cooperated with the South Side Community Committee to establish centers to fight juvenile delinquency; participated in war bond drives; raised funds for black students to study business management; and cosponsored an exhibit of black businesses.[46]

Another business organization that excluded black women was the biracial businessmen's association, the South Side Merchants Association. This association was organized in 1944, and 80 percent of its members were white businessmen who lived elsewhere but had businesses in Bronzeville. Perhaps to be expected, there were sometimes tensions among the association's black and white members. The greatest source of tension probably resulted from the different kinds of businesses owned by black and white members. Generally speaking, most black businesses were small and service-oriented, compared to white businesses that were more lucrative because they sold real estate, general merchandise, automobiles, and clothing. As of 1938, blacks in Bronzeville owned at least 2,600 businesses, but most of these were beauty parlors, grocery stores, barber shops, tailors, dress shops, express-fuel-ice companies, and restaurants.[47] In contrast, whites owned and operated at least 65 percent of Chicago's southside businesses as of 1939.[48] Some of the businesses were located in the very heart of Bronzeville on 47th Street and South Parkway, such as the Walgreen Drug Store, the Regal Theater, and the Savoy Ballroom. This pattern of white ownership would persist through the 1950s in other black Chicago communities as well. According to one 1955 survey of 240 businesses in Woodlawn (adjacent to the University of Chicago), whites managed and owned most of the profitable ones. Conversely, those owned by blacks were mostly grocery stores, taverns, and dress stores, located in low-traffic areas.[49]

There were other reasons for tensions between black and white association members. Black members of the association were distrustful of the white members' motives. Black members expressed concerned that the original white members had invited them to join only after the bylaws had been written. Second, the association had disproportionately appointed as officers those blacks whose businesses did not compete with those of white members. Third, some blacks questioned white members' sincerity. Although white businessmen promised to improve schools, housing, and recreational facilities, they seemed to be motivated more by a fear of race riots and subsequent losses to their businesses rather than by a sense of community spirit.[50] Lastly, white businessmen's ideas of expanding housing opportunities did not include speaking out against restrictive covenants.

It was more than likely that black women were familiar with both men's organizations and their activities. Ironically, not unlike the early twentieth century, black women were excluded from both associations, even though some black businesswomen were prominent in the community. To some extent, then, organizations remained bifurcated by gender. But black women, too, had their own organizations, such as clubs affiliated with the CNDA and the National Association of Colored Women (NACW), the National Council of Negro Women (NCNW), sororities, and professional black women's organizations. Victoria Wolcott has spoken of the predominance of a bourgeois female respectability in such organizations.[51] In Chicago, however, that preoccupation seems to have diminished by the 1930s, with the exception of the women's clubs. However, like black middle-class women in Detroit, Chicago women did evoke a professional discourse in their organizations to obtain leverage and employment. This gave them additional influence to protest the pressing problems of housing, employment, and schools, as well as national issues such as the *Scottsboro* and *Angelo Herndon* court cases and the Montgomery bus boycott.[52]

Secondly, black women belonged to black community organizations at large, such as black churches, the Chicago Urban League (CUL), and the CCNO. Although many of these organizations were headed by black men, there were influential black churches under the pastorships of women, such as Elder Lucy Smith, Mary Evans, and Dorothy Sutton. These women had tremendous organizational and fund-raising skills, thereby enabling them to establish social services for their congregations. Similarly, Irene McCoy Gaines was president of the CCNO from 1939 to 1953. The organization was successful because it worked with trade unions and labor organizations, such as the Negro Labor Relations League. For example, when the CCNO protested against dairies that refused to hire blacks, the group convinced several southside restaurants to not buy from those dairies. The CCNO and the CUL also organized a movie theater boycott to secure jobs for black projectionists, resulting in ten new hires.[53] More than likely, the trade unions' membership in the CCNO contributed to the organization's more direct strategies, as did the leadership of Irene McCoy Gaines.

Third, many middle-class black women joined interracial organizations, including the NAACP, the Council against Discrimination (CAD), the Committee of Racial Equality (CORE), the Chicago Council against Racial and Religious Discrimination (CCRRD), the Chicago Commission on Human Relations (CCHR), the Hyde Park-Kenwood Community Conference (HPKCC), and the CSC. In most cases, these organizations included both men and women as members, although one organization, the Women's Joint Committee on Adequate Housing (WJCAH), was composed of women only.

Memberships in these different types of organizations served varying purposes. In the cases of forming a voting bloc or protesting discrimination in employment, black organizations were often more effective. Here, race superseded social class. Since many blacks lived in Chicago's second and third wards, blacks could create a formidable bloc in alderperson elections. As such, black women worked in conjunction with black organizations and as precinct captains, informing black residents of political candidates and platforms.[54] However, when protesting overcrowded schools, poor housing conditions, or discrimination in public housing, black women found that interracial coalitions were often critical to their efforts. In these cases, social class superseded race for several reasons. First, black as well as white women realized the importance of being "connected" to those who effected policy and law, including politicians in city hall and the state legislature. Irene Mc-Coy Gaines, Cora Watson, and Loraine Green were examples of black women connected to such powerful political structures.[55] Second, black and white women were acutely aware that these were pressing national issues, not simply local concerns. Coalition building was, therefore, imperative at all levels. Third, middle-class women believed that their education and professional experiences were requisite for membership in these organizations. As such, their form of "trickle-down" activism, with later benefits for all, justified the more formal strategies of committee meetings, ad hoc committees, and commission reports.

The CNDA, the umbrella organization of black women's clubs in Chicago and its surrounding communities, fits the first model of an all-female black group. The CNDA worked on a number of issues, for example, advocating for black representation on the school board, protesting discrimination in wartime employment of black women, circulating petitions to free the Scottsboro boys, and raising monies to support community institutions such as the Phyllis Wheatley Home for working women.[56] However, similar to the first generation of Chicago clubwomen, much of their activism was circumscribed around the issues of the welfare of children and youth. As such, the CNDA expressed alarm at the number of children involved in the illegal game of policy and other "social evils" during the 1930s. Indeed, because of massive unemployment during the Depression, a strong underground economy had developed. In 1930 alone, there were as many Chicago blacks "employed" as writers, runners, clerks, and checkers of policy games as there were black doctors, dentists, teachers, social workers, and lawyers.[57] One newspaper reported that as of 1939 there were at least 4,200 policy stations that thrived on Chicago's southside, including the "fronts" of barber shops, beauty parlors, barbecue stands, cafes, and storefront churches.[58] Gaines, then president of the CNDA, wrote a letter to Mayor Edward Kelly, informing him that the CNDA had formed a committee to discuss southside crime conditions with city officials. The women were especially concerned about taverns, prostitution, and policy games that even children played. But when she requested Kelly's cooperation, he was evasive.[59]

The CNDA was somewhat more successful in fighting tavern owners who sold liquor to minors during the 1930s. Here, they relied upon the second model, working with black community organizations. Working in conjunction with the CUL, black churches, and the *Chicago Defender,* the clubwomen organized a campaign to protest against taverns frequented by prostitutes, youth, and even children. Prominent clubwomen Gaines, Cora Watson, Jeanette Smith, and Belle Fountain took the lead in distributing over 4,000 pledge cards to endorse enforcement of the city's liquor laws. Although only 800 were returned, some citizens wrote the names of taverns that needed to be investigated. As a result, two drinking establishments, the Savoy and the Palais de Gardes, posted "no sale of liquors to minors." Whether the police actually enforced the law, though, was not clear.[60]

Similarly, clubwomen worked with other black institutions to battle prostitution and drugs on Chicago's southside. As of 1931, 87 percent of Chicago's prostitution houses were located in the poorer black neighborhoods. Lured by jazz clubs and "black-and-tans" (the slang term for bars and clubs where blacks and whites socialized), many white clients frequented these places. When city officials and police ignored the problem, the *Chicago Defender* responded by listing neighborhoods where "places [were] infested and vice flaunted openly."[61] The 20th Century Neighborhood Club, too, "declared a war" upon the "undesirable element" who sold their "wares" openly.[62] Again, though, it was not clear whether the police cooperated.

Of those black community organizations headed by women, most were churches. Many poorer black migrants attended storefront churches, whose numbers had increased to over 250 by 1939, with an average congregation of forty members. Lucy Smith was one of the most popular of all evangelical preachers of Chicago. Dissatisfied with the A.M.E. church, she had joined a white Pentecostal church in 1914, where she had received her calling. She then started a church in her own home where she healed and assisted poor migrants. In fact, Smith claimed to have healed at least 200,000 people during her thirty-eighty-year career as a preacher through direct healings, her "anointed" handkerchiefs which she gave to people, and her radio program broadcast three times a week.[63] By the late 1930s, she was able to build her All Nations Pentecostal Church on a "fashionable" street, where she concentrated on giving people "good news about salvation."[64] She was so popular that one pastor noted, "If you want to see my folks on a Sunday night, go to Elder Lucy Smith's."[65] But Pastor Smith probably had a strong following as well because she set up soup kitchens during the Depression.

Better educated and wealthier blacks attended churches such as the Cosmopolitan Community Church under the pastorship of Mary Evans. A graduate of Payne Theological Seminary and the University of Chicago, she had become minister of the church in 1932. Then comprising only 100 members, the congregation grew to 900 by 1940. This was accomplished in part through the church choir, which broadcast over Chicago's radio, as well as Evans's leadership in clearing the church of its debts through tithings. By 1936, the church's debt of $36,000 was clear.[66] As one member's testimonial claimed, "Significantly, this sum was raised without resorting to pay entertainments, bazaars, teas, or other forms of money-raising events."[67]

The large congregation built a new church in 1948. That allowed Evans to further enlarge the church's services to include a nursery, health clinics, scout units, playgrounds, and a Bible school. Unlike other black nurseries, which faced closure in the 1950s, Cosmopolitan's nursery thrived. This was because, unlike other nurseries, it did not have to rely on external funds. Accommodating up to 100 children, the nursery had two large playrooms, a gymnasium, rooms for small-group activities, two private playgrounds, dormitory rooms, and an "isolation room" for first aid. Two doctors were on call and a graduate nurse was on duty all day. Combining methods of social group work and psychoanalysis, the staff developed a "modern" work-play program that focused on habit formation, social training, handicrafts, music, storytelling, and physical training.[68]

A protégée of Evans, Dorothy L. Sutton became minister of the Commonwealth Community Church in the late 1930s. Having apprenticed at the Cosmopolitan Community Church under Evans's tutelage, Sutton undoubtedly drew from Evans's resourceful skills and strategies. Within two years' time, her congregation grew to 325 members, most of them young professionals. Like Evans, Sutton established programs for children, including a Sunday school, choir, drama guild, and boy scout troop.[69]

Besides churches, perhaps the most influential black organization headed by women was the CCNO. Indeed, the CCNO was able to leverage a great deal of power because it unified the voices of so many black activists and because of its more radical protest strategies, including mass marches, rent strikes, "don't buy where you can't work" campaigns, and rallies.[70] In fact, as president of the CCNO, Gaines had preceded A. Phillip Randolph in his threat to organize a mass protest in Washington, D.C. unless more blacks were given war-related industry jobs. In 1941, she and fifty members of the CCNO had traveled to Washington to protest discrimination in employment from government defense contracts. As Cheryl Johnson-Odim has suggested, the CCNO's presence may have actually helped to further persuade President Roosevelt to issue Executive Order 8802, which outlawed discrimination in employment by those businesses that procured government contracts.[71]

During the 1940s and 1950s, black organizations increasingly formed coalitions and utilized the third model: interracial organizations. For example, the NAACP, an interracial organization since its inception, continued to be so through the 1950s, although black membership increased substantially to support litigation for desegregation. In Chicago, many black women were active NAACP members. For example, pastor Mary Evans and schoolteachers Ethel Hilliard and Margaret Flagg Holmes assisted in the Chicago chapter's membership drives and fund-raising events. So did clubwomen Nannie Reed and Josephine Walker; Annie Malone, founder of Poro College; and Isabel Joseph Johnson, a gospel radio host of Sunday afternoon programs during the 1940s. Some women held NAACP offices, such as Cora Watson and Geraldine Glover, the latter a president of the Flying Squadron, a youth auxiliary of the Chicago branch.[72]

Further, these women contributed to the NAACP chapter's mass protests, "don't buy where you can't work" campaigns, and litigation relating to the desegregation of public housing. As early as the 1930s, the Chicago NAACP had organized a "don't buy where you can't work" campaign, targeting a southside Woolworth's. They also protested the shoe department at Sears for discriminating against black women. In 1933, to protest against the jailing of the Scottsboro boys, they organized a march in which 20,000 Chicago residents participated. The youth council, too, organized a parade in the downtown Chicago Loop to protest lynching. During the 1950s, the Chicago NAACP led a group of 5,000 to protest white mob violence against the integration of the Trumbull Park Homes. They then sued the Chicago Housing Authority (CHA) on behalf of the thirteen black applicants denied admission to the Trumbull Park Homes. Watson and Gaines were particularly active in this last endeavor.[73]

The Chicago NAACP chapter also collaborated with the CCARRD. Formed after the Detroit race riots of 1943, the CCARRD acted as a clearinghouse and also assisted public agencies and research institutions in eliminating racial and religious discrimination. Their projects included supporting a permanent Fair Employment Practices Committee (FEPC) at the national level as well as protesting the overcrowding of black schools, segregated blood banks of the American Red Cross, and substandard housing.[74] Similarly, the NAACP chapter and the CNDA worked in conjunction with the interracial Commission on Human Relations (CHR) and the Council against Discrimination, both of which collected and reported incidents of discrimination in housing and employment. Most racial violence, the CAD reported, had resulted when blacks attempted to move into white neighborhoods or public housing. As one researcher aptly noted, "[Black] move-ins [we]re most important as a measure of the state of race relations in the city."[75] The CAD was especially involved in fighting discrimination at Woodlawn Hospital in the early 1950s, and the organization published a fact-finding report from its investigations. The hospital, located in an interracial neighborhood, "still drew a deep color line" in hiring doctors and nurses, as it also did in accepting patients. As one CAD report documented, "We could scarcely believe that a Negro patient with a skull fracture was turned away from Woodlawn—to die a few hours later."[76]

One of the most activist-oriented, all-female, interracial organizations was the WJCAH, formed in 1940. Composed of over ninety Chicago women's civic groups—including both black and white women's clubs—its goals were to educate the public on Chicago's housing issues, including slum clearance and housing projects, and most importantly to confront landowners' noncompliance with housing codes. As such, the WJCAH conducted surveys, sponsored exhibits, conducted tours of public housing and slum areas, and attended the housing court's weekly sessions and city council hearings. The group recommended the following basic reforms: that minimum safety and sanitation housing standards be enforced by city officials; that families on public relief be given an "adequate" allowance for rent so they could live in safe homes; and that more public housing be built, since many families could not secure decent housing at affordable prices. Evoking the patriotic sentiments of World War II, they claimed, "Every Chicagoan has a country worth defending, but not every Chicagoan has a home worth defending."[77]

The WJCAH targeted the Wells Homes as one site for their protests. Initially, they toured the project, among others, to gain a better understanding of community and home life there. They also sponsored talks by professionals who worked with the Wells Homes' tenants, including Miss Butler, a recreational worker, and Frances Duggan, an elementary teacher of the children at the Wells Homes. Having taught in many poor neighborhoods of Chicago, Duggan stated how impressed she was with the Wells Homes children. They came to school clean and properly dressed, and their attendance rates remained high. All of this, she argued, was because of the excellent facilities at the Wells Homes.[78]

Following their tours and talks, the WCJAH devised a questionnaire to pass out to applicants who had been accepted to the Wells Homes, asking them about the conditions of their previous housing. Noting the dilapidated and unsanitary conditions that most reported, the women recommended that no one reoccupy those buildings until they were repaired. Further, the women intended to present these cases to Chicago's department of health and to subpoena the records of the sanitary and building departments.[79] It was not clear, however, whether these events actually transpired. The second occasion for the WJCAH's protests at the Wells Homes involved hearings related to a case in which two women burned to death because of a house fire in the neighborhood. The WCJAH drafted a petition protesting the inconsistent evidence presented by health, building, and fire department officials. Almost 650 women from various clubs and organizations signed the petition at the Wells Homes, which was then presented to the Chicago City Council.[80]

Despite their activism, the women of the WJCAH were not as successful in their litigation and protest efforts as they had hoped. Their goals—to centralize the health, building, and fire departments and to have noncompliant landlords fined for their violations—were resisted by city officials, judges, and lawyers. Nonetheless, the women did raise public awareness, and they created interracial and cross-class social protest coalitions.[81]

The problem of substandard housing for blacks, compounded by a severe housing shortage, worsened after World War II. The mayor and city officials recommended public housing and "slum clearance," solutions that exacerbated the availability of housing.[82] Unfortunately, other solutions, such as private ownership and renovation of older homes, had been dismissed. As early as 1944, the Chicago Housing Authority (CHA) had funded a study to determine whether these solutions were more economically feasible than slum clearance. They discovered that most buildings were in such disrepair that it would have been too costly for landowners to comply with legal minimum standards.[83] Clearly this finding underscored how substandard and unfit housing was for many blacks in Chicago.

When Mayor Martin Kennelly recommended a broad program of slum clearance and redevelopment, private industry leapt at the opportunity, for public funds were available and land was sold for less than its original cost. The New York Life Insurance Company was one of the key bidders, assuring city hall and black residents that they would build affordable private apartment complexes, parks, and shopping centers. Blacks remained skeptical, concerned that rent would be too high for them and that many well-kept houses would be destroyed in the process.[84] Many prominent, middle-class black citizens, including Gaines, lived in these areas. She and others were critical of slum clearance, especially since not all housing was substandard and housing opportunities remained limited for blacks.

To complicate matters, a new expressway was slated for construction in the 1950s. Cutting directly through the heart of Chicago's black community, the expressway alone would dislocate more than 3,500 families and 900 single people, in addition to demolishing businesses, community institutions, and public schools.[85] Destruction was slated not only of people's homes but also of the very infrastructure of black communities. Despite the prodigious activism and protests by blacks against the expressway, they were not successful in fighting city hall.

Conclusion

Clearly black women's activism was prodigious. Yet the question still remains: How effective was their activism? Given the perseverance of restrictive covenants and discrimination in employment, one might rephrase the question: How effective could black women activists be? In terms of judging black women's social and political work described thus far, I would contend that any gain, no matter how small, demonstrated effectiveness to some degree. For example, the CCNO was able to make some gains in black employment. But admittedly, as discussed later in chapter 4, their fight for black representation on the school board was less successful. The CNDA, in its efforts to stop youth from drinking, did receive some cooperation from several establishments. But they were less effective in their attempts to discuss with the mayor children's participation in illegal policy games. In terms of Chicago's NAACP branch, the organization was somewhat successful in helping to achieve integration in some public housing projects. Further, its increased membership most likely contributed more to the larger national goal of desegregating higher educational institutions and public schools. However, it is often difficult to gauge the "success" or "effectiveness" of the Chicago NAACP or any one organization because, more often than not, they worked in conjunction with others. And even if an organization worked alone, its members often built upon the efforts of its preceding generation of members.

Nonetheless, I would argue that black women's involvement in pan-African intellectuality and social uplift, either through their own black women's organizations or through those that black women headed, were remarkably effective. For example, five black women had the vision and determination to start the first black art museum in the country; black female teachers conducted research and implemented black history and literature into their curricula; and black playwrights directed Chicagoans' attention to the problems that blacks faced in the city. As ministers, black women provided child care, recreational programs for children and youth, and facilities for working women and the elderly. As clubwomen, they engaged in many successful social-uplift activities. As detailed later in chapter 5, black clubwomen provided a great deal of "relief" to the community during the Depression. For example, they founded a home for dependent and orphaned black children, while continuing to fund-raise for the all-black institutions of the Old Folks Home and Provident Hospital. At the same time, they started a health clinic and a relief committee that sewed clothes for children and mothers in need. They accomplished all this and much more during a decade when volunteerism and service were the most available means of capital for many.

Historian Robert Cook has cautioned that current scholarship has popularized the myth of strong black community institutions successfully fighting for civil rights. He argues instead that, despite grassroots black organizations' prodigious efforts, racism often wielded the greater power.[86] This was true of many Chicago black social protest organizations, despite their commendable spirit and sense of empowerment. However, Cook has not fully considered the first two models of social activism: a pan-African intellectuality and the promotion of the expressive arts. The endorsement of black curricula by the superintendent of the Chicago public schools for three years was one example of a widespread and successful change. Similarly, the institution of the SSCAC, which still thrives today, is another example.

Because of the complexity of black women's activism, we should not polarize Chicago black organizations as separatist, integrationist, or accommodationist, as some scholars have done.[87] Black women used various strategies and approaches; for example, they joined both black and interracial organizations in protesting overcrowded schools, substandard housing, segregated public housing, and racial violence. Together, these organizations effected change, although such change was often piecemeal and gradual. Thus, those who celebrate the social protests of the 1930s but accuse blacks of accommodation and conservatism during the postwar years need to include the prodigious activism of middle-class northern women in their analyses. To be sure, Chicago black women continued to engage in marches and other forms of active protests through the 1950s. In using the three strands of activism—a pan-African intellectuality, the expressive arts, and social protest—black women showed a spirit and cultural identity that cannot be captured fully in applied categories of separatist, integrationist, or accommodationist.

The next chapter examines black women's involvement in one central Bronzeville institution: the PCH. Although the name of Horace Cayton is most often associated with the settlement, the female staff was largely responsible for developing and implementing its outreach programs. Similarly, a cadre of female volunteers engaged in literacy programs and other social projects. The professional and volunteer work of women helped to make the PCH a model black community center.

2

Parkway Community House

The Good Shepherd Community Center

In 1936, members of the Good Shepherd Congregational Church launched a funding campaign to open a community center for poorer blacks in and near Washington Park. The middle-class black congregation wanted to ameliorate the conditions of rising crime, delinquency, and infant mortality in the neighborhood, as well as to eradicate policy gambling and prostitution.[1] Over time, Washington Park, adjacent to Hyde Park and the University of Chicago, had become increasingly black, despite protests by restrictive covenant associations. As noted in chapter 1, when the Supreme Court ruled in favor of Carl Hansberry, middle- and working-class blacks moved into the area. Black parents not only wanted to have more affordable housing but also hoped their children could attend school full-time rather than for half days. Since 1933, black parents had protested overcrowded black schools in Washington Park, boycotting the elementary school on the first day of classes. The boycott was a success, resulting in textbooks for all children and a new kindergarten. Parents continued to monitor the school through their newly formed Fifth Ward Citizens Protective Association.[2]

Members of the Good Shepherd Congregational Church were aware of these issues, which were addressed in the church's lecture series and discussions. Church members actively studied community issues, then sought resolution through outreach. Female church members were particularly active in the funding campaign for the community center, raising $10,000 toward the $60,000 needed to purchase the property.[3] Two years later, in 1938, the

Good Shepherd Community Center (GSCC) opened. Originally, the board of directors was made up of sixteen men. But within a short time, at least seven board members were black women, all known for their involvement in child welfare issues. As early as 1924, clubwoman Ada McKinley founded the South Side Settlement House (SSSH), which offered outreach programs to mothers, children, and youth. Irene McCoy Gaines, a president of the Chicago and Northern District Association of Colored Women's Clubs (CNDA), had worked as a social worker for the Chicago Urban League (CUL) and the Cook County Bureau of Public Welfare. Mattie Elliott Bryan, as head of the Big Brothers, had a great deal of experience working with the Cook County Juvenile Court and affiliated community institutions. Lawyer Edith Sampson, a former juvenile court probation officer, continued to work with the court system, and she also became deeply involved in a new national black women's organization, the National Council of Negro Women (NCNW). Ruth Moore Smith, a former elementary schoolteacher turned principal in 1935, worked with the South Parkway YWCA (SPY), as did Charlotte Jackson and Pauline Jackson Lawrence.[4]

The community center offered a comprehensive program for children and youth as well as adults. For children, there were clubs, craft and shop classes, summer camps, health and sex education, and a reading room. The last was especially important, given the crowded conditions and double shifts at black schools. For working-class mothers, there was a nursery, as well as mothers' clubs and classes in parenting education, cooking, sewing, and knitting. The center also started a fathers' club council, an unusual program since most community centers neglected fathers in their parenting education. There were cultural activities in drama, music, painting, art, and dance for all ages. The center offered adults classes in economics and sociology, providing community members with conceptual frameworks for understanding social and economic problems.[5]

The Works Progress Administration (WPA) was instrumental in the development of the center's activities. Black sociologist Horace Cayton had been named director of a WPA-funded study of black culture in Chicago in late 1936. Given his work and research experience, Cayton was well qualified as project director. He had been employed as a longshoreman, cook, sailor, shoeshiner, and railroad worker, and his experiences sparked his interest in labor problems and applied sociology. As a fledgling sociologist, he had worked with University of Chicago professor Harold Gosnell on a study of black Chicago politics, which further informed his later co-publication *Black Metropolis*. He also investigated Chicago's black communities with University of Chicago sociologist W. Lloyd Warner. But in order to obtain WPA funds, Warner and Cayton claimed that their study focused on the salient issue of juvenile delinquency.[6] Indeed, at that time there was a disproportionately high percentage of black delinquents in Chicago, nearly 22 percent of the total delinquent population.[7] Fittingly, the Good Shepherd Community Center housed the WPA Project in 1938, so that Cayton could conjoin research to outreach and community education.

Examining the cultural and social causes of delinquency gave Cayton and Warner further opportunity to theorize about caste, race discrimination, and social disorganization. Throughout their study, Warner and Cayton underscored the idea that blacks and their institutions could not be understood without considering the dire effects of discrimination and caste-like status. They argued that black and white social-class structures in southern and northern churches, families, and community associations on the whole were separate or "bi-racial."[8] Warner and Cayton thus extended the Chicago School of Sociology's race-cycle theory to emphasize the reciprocal influences of migrants and associations. That is, they claimed that not only did community institutions influence migrants' behaviors and adjustments but also that migrants influenced the expectations and outcomes of institutions.[9] Parkway Community House (PCH), an outgrowth of the GSCC, was to become an example of this organic process.

The WPA project had a visible presence in the GSCC and the black community at large. Its staff included at least twenty University of Chicago graduate students, who collected and organized materials on black life for the "Negro in Illinois" project. A field staff of 150 WPA workers conducted interviews, typed, and performed clerical and statistical work. They conducted literally thousands of interviews and also examined newspapers, census data, and other public documents for pertinent information about black life in Chicago. But given the high rate of black unemployment during the Depression, Cayton was displeased that most of the research assistants were white, as were 20 to 30 percent of the other WPA staff. As of 1935, nearly 38 percent of Chicago's black population was on relief because of unemployment, compared to only 10 percent of whites.[10] Cayton also may have been concerned that white researchers could not establish rapport with black informants and accurately represent their experiences. After all, if theories of caste and biracialism were true, how could whites fully understand the separate world of blacks?

For Cayton and the community center, the WPA project became a catalyst for social activism. For example, Cayton was greatly concerned about

Chicago blacks' high rate of tuberculosis, which resulted in 38 percent of total deaths from the disease, even though blacks comprised only 7 percent of the city's population. Consequently, he requested help from the WPA to provide a tuberculosis clinic in the center. To alleviate black unemployment during the Depression, the center planned to develop a training project for domestic workers, similar to a project administered by the WPA and the Illinois State Employment Service. Given the lack of affordable housing for blacks, Cayton planned to remodel two buildings as "residence halls" for unmarried black female workers.[11] Although the training project did not materialize, the dormitories would later house wartime female workers. These dormitories would also become sites of activism, for residents were required to participate in community betterment.

In order to expand its programs, in 1940 the center acquired additional facilities at 51st Street and South Parkway, in the heart of Bronzeville. Although dilapidated, the Chicago Orphan Asylum was a complex of six buildings, including a schoolbuilding with a gym. As such, the asylum could house the nursery, theater, and classes for children and adults. Two buildings were designated as residence halls; the others became rental properties for organizations engaged in community projects. Securing these properties was critical to the GSCC's survival, as rental fees accounted for nearly half of the Bronzeville center's income during some years. In turn, organizations renting rooms there—including the Christian Science Church, with a war-relief sewing project, and the Municipal Tuberculosis Sanatorium—provided needed services for Bronzeville's poorer residents.[12]

Cayton—as researcher, activist, and board member—had been pivotal in developing the center's programs. Not surprisingly, he was offered the directorship of the Good Shepherd Community Center in Bronzeville. From the very beginning, however, Cayton and the board of directors disagreed, especially about his salary and responsibilities. Cayton countered the board's initial offer of $3,000, claiming that the Carnegie Foundation had offered him a one-year assignment at a higher salary. The Carnegie Foundation at the time was funding a large project, "The Negro in the U.S.," under the directorship of Gunnar Myrdal. The WPA project had certainly given Cayton visibility as a researcher. But in the end, Myrdal did not hire Cayton, perhaps because of Cayton's changing demands.[13] Regardless, the directorship of the Chicago center promised Cayton the possibility of further social change and development of a truly indigenous black community center.

The center's personnel committee, however, found Cayton's conditions for accepting the directorship "so complicated" that they requested that he submit in writing the conditions under which he would accept the position. Using both job offers to his advantage, Cayton was indirect. He countered that he would refuse the Carnegie offer if he became the center's director immediately. He was especially concerned that the WPA project not lose its momentum. However, if he didn't accept the Carnegie position, he wanted to use the Julius Rosenwald Fellowship he had just received to complete his doctorate. Graduate classes, he argued, would actually help him with his work at the center. What he didn't acknowledge to the committee was that a doctorate was essential for other professional opportunities if the directorship did not work out. When he met with the committee again, he raised further conditions. Since he had accepted the Rosenwald Fellowship, he would need an assistant. But the committee responded that they could not afford two salaries. In the end, the committee compromised and gave him his requested salary and an assistant.[14]

However, the committee stipulated that fund-raising was to be one of Cayton's main responsibilities. After all, the committee argued, how could the center survive without external money? Again Cayton hedged. He knew how difficult fund-raising would be, especially since he would have to approach white donors. In fact, one year earlier, he had offered to compile a list of black employees at steel industries so that they could be approached for financial gifts to the center. But he suggested that the white members of the campaign committee approach the executives of the steel companies.[15] Cayton knew that the center's funding already relied heavily upon foundations staffed by white administrators, as well as upon white Congregational churches and women's clubs. He also knew that fund-raising would take time away from the more pressing work of community outreach, education, and his own writing.

The committee finally agreed that Cayton be given a contract immediately, with the stipulation that his duties would include developing programs and fund-raising. Cayton accepted and became director in December 1939. As he later remembered: "I plunged myself into community work, secure in a position which would not mean living in the South and which assured a good living."[16] Cayton immediately visited black community centers and settlements in other cities: the Bethlehem Settlement in Nashville, Karamu House in Cleveland, the Robert Gould Shaw House in Boston, and the Dunbar Community League in Springfield, Massachusetts.[17] Cayton not only wanted to broaden the center's programmatic activities but also to do so from a black perspective.

In this regard, he carried on the vision of Ida B. Wells, the prominent black Chicago journalist and activist, who had founded the Negro Fellow-ship League in the heart of Chicago's Black Belt in 1908. Wells had firmly believed in the collective power of the black community, whether through social protest, economic boycotts, or community institutions. As such, her social settlement conjoined social, political, and economic issues through legal advocacy, an employment bureau, a reading room and library, and other educational resources. Perhaps Cayton was also influenced by the High-lander Folk School in Tennessee, founded in 1932. Similar to Highlander, the Bronzeville center became involved in labor issues, started a citizenship school to teach literacy, and organized a people's forum that promoted dis-cussion and corresponding activism.[18]

Although Cayton was inspired by his visits to other black community centers, he was not as successful as he had hoped in recruiting black social workers for group work. This model of social work had become popular during the Depression, especially through federal programs such as the WPA and the National Youth Administration (NYA). According to professionals in group work, participants developed healthy social relationships through group activities, such as games, arts, crafts, drama, and other recreations. Through group interactions, individuals resolved their conflicts and formed allegiances beyond their primary group, which were considered signs of developed personalities. Although some professionals argued that group activities could lead to greater intercultural understanding and participatory citizenship, there were other professionals who recommended that com-munity facilities focus instead on socially and economically disadvantaged persons, whom they considered "maladjusted."[19] Such was the case with the Abraham Lincoln Center (ALC), an interracial social settlement. There, Dr. Rudolf Dreikurs, an Adlerian psychiatrist, had established a child guid-ance clinic in 1939 that used both psychiatric and group work methods with parents of "maladjusted" children. Although the clinic closed by 1942, over half of its clients were poor blacks.[20]

Cayton subscribed to a very different model of group work, one that fostered the development of skills necessary for critical citizenship. This entailed the study and discussion of, as well as participation in, groups that questioned the established social order and encouraged marginalized citizens to enact social change. Instead of treating poverty as an indication of an "inadequate" personality, Cayton and his staff prompted the working class and the poor to question the economic and social structures that influenced substandard housing, overcrowded schools, and underemployment in their communities. The center especially utilized this type of group work in youth and adult classes, the lecture forums with group discussions, and the outreach activities of its dormitory residents.[21]

Cayton decided that if he could not find qualified black social workers in group education, he would have them trained at the center. At one 1940 meeting, the name of Neva Boyd, a white social worker, was mentioned. She certainly had the necessary qualifications for group work, given her long history in recreational and group work. In 1909, the Chicago Woman's Club had hired her to direct social activities at a westside park, where she had organized social clubs for youth and adults and also directed plays, dances, and other recreation. In 1911, she founded the Chicago Training School for playground workers, which became a department of the Chicago School of Civics and Philanthropy (CSCP) in 1914. When the CSCP later became the School of Social Service Administration at the University of Chicago, the Chicago Training School became independent until 1927, when it then became part of Northwestern University's Sociology Department. Cayton decided to hire Boyd to train staff and volunteers in group work, as well as to develop intercultural activities at the center.[22]

Cayton realized, however, that he could not rely upon too many volunteers. At the same time he knew that the center did not have enough funding to pay for the number of trained group workers needed in the Bronzeville community. The center's funding had been complicated by a fund-raising arrangement in which the black community, the Chicago Congregational Union, and the Chicago Community Trust were to contribute equally. But the black community did not have the same resources as the Chicago Community Trust or the Chicago Congregational Union. In some years, the wealthier white Congregational churches of Hyde Park, Winnetka, and other Chicago suburbs contributed more than Kingsley's congregation. Although all donations were critical, especially for expansion of the Bronzeville center, the monies carried the additional complication of white representation on the center's board of directors. Although Cayton was able to eventually redistribute the board's membership to include more blacks, that did not solve the center's financial problems.[23]

The center's problems, though, were greater than financial issues or board memberships. There were ideological differences between Cayton and Pastor Kingsley. Cayton's vision of a community institution had included the participation of a cross section of Chicago's black community, including artists, intellectuals, labor unionists, and political groups (sometimes suspected of being communist). At one committee meeting in 1941, Kingsley talked at length about communists using the Bronzeville center and worried that the center might gain a reputation for being radical. Kingsley was referring in particular to a recent visit by black novelist Richard Wright, who, although he was a communist sympathizer, was not actually a party member. Wright had worked with Cayton on the WPA project, and they had become close friends. Ironically, Wright was visiting the center to assist Cayton in a fundraiser. Kingsley's concern, however, prompted another board member to ask if a person "such as Richard Wright or Paul Robeson" should be allowed to stay at the center, given their "radical sympathies."[24] Cayton replied that any group or person should be allowed to rent the center's rooms, including communists, until the center created an exclusionary policy or until communism was declared illegal.

But Kingsley did not let the matter rest. He later raised the idea that subversive groups at the center were under the surveillance of the FBI. When Cayton contacted the FBI, they replied that they had no knowledge of any such investigation and that anyone who presented himself as an FBI agent was an impostor. Cayton then asked the FBI to make a thorough investigation and wrote to Kingsley about his actions.[25] Kingsley replied by letter to Cayton: "Various officers have been to me three times about activities on the Southside. Naturally they did not reveal their whole purpose or methods about a meeting at the center some time in the fall where the remnants of the Trotsky group . . . had come to the Southside to agitate among Negroes and foment disorders. It was a mixed meeting and distinctly subversive. The reason they came to me was that they thought of me as the one responsible for the Center. I referred them to you. We must be careful about the types of people who come in and their programs and objectives. It is incumbent upon us to have personal contact and be able to pass judgement on what is going on. This is the extent of my knowledge of the affair."[26] The dispute was resolved in 1942, when the Bronzeville center dissolved its association with the Good Shepherd Congregational Church. Consequently, the center was renamed Parkway Community House (PCH), with Cayton continuing as its director.

Parkway Community House's "Applied Sociology"

Cayton's goals remained steadfast in the operation of the "new" center's educational, social, and recreational services and in solving social problems through discussion and community projects. As such, the PCH continued its activities to meet the needs of all community members: children, youth, young workingwomen and mothers, labor union organizers, and activists. This was largely possible because of the center's nearly all-female professional staff. Dorothy Rogers and Emily Miller, respectively director of programs and director of community activities, coordinated a largely female staff of program staff, nursery school staff, teachers, and volunteers. Business manager Suzanne Tory deftly handled the PCH's accounts. Women's organizations—including Delta Sigma Theta Sorority, the DuSable Senior Girls' Club, the Douglass League of Women Voters, the Phi Delta Kappa Sorority, and the Metropolitan Council of Negro Women—were especially active as volunteers in the center's fund-raising bazaars and benefits, as was the Friends of Parkway Organization.[27]

Additionally, an all-female staff was in charge of the nursery school that assisted working mothers, many of whom were domestic, laundry, and factory workers. Although the nursery had only three rooms, its teachers cared for up to sixty children. Costs to parents were minimal, as tuition accounted for less than $100 of the PCH's 1941 budget. Yet some board members were concerned that the nursery wasn't reaching out to the "most under-privileged." Cayton was in a difficult position: he wanted to reach out to more parents but also thought that the PCH needed to charge "a relatively high tuition" or its debt would increase.[28] As of 1942, the PCH's overall expenses had already exceeded its income by over $5,000; a year later, the PCH was $7,000 in debt. Yet in order to get funding from the Chicago Community Fund, the nursery was required to serve low-income and working mothers, those who could least afford to pay higher tuition.[29] The PCH had reached out to the community, but in doing so it risked financial instability.

Realizing there was a dilemma regarding the nursery, the board decided to close it temporarily and studied various plans. The staff reasoned that if the nursery was closed, then the staff would have more time to do group work. Clearly, the staff could not manage both the nursery and the increased number of walk-ins. The financial problem of the nursery was resolved in 1943, when the PCH received federal monies through the Lanham Act to fund the nursery and an after-school child care program for over 150 latchkey children. In the latter program, children aged five to thirteen enjoyed a game room, arts and crafts activities, a children's theater, storytelling sessions, and the library's growing collection of books by and about blacks.[30]

During the 1940s, the PCH also developed programs for youth. With the assistance of National Youth Administration (NYA) instructors, boys enrolled in an after-school woodshop class and made furniture. In the evenings, teens danced to jukebox music, attended club and council meetings, and enrolled in sewing, drama, and dancing classes. Eventually, the dances became so popular that the PCH needed more adult chaperones. As a remedy, the PCH cosponsored the dances with SPY and the Wabash YMCA, both Bronzeville facilities. Teachers and school librarians Frances Clark, Ora Green Morrow, Virginia Frazier, and Lena White volunteered, as did Irene McCoy Gaines, then employed as a SPY social worker. Yet the PCH did not have the facilities for the 150 youths who flocked there to practice the latest dance steps. They relocated the dances to the Wells Homes' recreation center but encountered another problem. Many parents wouldn't let their daughters attend these dances because of purported gang activity. Because of reports of alcohol, fights, and weapons, the PCH moved the dances to the Sheil House, a Catholic center ten blocks away.[31] Indeed, the Sheil House had long attracted youth through its programs. As Cayton had noted earlier: "Area Projects are scientific. The Catholic Center here is doing the thing we talk about and better than the area project. They get empty stares, attract the young people by tap dancing, and boxing and the like, and really work with them."[32]

In addition to providing wholesome recreation, the PCH's staff members wanted to encourage teenagers to dress and behave appropriately. Under the direction of a black high school principal, Maudelle Bousfield, a youth committee met and decided on the appropriate clothing for the dances: suit jackets and ties for boys and dresses for girls. Rules for the dances included no smoking, drinking, or fighting. Cayton recommended that photographs be taken of teens behaving properly at the dances and that they then be posted at movie theaters, including the popular Regal Theater. He was also conducting a survey of commercial dance halls to determine how many youths attended.[33] His main concern was teens' consumption of liquor. Although there were age limits for consuming liquor, the dance hall owners and the police did not always enforce these laws.

One of the PCH's most innovative programs was a "community-wide project," in which over 100 young migrant women, many of whom worked in defense plants, engaged in community outreach. Cayton's earlier dream of converting two buildings into dormitories for workers had finally come to fruition. Residents performed various activities. For example, some helped migrants retrieve copies of their birth certificates, necessary for obtaining work in the defense and war-related factories. Other residents helped teach an Army literacy training course for young men who wished to enroll in the Army. This course was important, as 75 percent of those who failed the Army Classification Test in Chicago had arrived from the South and border states. The course was successful, at least for the 150 older boys who became eligible for the armed forces. Another group of residents worked for the Red Cross Canteen Unit, housing referral services, a clearinghouse that documented incidents of discrimination, or a victory forum that provided information on food rationing, draft registration, and other war-related efforts. The residents' two-hour weekly commitment was integral to the community service component of the PCH.[34] In effect, the residents became a cadre of group work volunteers, engaging in dialogue and problem solving "in new and as yet untried patterns."[35]

The dormitories also helped to alleviate the PCH's financial problems. The residents' volunteer services were critical, as WPA funding for employees and services had been discontinued. The residents' rent also brought in much-needed revenue. But the PCH's budget was still in the red. To secure additional funds, Cayton negotiated a $3,000 contract with the federal government to house fifty-five black WACs (at $1.25 daily per person).[36] Originally, the WACs were to have been stationed at Gardiner Hospital in Hyde Park. But some white residents were so concerned about their property values that they protested any attempts by the women to live there. The Oakland-Kenwood Association, a restrictive covenant association, recommended that the WACs be stationed instead in Washington Park, the adjoining black area. When neighborhood improvement and restrictive covenant associations still protested, the PCH became the solution.[37]

It is likely that in the evenings dormitory residents and WACs attended the people's forum, whose aims were "to probe relentless for the truth; to suffuse action with precision and understanding."[38] The format of lectures, guest speakers, and discussion linked international and national issues to local ones. For example, there were lecture series and discussions about Myrdal's *An American Dilemma* and St. Clair Drake's and Cayton's *Black Metropolis*. Discussion of the latter was especially useful because it gave community members sociological knowledge for understanding local issues. The concepts of democracy and freedom, so critical to the Chicago Black Renaissance, were debated at the forum, especially by speakers who emphasized the larger politics of the "colored races of the world."[39] Pan-Africanism had, in large part, prompted black Americans to conceive of their caste-like subordination as part of a worldwide process of colonialism and imperialism. The center's "Guide Right" lectures, which presented a series of twenty lectures on citizenship, democracy, and government, also conjoined local concerns to international ones. For example, when anthropologists from Chicago universities lectured on European imperialism in Africa, discussions brought the subject back to the home front.[40]

Foregrounding these issues was the fight for "first-class citizenship" through participation in the war effort. Segregated camps and even blood banks prompted many black Americans to question their own hopes for a more equitable future. Regarding blacks' involvement in World War II, Cayton was equally skeptical, pointing out that any discussion had to first consider the dual position of blacks in American society. He noted how the hopes of blacks had been dashed during World War I. Why, he asked, would it be any different for World War II? Further, he questioned who the enemy was. Blacks, he countered, did not hate Hitler or the Germans, despite their treatment of black athletes and artists. Rather, Hitler had made blacks laugh because Hitler felt superior to white Americans. Cayton thought that Hitler's hatred was no worse than that of white Americans or Britons. But Cayton was not alone in these sentiments. Other blacks had baldly asked why a black man should fight a white man's war against yellow men. Cayton concluded that despite the use of propaganda to lure blacks into the service, there would be no significant postwar improvements.[41]

Indeed, blacks had made significant gains in employment during World War II. In 1944, an estimated 541,000 wage earners were employed in Chicago, with an increase of almost 200,000 factory jobs reported in 1939. The color line in Chicago had finally started "to bend" in the iron, steel, and meat-packing industries.[42] Black women had been hired at the Swift Company, the American Maize Products Company in nearby Hammond, Indiana (where 30 percent of employees were black), the RCA-Victor Division of Radio Corporation of America, and International Harvester (where almost 19 percent of employees were black).[43]

As such, the forum discussions focused on whether blacks would keep their jobs once the war ended. One labor organizer at a panel discussion forewarned that blacks, and black women especially, would be the first to lose their jobs. He recommended that blacks form coalitions with international groups instead of isolating themselves. Such an approach, he argued, would lead to a more full-fledged democracy and worldwide citizenship. Marjorie Stewart Joyner, a founding member of the National Council of Negro Women (NCNW) and an active member of the Cosmopolitan Community Church, likewise anticipated the displacement of black women from factory work and encouraged them to take up careers in beauty culture, as she herself had. At least then they would have more autonomy and be of service to the black community. There were discussions on other relevant topics, including the color line (who "drew" it and how to "smash" it through politics), labor unions, and interracial and black organizations. Participants took a hard look at Bronzeville's businesses and community institutions, asking how they would help blacks during the postwar transition. The ambivalence of postwar hopes and fears sought resolution, then, through discussions and cross-class solidarity. Unfortunately, the predictions by Joyner and others would become true. Even though the hiring gap in manufacturing had narrowed, black women would still dominate the domestic service sector as of 1950. Further, unemployment for nonwhite women would be as high as 13 percent in 1950, compared to only 3 percent for white women.[44]

The issues of citizenship and democracy, so central to the PCH, were embodied in its theater productions as well. Not unlike the Federal Theatre troupes, discussed more fully in chapter 3, the PCH's Skyloft Players conceived itself as a community theater. Its first director, Helen Spaulding, was one of many examples of a professional migrant. A graduate of Tennessee State College, Spaulding taught high school in West Virginia. Upon arrival in Chicago, she worked at the Goodman Theatre, while also attending Northwestern University.[45] Assisting her was a cadre of black female professionals. The Skyloft Players' managers for publicity and business, as well as the entertainment chair, were women. Artist Margaret Goss Burroughs, Gaines (whose husband was an actor with the Skyloft Players), social worker Irma Cayton, clubwoman Elizabeth Lindsay Davis, and librarian Vivian Gordon Harsh were patrons of the Skyloft Players, as were the Delta Sigma Theta and the Alpha Kappa Alpha sororities.[46]

Undoubtedly, Spaulding's experiences in the South informed her philosophy of theater, as did the writings of W. E. B. Du Bois and Alain Locke. As she proclaimed: "This is a theater OF the people, FOR the people, and BY the people."[47] The Skyloft Players carried out this manifesto by producing plays for local churches and organizations and also performing radio plays for the CUL and its Junior League. They sponsored playwriting contests that focused on community issues; the 1946 theme, for example, was southside housing conditions. During Negro History Week, they recommended authors for readings, including Langston Hughes, Roi Otley, and William Faulkner. Troupe members also taught classes in acting and stage production, as well as sponsoring guest speakers in theater. Of special note was a talk by film critic Marie Seton, who discussed the deprecating roles that black actors and actresses often had to perform in theater productions.[48] Concerned about finding new talent in the community, the Skyloft Players sponsored talent contests. Helen Spaulding encouraged potential actors and actresses: "Those who abhor the crap-shooting roles given to Negro actors on stage and screen should use this opportunity to show the true side of our current problems and living conditions, and to portray a more equalized racial representation to the public."[49]

Although the Skyloft Players' budget was minuscule during the 1940s, a mere $30 per month, it produced an impressive number of plays. Langston Hughes's plays were regularly performed, and Hughes often took part in the productions. The cast for one of his plays included artists Margaret Goss and Charles Sebree, plus Cayton's wife, Irma Cayton, with Hughes singing in the play's chorus. Bertha Moseley Lewis, a prominent black clubwoman and founder of several theater troupes, directed the play. The Skyloft Players also performed classics such as *Our Town* and *Emperor Jones*, as well as original works by troupe members that focused on interracial issues.[50] Of all of the PCH's programs, the theater was the most interracial. This may well have been due to the influence of the community theater movement and the Federal Theatre Project (FTP), both of which encouraged the production of plays by historically excluded minorities.[51] As such, the Skyloft Players stretched the PCH's pan-Africanist ideology to include all "colored races of the world."

Similar to the FTP, the Skyloft Players enacted community activism through its children's theater and youth contests. They performed children's plays by black dramatists Langston Hughes and Arna Bontemps, and also produced international folk plays in schools and parks. The troupe collaborated with the *Chicago Sunday Bee* in cosponsoring a children's essay contest. Awards for the 1945 essay were handed out at the Phi Delta Kappa's Children's Theatre production *On Freedom Road*, performed at the PCH. The Skyloft Players sponsored a high-school speech contest in 1945, with the timely topic of "The Negro in the Post-War Period." The purpose of these contests was expressly to "stimulate an awareness of civic problems and an intellectual approach to such problems, as well as to give young people an outlet for constructive presentation of their conclusions."[52] Langston Hughes and Richard Wright were among the judges of the contests.

The peak of the PCH's success occurred during the war years because of available federal funding, Cayton's directorship, and a capable staff. Yet the PCH's activities continued to expand after the war because of increased migration and the return of veterans. For example, the PCH had started an interracial camp to break down racial barriers, as well as classes in tap and interpretive dance and photography. The PCH also developed a record music series that featured protest and folk songs by Woody Guthrie, Osco Houston, Josh White, and Leadbelly. It is not clear which services were most used at the PCH then, although the 1946 annual report claimed that over 64,000 persons used the PCH's services. (Most likely they tallied each individual's use of services, not individuals per se.) This may have reflected working mothers' concerns about child care, as many of the nursery schools in Chicago had closed due to the cessation of federal funds. Nonetheless, the staff was not able to handle all of their programs, plus the new ones. And once again, the board expressed concern about qualified black group workers.[53]

Although the PCH had been $7,000 in arrears before the war, postwar funding was even more of a problem. The traditional community fund-raising events of annual teas, fashion shows, letter fund-raisers, and tag days were of little help. The loss of federal monies for the nursery and WAC housing undoubtedly contributed to the PCH's increased debt. Further, the rentals from wartime projects had ceased. It is not clear whether Marshall Fields, Swift and Company, the Weiboldt Foundation, and the *Chicago Tribune* Charities continued to contribute to PCH after the war.[54] Nor is it clear why the PCH's deficit increased to over $20,000 by 1955, since records are sparse from 1947 to 1953. Slum clearance and its attendant problems probably taxed the PCH's services, although there are no indications that the PCH directly helped displaced black residents find alternative housing.[55] When the PCH decided to sell its property in 1955, it probably did so at a financial loss. As a result the nursery, which once cared for so many children, took in only fourteen children from outside of the area in 1955.[56]

Shouldering the center's fiscal responsibilities of the PCH and bowing to the endless concessions of white board members took a psychological toll on Cayton. He had referred to the center as "a sop thrown to the Negro community by wealthy and middle-class whites, who felt virtuous by supporting it but who would resist with all their strength any move on the part of Negroes for better jobs, housing in white areas, or the free exercise of civil rights."[57] Haunted by nightmares of white men and bouts of alcoholism, Cayton became a patient of psychoanalyst Helen McLean at the Institute of Psychoanalysis. He resigned as director of the PCH in 1949.

But Cayton had suffered from psychological problems for many years. In fact, he had attributed his breakdown to the "psychological scars" of a caste system and its corresponding social and economic constraints.[58] Certainly Cayton's directorship of the PCH had placed him in difficult circumstances, as he had to constantly mediate among the power of white board members, the administrators of philanthropies, and city officials. At the same time, he found it difficult not to speak out against the injustices of white power: restrictive covenant associations, "slum" landlords, and corrupt police. In one situation, where he had served on a jury to determine why twelve blacks had burned to death in their "crammed" kitchenettes, he accused the police of concealing evidence. As he sadly concluded: "Twelve Negroes had escaped from the South only to be burned on an altar of neglect, indifference, greed, and racial bias."[59]

These social tragedies, coupled with personal ones, caused Cayton to suffer from the depersonalization that black psychiatrist Frantz Fanon has so poignantly described. As Cayton reflected: "My illness is a sickness of the soul, something beyond religion or psychiatry. It's the sickness of the age. It's a form of alienation—or better, the result of alienation. It's a loss of identity, a lack of at-homeness. I'm not at home in any place or with anyone."[60] Although it is beyond the scope of this chapter to discuss this aspect of Cayton's life, what is pertinent is how the community that the PCH served underwent even further deterioration, conditions which I believe partly contributed to Cayton's own sense of hopelessness.

How did the PCH fare with other community centers serving the Bronzeville neighborhood during the 1950s? Both the ALC and the SSSH shared somewhat similar fates. Like the PCH, both of these settlements had offered a variety of services to their respective communities of Grand Boulevard and Oakland from the 1930s through the 1950s. These areas were impoverished with high delinquency rates and crowded kitchenettes and schools. Like the PCH, the ALC and the SSSH offered music, art, drama, and home economics classes; clubs for different ages; a nursery school and playschool (both supported by the WPA); and adult education.[61] But unlike the PCH, the SSSH worked directly with residents of public housing. The center was especially proud of its program for elderly residents at Prairie Courts Housing; it was the only program that used group work with the elderly. They also assisted displaced residents in finding housing during the urban renewal of the 1950s.[62]

Like the ALC and the SSSH, the PCH relocated farther south to one of Chicago's most congested neighborhoods in 1956.[63] The PCH's financial problems remained unabated, aggravated by the push-and-pull factors of the neighborhood's transition and the city's reluctance to more fully assist the center. At a committee meeting of group workers employed by the PCH and the SSSH, one social worker noted that many people in the community had been on relief since the 1930s. She pointedly asked, "Are we in a way of life that is not American?"[64]

Cayton and his largely female staff had succeeded in providing an intellectual and social center for residents for over fifteen years. But following the closure of the PCH and its subsequent relocation, the center could not reestablish the political radicalism and artistic vigor that had characterized its heyday.

3

Community Sponsorship of Literature and the Arts

The Cultural Roots of the Chicago Black Renaissance

The expressive arts of the Chicago Black Renaissance drew their energy from a variety of sources: a pan-African intellectuality; expositions and exhibits that showcased race progress; the stewardship of women's organizations, including sororities, clubs, and study circles; community institutions that sponsored exhibits, lectures, readings, and discussions; and the black migration. Indeed, a steady stream of black migrants came to Chicago, mostly from the cotton states of Mississippi and Arkansas. The migrants' dialects, songs, and laughter filled Chicago's southside streets. Chicago's black writers heard the migrants' blues music, dialects, and church shouts and responded to these rhythmic intonations. As Langston Hughes described the experience: "They live on Seventh Street in Washington or State Street in Chicago and they do not particularly care whether they are like white folks or anybody else. Their joy runs, bang! Into ecstasy. Their religion soars to a shout."[1]

The experiences of migrants resonated for many Chicago black writers, as did the natural and psychological landscape of the South. In *For My People*, Margaret Walker wrapped images of Africa around those of the southern Delta, expressing a deep yearning for a home fertile with the joys and agonies of her people. Richard Wright, too, never forgot the South. When he created characters like Bigger or described a rat-infested kitchenette, he was mirroring images of both the South and Chicago.[2] Other writers created characters spun from black southern folk traditions, such as Hughes's "Simple," a trickster par excellence. As Arna Bontemps described him, "Simple is the kind of funny man who will not make Negroes ashamed. He is the very hipped, race-conscious, fighting-back, city-bred great-grandson of Uncle Remus."[3]

Black community institutions became havens for writers to read one another's works, for artists to exhibit their paintings and sculptures, for readers to share their interpretations, and for children to recite and perform black poetry and theater respectively. To illustrate, during the 1930s and 1940s, there were a number of Black community theaters that produced plays by black writers. Similarly, at the George Cleveland Hall Library, black writers read their latest works to appreciative audiences, many of whom had joined the library's book and history clubs. Black newspapers, too, promoted literature and the arts through advertisements, announcements, reviews, and serializations of novels. Their editorial pages also featured columns by prominent black leaders and writers, such as Hughes and W. E. B. Du Bois. Black Chicago literary and cultural magazines, especially *Negro Story Magazine* and *Negro Digest,* published poetry, fiction, and essays by Chicago black writers, and they also showcased black photographers and graphic artists. As noted earlier, the South Side Community Art Center (SSCAC) exhibited black American and African art, while also offering art, writing, and theater classes to adults and children.

Not surprisingly, the Chicago Black Renaissance had a mix of patrons. Generally, black community institutions in Chicago offered more support to artists and writers than did those of the Harlem Renaissance.[4] The SSCAC, for one, sponsored a number of fundraising events to ensure that the center remained a black community institution. The *Negro Story,* too, relied upon the support of black Chicagoans, such as lawyer Edith Sampson, cosmetologist Majorie Stewart Joyner, artist Rex Gorleigh, writer Frank Marshall Davis, and newspaper editor Claude Barnett. Of course, federal agencies—including the Works Progress Administration (WPA), the Federal Art Project (FAP), and the Federal Theatre Project (FTP)—were critical for financial support during the Depression and early years of World War II, as were Chicago philanthropists and the City of Chicago. For example, the George Cleveland Hall Library relied upon city monies, although librarian Vivian Harsh also used her own resources to build the library's collection of black history and literature. The Chicago Community Trust supported Parkway Community House (PCH) and its Skyloft Players for many years. The Rosenwald Fund's fellowship program likewise supported many Chicago black artists, writers, and intellectuals, including Horace Cayton, St. Clair Drake, Margaret

Walker, Richard Attaway, Richard Wright, E. Franklin Frazier, and Katherine Dunham.[5]

But it was the WPA that gave a start to many black Chicago writers and artists. The WPA not only provided an income during lean times but also offered camaraderie for both black and white writers. Arna Bontemps and Richard Wright met Jack Conroy through the Illinois Writers Project (IWP). The friendship between Bontemps and Conroy became a fruitful collaboration with the novel *They Seek a City,* later *Any Place but Here,* and a juvenile story *Slappy Hooper.* Wright also worked with Margaret Walker on a WPA project, supervised by sociologist Louis Wirth. The two writers became close friends, and Walker sent Wright research materials for his novel, *Native Son.* Fenton Johnson and Frank Yerby also worked together on the IWP under the direction of Katherine Dunham and Horace Cayton. In Bontemps's estimation, no other writers' project in the country produced such comparable black talent during the Depression. "Chicago," he extolled, "was the center of the second phase of Negro literary awakening."[6]

Moreover, the WPA broadened writers' understanding of black Chicago history and also sharpened their research skills. Writers were encouraged to use the sociological methods of interviewing and participant observation to "get at" community perspectives. In fact, Alan Lomax, then national advisor on folklore for the Federal Writers Project (FWP), recommended that WPA writers study communities by talking to persons from all walks of life. This approach was not unlike that used by black sociologists Charles Johnson, Horace Cayton, and Earl Moses.[7] Using sociological strategies, the WPA writers produced remarkable collections, such as the *Negro in Illinois.* Further, these experiences provided black writers with materials for their creative writing. (Because WPA writers were required to write only 1,200 to 2,000 words per week, they had plenty of time to work on their own projects.)[8] Subsequent publications of Bontemps, Conroy, Wright, Walker, Drake, and Cayton attest to the influence of their WPA experiences.[9]

Additionally, the WPA required that writers work in genres they might not have used otherwise, such as reportage, travelogue, and historical narrative. This genre-crossing may have led some WPA writers to further experiment with their own writing. In fact, many black Chicago writers wrote across genres, thereby reaching out to a larger readership. Although we may think of Hughes as a poet, he was also a playwright (for both children and adults), a biographer, a short story writer, and a journalist. Margaret Walker, the first black poet to win the Yale Prize for Poetry, was a novelist, a children's story writer, and a historical writer. Shirley Graham wrote not only historical bi-ographies (for children), short stories, and plays but also operas. And poet and playwright Arna Bontemps wrote both adult and juvenile fiction.[10]

In addition to their work in the WPA, black writers influenced one another through their own writers' groups. At least fifteen members of the Southside Writers' Group met twice a month at the Abraham Lincoln Center (ALC), where the IWP was housed. Led by poet Margaret Walker, the group included Fenton Johnson, Theodore Ward, Richard Wright, Garfield Gordon, Frank Marshall Davis, Dorothy Sutton, Julius Weil, Russell Marshall, Robert Davis, Marion Perkins, Arthur Bland, Fern Gayden, and others. Many of its members were established writers, at least in Chicago. For example, Fenton Johnson had already written four volumes of poetry and two books of prose. Wright was revising his first novel. Frank Marshall Davis had written two books of poems; Perkins had written two plays. Dorothy Sutton, a law student and minister, had published some of her poems in literary magazines.[11] Unfortu-nately, little else is known about this writers' group, because the prodigious notes of one member were accidentally destroyed.

There were, of course, other prominent black writers not affiliated with the WPA or the Southside Writers' Group who lived in and wrote about Chicago, such as short story writer Marita O. Bonner and playwright Lor-raine Hansberry. Pulitzer Prize–winning poet Gwendolyn Brooks did not get her start through the WPA or the Southside Writers' Group, yet she drew heavily from the images of Bronzeville. Black journalists Era Bell Thompson and Thyra Edwards did not belong to either group, but Thompson would become co-editor for the *Negro Digest* and managing editor for *Ebony* (and later its international editor). Thyra Edwards (later Gitlin), a Chicago social worker involved in the Spanish Civil War, joined popular front organizations, while publishing in *Negro Digest* and the "People's Voice." And Margaret Burroughs wrote for the Associated Negro Press.[12]

Radio became another medium of expression for black Chicago literature and history. Perhaps one of the more experimental black radio programs in Chicago was Richard Durham's "Destination Freedom." Airing from 1948 to 1950, the program's opening announcement reflected the postwar disil-lusionment felt by Durham and many other blacks: "D. F., dramatizations of the great democratic heritage of the Negro people is brought to you by station WMAQ as a part of the pageant of history and of America's own DESTINATION FREEDOM!"[13] Durham's historical episodes dramatized how Harriet Tubman, Frederick Douglass, Sojourner Truth, Ida B. Wells,

Mary Church Terrell, and Carter G. Woodson, among others, had traveled the road to freedom. Other episodes portrayed those who had followed in their footsteps: Langston Hughes, Joe Louis, Marian Anderson, Duke Ellington, Richard Wright, Lena Horne, Gwendolyn Brooks, Mary McCleod Bethune, Paul Robeson, and W. E. B. Du Bois. Yet none had arrived at their true "destination freedom." Freedom, in Durham's view, would not be realized until blacks had the freedoms enjoyed by most Americans: voting rights, equal opportunity in employment, and the right to buy a home in a non-black neighborhood. In one 1949 radio play, Durham dramatized blacks' limited housing choices through the conversation of two European men visiting Washington, D.C. One observed how the black neighborhoods there reminded him of "Nazi ghettoes." The narrator followed with the commentary: "It might surprise the people we liberated from Nazi ghettoes to know that race segregation is defended as both 'natural' and 'American' by the business and property interests that dominate the Nation's Capital."[14]

Durham also drew from experiences of Chicago's southside to depict segregation and substandard conditions in black housing. In a 1949 radio play, "Slums" was personified as a character, and black politician Archibald Carey was "after him." Durham was referring to Carey's support of an ordinance to outlaw discrimination in public housing, which did not pass. As the radio script concluded: "The slums are the cemeteries of the living. Jim Crow is the undertaker. Both must disappear from American life."[15] In yet another play about housing, he stressed how veterans had no decent housing for their families.[16] Although there is no record of how many people listened to "Destination Freedom," radio was certainly a popular source of jazz, spirituals, and church sermons for many blacks. It is thus likely that "Destination Freedom" had a wider audience than some of the black cultural institutions in Chicago, such as the SSCAC or the George Cleveland Hall Library.

In essence, Chicago black writers and artists created a cultural and political front during the Chicago Black Renaissance, drawing from the social injustices of Chicago's southside and connecting them to the historical racism in the South and the exploitation in African countries. At the same time, the performative elements of black Chicago's drama, poetry, and dance celebrated the joys and tribulations of migrants and the pride and dignity of Africans. Indeed, the South and Africa were not merely tropes; as subjects they were ritualized and enacted to honor and confirm a collective black identity. Chicago's black cultural institutions and the prodigious activism of the women affiliated with them were largely responsible for this renaissance.

Black Theater

Like many American cities, Chicago had its own "little theater" movement in the 1920s and 1930s. One of the movement's major tenets was the practice of democracy through ethnic theaters and interracial collaborations. In this vein, little theaters offered ethnically disenfranchised actors further opportunities to perform experimental and political plays. W. E. B. Du Bois had helped to launch the Krigwa Little Theatre Movement in New York City, with the performance of his play *Star of Ethiopia* in 1913. Thereafter, the Krigwa movement branched out to other cities, including Chicago. Hughes, too, was influential in the little theater movement in the 1930s through his directorship of the Harlem Suitcase Theatre (so named because all of their property fit into a suitcase). Backed by labor unions, this "people's theater" performed plays by Hughes and Paul Green, a white southern playwright whose controversial plays vivified the injustices blacks faced.[17] Black Chicagoans, too, established little theaters during the 1920s and 1930s, including the Ethiopian Art Theatre, the Little Princess Theatre, and the Masque Players.[18] The movement would continue through the 1940s with the Skyloft Players; the Chicago Negro Art Theatre, started by Frank Greenwood, a Skyloft actor; the Sheils Players Group, based at Sheils House, the Catholic settlement house; and the People's Theatre, an interracial group that was launched by Harvey Cogbill and Bill Moore.[19]

Democracy was at the very heart of the black little theater movement. The movement was especially important for black actors and actresses, who were given more serious roles instead of caricatures of black stereotypes. As W. E. B. Du Bois poignantly wrote in 1920: "It is not that we are ashamed of our color and blood. We are instinctively and almost unconsciously ashamed of the caricatures done of our darker shades. Black *is* caricature in our half conscious thought and we shun in print and paint that which we love in life. . . . Off with the thought of chains and inchoate soul-shrinkings, and let us train ourselves to see beauty in black."[20] Another black writer concurred with Du Bois: "The lazy, indolent, crap-shooting, singing and dancing, carefree 'colored brother' is no more representative of the Negro in America than is the Ghetto Jew symbolic of the American descendants of Israel."[21] For this writer, the little theater movement provided actors with more dignified and authentic characters. Likewise, black directors were given more autonomy to produce plays that focused on black experiences, including those of migrants. In order to authentically capture migrants' experiences, one black dramatist encouraged black actors and directors to study black folklore and folk drama. He believed that such productions, often performed before an interracial audience, would teach whites about the racism experienced by blacks.[22]

Bertha Moseley Lewis was one of the better-known black directors of Chicago's little theater movement during the 1930s. With degrees from Northwestern University and the University of Chicago, Lewis had tried to start a little theater group in the 1920s, when Eugene O'Neill and Sherwood Anderson came to the southside for a production of Oscar Wilde's *Salome*. Lewis was a young actress at the time, and her father refused to let her act in the play, perhaps because of its purported sensuality.[23] She then started the Masque Players with young members of the Grace Presbyterian Church, whose first performances so moved several University of Chicago black students that they approached her to present plays about black "folk life" at the Cube Theatre. The Cube was a vibrant black storefront theater on 57th Street and Stoney Island, which was started by Katherine Dunham's brother. There, Lewis met writers Hughes and Bontemps, artists Charles White and Charles Sebree, anthropologist St. Clair Drake, and dancer Katherine Dunham.[24] Under the auspices of Lewis, the Masque Players performed two plays with black themes: *Porgy* and *In Abraham's Bosom* by Paul Green, who had received the Pulitzer Prize for the latter play. At one of these productions, Alain Locke, champion of the "New Negro," made the curtain speech. Locke's endorsement of the plays marked Lewis and Cube as rising stars in Chicago's theater community. Soon thereafter, Cube was forced to relocate to Poro College, yet it still advertised itself as an "experimental theatre."[25] Because of the Masque Players' success, Lewis then set up a new theater in a garage, which was named the Book Nook and Show Shop. (It was also a lending library and a shop.) Then Lewis started yet another theater group, the National Negro Folk Players. In their performance of *La Guiablesse*, Lewis collaborated with Dunham, who performed Haitian ceremonial and Moorish dances.[26]

Dunham made her first public appearance at the Chicago Beaux Arts Ball in 1931, then shortly thereafter at the Chicago World's Fair in 1933. In 1933, she also became co-director of the Negro Dance Art Studio with black composer and pianist Florence B. Price. One year later, Dunham started another school of dance, the Chicago Negro School of Ballet, and her pupils formed the Negro Dance Group, which performed ballet as well as African dance.[27] Dunham's interest in the study of African dance had been fueled by Lewis and also by her mentor, Melville Herskovits. In 1932, she had written to Herskovits to ask whether a comparative study of African dance might not be a valuable contribution to anthropology. But she had another, more immediate, purpose for writing. She was organizing a library for Provident Hospital and asked Herskovits if he would donate social science books. Herskovits encouraged her to study anthropology and also to contact the Rosenwald Fund for book donations. Dunham's contact with Herskovits would prove invaluable, as later she would receive a Rosenwald Fellowship to study Caribbean dance through his recommendation.[28]

Herskovits continued to be Dunham's academic mentor; he attended her dance performances, and she attended his lectures. At one point she borrowed his lecture slides so that her dances would be more authentically African. Herskovits was probably also responsible for helping Dunham to procure work with the WPA, where she conducted anthropological research about religious cults, including the Temple of Islam. Yet even though Dunham was interested in anthropology, she saw it as a means to better understand African retentions in black American dance, not as a future career. But Herskovits wanted her to be more studious. He was disappointed when she had not registered for fall classes in 1936 because she was working on a dance recital. At that time, she had her own studio and was collaborating with black composer William Grant Still, among other projects.[29]

When Dunham was awarded a scholarship from the General Education Board to study anthropology at the University of Chicago in 1936, Herskovits was again disappointed that she chose not to study with him.[30] Dunham explained that she needed her job, and that even though she would have preferred to study under Herskovits she could not live in Evanston and travel daily to the southside for dance rehearsals. In conclusion, she said, these reasons, "coupled with a feeling of not belonging which I have always felt toward Northwestern, prompted my choice."[31]

Increasingly, Dunham's dance and theater work pulled her toward her own creative work and not in an academic direction. Not only was she busy with her dance studio and classes, since 1934 she had collaborated with Lewis on a number of children's plays, based on the fairytales "The Steadfast Tin-Soldier," "Alice in Wonderland," "Hansel and Gretel," and "The Rescue of Old Nick." Black sororities and women's clubs assisted with the play productions—sewing costumes, creating stage designs, promoting productions, and writing the plays' narration.[32]

Graham had come to Chicago late in 1936 when there was a reopening of the director's position at the FTP's Negro unit. Before then, there had been two white directors, both of whom lasted only several months. The first director, Mary Merril, had the unit perform mostly classical plays, with a "twist" of race. When Jewish director Charles de Sheim was hired to take her place, instead of black actor and playwright Robert Dunmore, there was resulting tension and de Sheim had to leave.[33] Graham was an ideal replacement. She had completed a master's degree at Oberlin College, with a thesis on "Survivals of Africanism in American Music." She also studied at the Institute of Musical Art and Parisian Study, then returned to the United States for the premier performance of her African-based opera, *Tom-Tom*. As the first black woman to have her own opera performed, she had already achieved some degree of notoriety.[34]

Herskovits was instrumental in helping Graham get the directing job.[35] Graham continued to write him to garner his support, as well as confiding her problems with the unit. At first, she was enthusiastic because the Negro unit was "going strong." She was not bothered by the fact that it was a segregated unit, nor that some directors or actors thought such practices were discriminatory. Instead, Graham considered it an opportunity to showcase the natural talents of black performers. As she stated: "I believe that the American Negro is primarily fitted for the theater; that the age old wisdom, burning sun of the tropics, pulsing rhythms, have been refined and purified by these three hundred years of pain and suffering, until tears and laughter mingle in our hearts and make us artists."[36]

The Negro unit worked with several Chicago black community theaters, including the Princess Theatre in Chicago's Loop. When Graham asked Herskovits to serve on the theater's advisory board, he agreed. He was unable to attend most meetings, but that was of little consequence because Graham communicated with him frequently. Indeed, having Herskovits's name on the theater's letterhead gave the Princess Theatre more prestige.[37] But Graham's choice of plays would get her into trouble, for she eschewed the merely entertaining and focused on political messages. Following her first production of *Mississippi Rainbow,* which received good reviews, she decided on Paul Green's controversial play, *Hymn to the Rising Sun.* The play's setting was a southern prison, where a white warden cruelly beat a young black prisoner to death. Green had expressly written the play to advocate for prison reform after he read about prison conditions in North Carolina, where two black prisoners suffered gangrene when they were chained in an unheated cell and as a result their feet had to be amputated.[38] The play had just been performed by an all-white cast with the FTP in New York City. But Graham thought that "[her] people could do a much better job of it."[39]

Despite the FTP's caveat to avoid "problem plays," Graham rehearsed

Green's play for three months, with the assistance of Theodore Ward and Richard Wright. However, the production closed on opening night. Although the politics surrounding the event were not disclosed, Graham ruefully remarked how the unit had become a "black eye" in Washington, D.C. Consequently, her troupe began to rehearse another play by Green, which did not have the political content of his other plays.[40] Wright, on the other hand, went on to collaborate with Green on the dramatization of his novel, *Native Son*. Directed and produced by Orson Welles, that play became a success.[41]

Although Graham was again told to avoid "problem plays," she went ahead and directed another one with political content, Theodore Ward's *The Big White Fog*. Situated in Chicago, the play featured a black character who attended a Chicago college but had to drop out because of poverty. Another character, discussing her difficult migration to Chicago, concluded that if she had to make the decision again, she would remain in the South. University of Chicago officials asked the mayor to cancel the production, because they feared the play would contribute further to racial tensions.[42] At that time, the University of Chicago was implicated in restrictive housing covenant associations and certainly did not want more egg on its face.

Given the situation, Graham decided to solicit input from black community groups, including the Chicago NAACP, the Chicago Urban League (CUL), church groups, and women's clubs. The Chicago NAACP responded that the play was "communist propaganda" and should not be performed.[43] Lewis, then chair of the drama committee of the Chicago and Northern District of Colored Women's Clubs (CNDA), was also asked about the play. She responded that a white audience would not be interested in black life and problems. But this discreet response perhaps camouflaged greater concerns for Lewis and other black leaders. They may have been reluctant to present portrayals of a black family before a white audience, believing that whites couldn't possibly understand the complexities of blacks' economic distress, intergenerational discord, and mixed ancestry. Given the then-accepted sociological theories about black families as "disorganized" and "pathological," as well as the impoverished conditions of many black families, Lewis's response was perhaps well founded.[44] Lewis was certainly aware of how black theater could be a vehicle for activism and change. But she was also well aware of how a play's message could be misinterpreted and distorted.

This controversy, as examined by Rena Fraden, centered around the issues of representation and authenticity. The troubling question to the actors and the community leaders was this: To what extent would Ward's play be perceived as representative of the "typical" black family in Chicago? This was an especially contentious issue, because Ward had wanted the play presented in a downtown theater before an interracial audience. As he envisioned the performance, the play would be especially instructive for whites about the daily difficulties faced by black families. But an unsettling question remained: Which black families would be represented? The play ran for less than two months, then subsequently for several days at a black high school.[45] Graham became disillusioned with Chicago blacks, saying they cared only about money. Further, she concluded, "The city as a whole is utterly devoid of cultural interests."[46]

Graham was also criticized for the performance of a children's play by Charlotte Chorpenning, a white instructor with the Sociology Department at Northwestern University. Graham had decided to direct Chorpenning's adaptation of *Little Black Sambo* and set it to music.[47] She used puppets to tell the story, and though she had wanted to create a world of wonder for children, instead she was criticized for using puppets that were described as having "Black faces" and "thick red lips."[48] Katherine Dunham came to Graham's defense, claiming that the play was directed by "one of our most brilliant young Negro directors."[49] Although Graham may have conceptualized the puppets' faces as African masks, issues of representation again became contentious, especially in segregated Chicago.

Not all of Graham's productions, though, received negative reviews. *L'Ag'Ya*, with choreographer Dunham, and *Swing Mikado* were "box-office attractions." *Mississippi Rainbow*, performed at the Princess Theatre, received rave reviews from the *Chicago Herald* and *Chicago Examiner*.[50] Nonetheless, when the Chicago Negro unit was accused of political agitation in 1938, Graham left Chicago and went to Yale.[51] That same year, Dunham was hired as dance director of ballet for the Chicago Negro unit. That position, too, would be short-lived. She was released that same year purportedly because there was no work in ballet, although one has to wonder if it was because she came to Graham's defense. Still, Dunham tried to get her job back. She wrote to Mary McCleod Bethune, her mother's teacher, and asked her to present her case to Hallie Flannigan, then head of the FTP. Despite these efforts, she was not rehired. Like Graham, she left Chicago for the East Coast. But unlike Graham, she would return regularly to Chicago to perform.[52]

The Promotion of Black Literature and History

Until 1932, there were no public libraries on Chicago's black southside, despite Dr. George Cleveland Hall's campaign to establish a library. As a member of

Chicago's black elite in the early twentieth century, Dr. Hall was prominent in social and civic affairs. A close friend of Booker T. Washington, Hall assumed presidency of the Chicago chapter of Washington's Negro Business League just before World War I.[53] By the early 1930s, Hall had convinced Julius Rosenwald to build a library for blacks in Chicago, just as Rosenwald had done throughout the South. As the first director of the "Hall Library," Vivian Gordon Harsh was determined to build the southside library's repositories. Toward that end, she traveled throughout the South each summer, combing small towns for older books by and about blacks. Shipped back to the Hall Library, these books became part of Bronzeville's new "intellectual center."[54] By 1935, the library housed over 35,000 books. Through the Emergency Educational Program, the library also offered classes for adults in social sciences, civics, economics, government, foreign languages, parent education, social psychology, and black history. As of 1939, the Hall Library served 95,000 residents in Bronzeville and adjoining neighborhoods.[55]

Along with children's librarian Charlemae Rollins, Harsh organized a number of programs for the community: storytelling sessions, book and drama clubs, Negro history clubs, and black history and art exhibits, plus a series of lectures and book reviews that underscored black contributions to literature and the arts. Harsh was serious about librarians' "deep responsibility for intellectual and civic leadership in their communities."[56] She, along with Rollins, were members of a special committee organized to compile a bibliography of books and periodic literature on the history of black life in the western hemisphere. This ambitious task was undertaken not only to demonstrate black Americans' contribution to democracy and progress but also to further black Americans' knowledge about Africa, the Caribbean, and Latin America. Especially concerned that older books misrepresented black history and black Americans' achievements, such a task reflected, in one librarian's words, "a newer approach to the scientific knowledge and intelligent appreciation of the Negro race today."[57]

Harsh marshaled a staff of capable, mostly female librarians and community members to assist her in the promotion of black literature and history. Book reviews were published in the *Chicago Sunday Bee*'s columns—"George Hall Library News," "Tidbits about Books and Authors," and "Local Library News." Harsh also organized weekly discussions of recent books, moderated by Fern Gayden, including Zora Neale Hurston's *Dust Tracks,* Margaret Walker's *For My People,* and Richard Wright's *Black Boy.*[58] But Harsh was not exclusionary in selecting literary canons. In 1945, Harsh and schoolteacher Mrs. Theodore E. Crawley taught a course on the Hutchins-Adler method of studying "great books." Essentially, this method was an elaboration of the

Socratic method taught at the University of Chicago. Acting as facilitators, Harsh and Crawley prompted community members' ideas through questions about their readings of Plato, Aristotle, Marx, and Voltaire.[59] This study group was diverse, including teachers, lawyers, postal clerks, homemakers, social workers, and librarians. Moreover, Hall librarians taught a course for parents and teachers, "Guidance of Adolescent Reading." A number of PTA members completed this course, which was taught by Yolanda Yates, a reading specialist and children's librarian at the Woodlawn Regional Library. Among the subjects she discussed were the psychology of the adolescent and the adolescent in fiction.[60]

Certainly the Hall Library's staff played a significant role in cultivating readership of black literature and history. The breadth of the Hall Library's lectures and book review series, which lasted through 1953, was remarkable. Harsh worked with a literary advisory committee—which included Era Bell Thompson, actress Brunetta Mouzon, and Bontemps, among others—to invite prominent black writers to talk about and read from their work. Among the writers featured were Hughes, Hurston, Alain Locke, Bontemps, Wright, Attaway, Walker, Brooks, Willard Motley, and the cast from "Destination Freedom."[61] These events drew a responsive audience. As Hughes wrote to Bontemps about one of Brooks's poetry readings, "Hall branch evening was most delightful. Overflowing crowd filling two rooms, Gwendolyn Brooks well received and encored to read a second poem."[62]

Children and youth, too, were encouraged to read books about black literature and history, including blacks' contributions to World War II. As head of the children's department at the library, Rollins recommended children's books that portrayed exemplary blacks. In her estimation, there were two types of books for children: those written "for democracy" and those written "for fascism." The latter portrayed blacks as "superstitious" and "incompetent," thus undeserving of full citizenship.[63] In a 1945 Chicago Bee column, "About Books on the Negro," Rollins encouraged readers to question whether authors were writing appropriately about black life. Was the work realistic or nostalgic, harking back to a romantic past? Were the illustrations realistic or mere caricatures? Did the characters speak realistically or only in exaggerated dialect? Did the story contribute to the idea of democracy or was it patronizing?[64] Moreover, Rollins's stewardship of black history and literature extended not only to the local children but also to Chicago PTAs, the Chicago Public Library's advisory board, and national organizations.[65]

Rollins and other librarians cultivated children's appreciation of black literature through a number of activities. Since 1933, Hall Library's story hour was a drawing card, with over 2,700 children attending that year alone. There were also five children's clubs then, including boys' and girls' reading clubs and a debating club.[66] Other Chicago library branches in black neighborhoods promoted black children's understanding of black literature and music as well. At one children's program at the South Chicago library branch, children sang Haitian folk songs. For the final program, Hughes spoke and read his poetry, followed by a chorus composed of members from various churches. At the Oakland library branch, children from Oakland School participated in a program in which one speaker voiced the idea that those who did not participate in black history and improvement of black conditions "betrayed" the race.[67]

World War II stimulated other forms of activism for Harsh and her staff. She invited specialists to lecture to homemakers about consumer issues. Hall Library also offered classes in first aid and nutrition (the latter important because of wartime rationing). Librarians at southside locations—including the Hall, Oakland, and Washington Park branches—were concerned that soldiers had few reading materials, and so they organized book drives to collect works on black literature and history for the soldiers. While Harsh coordinated these "Victory Book Campaigns" for black soldiers, children helped to make toys for the British War Relief.[68] Talks, discussions, and exhibits at the Hall Library also focused on blacks' wartime contributions, such as one by *Chicago Sunday Bee* editor Olive Diggs, who emphasized black women's war efforts. Photographs of Chicago men serving in the armed forces were also on display at the Hall Library. The photograph exhibit most likely drew from the *Chicago Sunday Bee*'s prodigious photograph collection, which chronicled participation in war efforts by both black men and women.[69] This reportage, characteristic of much of the literature of the Chicago Black Renaissance, documented blacks' contributions to their country as mounting evidence for why blacks deserved first-class citizenship. Lastly, Harsh helped to organize the DuSable History Club, which met regularly at the Hall Library. By 1944, there were fifteen Negro History Clubs that met at the Hall Library and nearby schools, with over 800 persons attending the meetings. The Negro History Clubs were, in fact, among the largest clubs at the Hall Library during the war years, in large part because of the call for heightened patriotism against the backdrop of unrelenting black disenfranchisement.[70]

Annually, two weeklong celebrations also notably fostered black literature and history: Negro History Week (February 13 to 19), which was followed by Brotherhood Week (February 20 to 27). Negro History Week was an especially busy time for the Hall Library staff. Many people visited the special exhibits, such as the 1940 display of autographed works by famous black writers that included copies of rare books, newspaper clippings, and diaries. The 1946 exhibit included original photographs and illustrations of books by Bontemps, Graham, and other black writers. Other displays featured murals by art students from DuSable High School, created under the guidance of art teacher Ethel Nolan, and also a miniature African village built by art students at Dunbar Vocational School.[71]

With the Great Migration of the 1950s, the community of Bronzeville changed and so did the patronage of Hall Library. The number of clubs decreased; by 1953, the lecture and book review series was discontinued. In her annual reports to the Chicago Public Library, Harsh emphasized the legacy of Hall Library, such as twenty-two years of lectures and a book review series and twelve years of history clubs, among other contributions. But by the mid-1950s she increasingly referred to the neighborhood's demographic changes.[72] It was a time of increased migration and upheavals from urban renewal and high-rise public housing. Regardless, the Hall Library still continued to serve the Bronzeville neighborhood and to promote black history, literature, and the arts.

The *Chicago Sunday Bee* also worked diligently to showcase black literature and the arts. Like many other Bronzeville institutions, the *Bee*'s staff was mostly all-female. The newspaper was under the capable leadership of editor Olive Diggs. She had succeeded Ida B. Wells when she was hired in 1927 by Anthony Overton, the newspaper's founder and owner of Overton Baking Powder.[73] Diggs perpetuated Wells's legacy, most notably through the newspaper's emphasis on painstakingly thorough documentation. In Wells's case, the focus was on the enumeration of and conditions about lynchings; in Diggs's case, she and her staff recorded black men's and women's wartime work. As noted, the *Bee*'s full-page photographic spreads of black soldiers, pilots, nurses, and women on the front in Europe and at home documented how blacks fought for other people's democracy. Such evidence underscored black historian Charles Wesley's ironic contention that democracy needed to begin in America, not overseas.[74]

Like Wells, Diggs conceived of the newspaper as an agency of change. The *Bee* showed a remarkable breadth in its coverage. There was a steadfast focus on the connections among literature, art, history, and politics. "Labor News" and "Art Notes" were published side by side. Subscribers could read weekly installments of Wright's *Native Son* or order the book directly from the newspaper's book department. The editors conceived of the newspaper as not only reporting news but also educating the community. As part of that educational effort, women's accomplishments and activism were show-cased through front-page photographs of "socially awake" young women, the "Women's Section," and full-page photographs of women working in wartime factories, Red Cross canteens, and overseas.[75] This womanist per-spective intimated that full-fledged democracy did not discriminate because of gender or race.

The *Chicago Bee* collaborated with the Hall Library by publishing regu-lar columns about children's literature: Martha May's "For Your Child and Mine," Oneita Ferrell's "Browsing with Books," and "Juvenile Corner." But perhaps one of the most exciting activities for stimulating children's interest in literature and writing was the newspaper's essay contest, cosponsored by the Hall Library. The staff chose one topic, such as "What Negro Would I Most Like to Emulate and Why," to encourage children to read about black history. Observing that most children wrote about Joe Louis, Duke Ellington, and Ethel Waters, the *Bee*'s editors suggested as topics other blacks famous in the arts, literature, education, and science. Although the essay winner in 1945 wrote about Booker T. Washington, second and third prizes went to es-says about two women: soprano Marian Anderson and Maudelle Bousfield, the first black female school principal in Chicago and a prominent Chicago Urban League (CUL) board member.[76]

Another noteworthy literary undertaking was the *Negro Story Magazine.* Like the *Chicago Sunday Bee,* the journal was staffed mostly by women, including editor Alice C. Browning, a Chicago school teacher; Fern Gayden, a social work supervisor; and associate editor, Myrtle Sengestacke, sister of John Sengestacke, publisher of the *Chicago Defender.* But in order to give the magazine more prestige, the editors chose Langston Hughes, Chester Himes, and Ralph Ellison as advisors. Since the magazine's purpose was also to encourage new writers, these established authors were invaluable in helping to select works to be published, offering young writers feedback, and judging entries for the magazine's poetry and short story contests.[77] Further, aspiring writers could read and study the new and reprinted works by these three authors, published frequently in the magazine.

Although the magazine was short-lived, from 1944 to 1946, it published notable and new talents, including Gwendolyn Brooks (who won one of their poetry contests), Margaret Goss Burroughs, Grace Tompkins, Margaret Cunningham, Marion Perkins, Frank Marshall Davis, Margaret Walker, and Owen Dodson. Given its inception during the war, we should not be surprised that some of the stories and poems focused on the war experiences of black soldiers and WACs, and so included themes of discrimination and the tragedy of dying without obtaining full freedom. The editors, though, were not exclusive in publishing only black authors. One criterion for selection was that works should reflect "the struggle of the Negro for full integration into American life."[78] As such, there were some writings by white authors, including students of Jack Conroy, who wrote sensitively about black characters and themes. As the editors explained, there were the "Eleanor Roosevelts" and the "Lillian Smiths" who also fought against racism.[79]

To some extent, the magazine functioned as a kind of writers' workshop. Certainly the magazine created a community of young writers who took writing seriously and engaged in critique. Because the editors stressed the importance of writing a well-crafted story, not "propagandiz[ing]," the readers probably studied other writers' techniques.[80] Not surprisingly, because the editors encouraged new writers, the quality of selections was uneven. One might even question whether the editors' desire to publish writing about the black struggle compromised the quality of submissions. Nonetheless, selections by Brooks, Burroughs, and Walker did show how important such publishing initiatives were, especially since the editors encouraged experimentation. Further, the magazine contributed to the postwar momentum of challenging restrictions on blacks at home while freedom overseas was celebrated. The magazine's experimentation and protests were largely possible because of the entrepreneurial and creative spirit of its editors.

The editors probably realized that the magazine could be kept afloat only in the short term. As noted earlier, a number of black writers and Chicago community leaders financially supported *Negro Story Magazine.* But there were many other initiatives and institutions that relied upon community patronage, especially after the war. To some extent, the magazine competed with other black literary and artistic journals, including *Opportunity, The Crisis,* and *Negro Digest.* But *Negro Story Magazine* had a part-time staff who also worked full-time jobs. The situation worsened when one of the editors, Fern Gayden, had to give up her editorship because of her other obligations. Co-editor Alice Browning then was drawn to another publication venture, which may have taken some time away from *Negro Story Magazine.* In the summer of 1945, the Negro Story Press published the first issue of a children's magazine, *Child Play.* Although Browning included poetry and artwork from her students at Forestville Elementary School, she also included didactic pieces, for example, how to behave in a theater or museum.[81] That magazine, too, lasted only a short while. What Browning and the staff probably realized was that there was an abundance of promising work to be published but not enough resources to do so.

The SSCAC

The idea for the SSCAC began with five women in 1938. Pauline Kligh Reed had invited four friends—Frankie Singleton, Susan Morris, Marie Moore, and Grace Carter Cole—to meet Peter Pollack, owner of a downtown art gallery and the Illinois Director of the FAP. As Reed later explained, "Contrary to the custom at that time, we didn't ask any other women to join us."[82] But clearly other women assisted in the center's development. Irene McCoy Gaines attended the organizational meetings and gave her full endorsement. She, along with Margaret Goss Burroughs, Mrs. Gonzelle Motts, Pauline Jackson Lawrence, and K. Marie Moore became members of the first board of directors. Similar to the PCH's staff, most of the SSCAC's officers were professional women. President Pauline Kligh Reed was a social worker; second vice-president, Ethel Hilliard, was a schoolteacher, also known for her fund-raising skills with the Chicago NAACP. Margaret Goss Burroughs, an art teacher with recent degrees from the Chicago Normal College and the Chicago Art Institute, became the center's recording secretary and one of the "house" artists.[83]

The founders also realized the importance of including prominent men in the center's organization. As Reed recalled, "We went around the room and named twelve men each—sixty men—who together comprised a spectrum of the South Side society at that time."[84] One of those men was Golden Darby, owner of an insurance company and chair of the board of directors of the South Side Settlement House (SSSH). The settlement, among its other activities, had offered art classes attended by Burroughs and other aspiring young black artists. When Darby spearheaded the idea of a young artists' contest, with monetary awards and certificates, Burroughs was one of many contestants.[85]

Soon thereafter, the SSCAC became formally organized and chartered. From 1938 to 1939, the association held its meetings at the CUL's office and a local funeral parlor. But what the association really wanted was its own facility. In an effort to locate a place for the center, art teacher Ethel Mae Nolan chaired a committee to launch a "mile of dimes campaign." A cadre of mostly female volunteers collected dimes on street corners.[86] Their efforts paid off. In 1939, an organizing committee, of which Burroughs was a member, purchased the brownstone home of Charles Comiskey on South Michigan Avenue. This became the home of the SSCAC, which still stands today. When the FAP earmarked Chicago's southside for an art center in 1941, the SSCAC received an unexpected financial windfall.[87]

The FAP's sponsorship proved to be a mixed blessing. It underwrote the SSCAC's teaching and administrative staff. The government agency's philosophy, at least on paper, was similar to the staff's. The SSCAC staff had already embraced the FAP's central tenet, that art centers "return art to the people—to all the people."[88] The FAP's stipulation that art centers educate community members through free exhibits, lectures and films, classes, workshops, and cultural events was already in place at the SSCAC. Similarly, the SSCAC's facilities were available to other community groups for meetings. Finally, the FAP's intention to financially "jumpstart" community centers in hopes that communities would seek local support had already happened. The prodigious fundraising activities of the center's committees and the subsequent purchase of the brownstone demonstrated that the center could hold its own.[89]

As early as 1938, a fundraising tradition had been organized. The Beaux Arts Balls, or the Artists and Models Ball as it was more commonly called, was usually held at the Savoy Ballroom, and each year there were different themes, dances, music, and prizes. In 1939, the ball featured a mural by Charles White, with a stage setting by Margaret Goss Burroughs. Prominent community women chaired the ball's committees, such as Annabel Carey Prescott, an assistant principal and sister of Archibald Carey, Jr. Her work combined with other women's efforts were especially critical in 1942 when federal monies had expired. That year, the committee women enlisted the support of Marva Trotter Louis, wife of boxing champion Joe Louis, who coproduced the ball. The staff also started a membership drive, headed by Ora Green Morrow, a well-respected schoolteacher who had studied at the Art Institute, an art historian, and later a founder and president of the center's Book Circle.[90]

Burroughs also organized the Parnassains, a group of young black women concerned with cultivating black culture, especially at the SSCAC. Through the unflagging work of its members—Fern Gayden, Dorothy Sutton, Dorothy Malory Jones, Margaret Cunningham, and Violet Moten Foster—the group sponsored art, poetry, dance, and music programs. Keenly interested in finding new talent, they encouraged young artists to apply for sponsorship through Cunningham, the group's secretary. With the assistance of advisors Langston Hughes and painter Charles White, the group was able to present promising works by young artists.[91] But the Parnassains were not the only group of young women to sponsor cultural programs at the SSCAC. Black sororities were also active. For example, the Phi Delta Kappa Sorority hosted the opening of an art exhibit of Burroughs's paintings; the Sigma Gamma Rho Sorority cosponsored an exhibit of sculptures by Richmond Barthe.[92]

The center's directors and committee leaders were women, and many of its teachers were also women. Margaret Goss Burroughs, along with other artists, taught life drawing, commercial art, and conducted an artists' workshop. Gwendolyn Brooks taught poetry classes. Helen Forman, in charge of the children's art classes, frequently exhibited her students' work at the center. In part, this was to encourage parents' and the public's support of the center. This strategy was critically important after the war years, when federal Lanham Funds for nurseries expired and community centers pressed Chicago and Illinois officials to support preschool care.[93] This strategy was also effective since nearly four-fifths of the center's patrons were children. Monthly cultural programs for children had expanded to include a theater that presented recitations by poets, including Langston Hughes. Literature programs also featured writings by Charlemae Rollins and other children's authors.[94]

But the center did not only serve children. Because so few downtown art galleries exhibited black artists' works, before the opening of the center blacks had few opportunities to showcase their work, except at the southside YMCA or in church basements. Within a short time, the SSCAC became nationally known for its exhibits, many of which were organized by SSCAC committee members Pauline Kligh Reed, Margaret Goss Burroughs, and Fern Gayden. One was an exhibit and discussion of artwork by Rex Gorleigh, who had become the SSCAC's director in 1944.[95] Gorleigh had studied art in Chicago, New York City, Berlin, and Paris. He taught art at Harlem's YMCA and Utopia Neighborhood House, and later at Charlotte Hawkins Brown's Palmer Memorial Institute in Greensboro, North Carolina. An exhibit of Seman Hughie Lee Smith's paintings was also coordinated by the SSCAC committee, along with the Friends of the Armed Forces, a group of women recently organized to give encouragement and support to black soldiers through the promotion of art and culture. Mary E. Smith, an art teacher and staff member at the SPY, had donated his works to the SSCAC. The committee also helped to sponsor an art show of works by Margaret Goss Burroughs, including her silk-screen of Sojourner Truth that was later exhibited at the Library of Congress.[96]

One purpose of these wartime exhibits was to express blacks' dignity and accomplishments through black art. Margaret Burroughs was adamant that "racial solidarity" could only be achieved through race pride. Echoing Carter G. Woodson, she emphasized that children needed to learn black history, not "white history, white invention, white art."[97] As such, she believed that black art was one means of advancing racial pride. Alain Locke, too, thought that racial pride was necessary so that black artists could build on the "racial idiom of expression."[98] Their advancement of these ideas held special significance during the war years. As Burroughs stressed: "Now, in this critical war time period, we have our own plans for defense: a plan in defense of culture."[99]

Similarly, Locke and Burroughs looked to African art to inspire black artists and to help dispel notions of black inferiority. In fact, Locke had reminded white audiences of how modernist European art had drawn from African sculpture.[100] Both Locke and Burroughs played a critical role in the SSCAC's 1944 exhibit of African masks, carvings, horns, drums, weavings, and sculptures from Ethiopia, Sudan, the Ivory Coast, and Benin. Locke not only wrote the foreword for the exhibit's brochure but also served on the SSCAC's board of directors. Burroughs and other staff members assisted in securing the artwork from the Chicago Art Institute and other museums.[101]

During the postwar years, when FAP funds were no longer available, the SSCAC continued to exhibit black artists. One exhibit featured the paintings of William Carter and Virgin Island artist Ramon Gabriel, who then taught at the SSCAC. Another exhibit showcased book illustrations by Elton Fax, including those done for Shirley Graham's children's book, *George Washington Carver.* Photographs by Gordon Parks, the well-known black photographer of the Farm Security Administration, were also displayed. And the SSCAC, in conjunction with the Harmon Foundation, sponsored a portrait exhibit of twenty-seven "outstanding" black Americans, including Marian Anderson, Bethune, Carver, Du Bois, Jessie Fauset, Charles Houston, and Locke. The exhibit opened with invited speaker Locke, followed by speakers Jeanette Triplett Jones, then the dean of girls at DuSable High School; famous black artist Edouard Scott; and former SSCAC director Pollack, then on staff at the Chicago Art Institute. Again, a women's committee—with Henrietta Pelkey, Pauline Kligh Reed, Madeline Morgan, and Burroughs—helped to set up the exhibit.[102]

But the SSCAC staff did not only focus on black American and African art. They also turned their attention to the needs of the black community, especially those in public housing. The children's theater performed one-act plays at the Wells Community Center. Eve Cunningham, the theater's director (and considered by many to be a fine actress), was largely responsible for this project. Perhaps the children's theater reflected postwar concerns about pre-delinquency and delinquency, evident in one 1946 SSCAC flyer that advertised the arts as a sure way to readjust delinquent and problem children. This rhetoric, however, may also have been used to secure funding from Chicago philanthropies. That same year, various women's groups had met at the SSCAC for a "frappe sip" to raise scholarships for two public schools. Again, the purpose of the scholarship and apprenticeship programs was to prevent delinquency.[103]

In 1946, the SSCAC also sponsored an exhibit for kitchenette and public housing residents on how to remake a rental room into a "beautiful apartment." Here, the staff focused on the use of space and selection of furniture, with displays of wallpaper, floor coverings, curtains, and household accessories for persons of "average income." The SSCAC gave prizes and certificates from furniture stores to those residents with the most innovative décor. The Welfare Council of Metropolitan Chicago's endorsement of the SSCAC that year perhaps affected the SSCAC's activities, for it meant that the SSCAC was eligible for city funding.[104] But the SSCAC staff also realized that their neighborhood was becoming increasingly more overcrowded and impoverished.

Despite the neighborhood's poverty, the SSCAC was able to remain a vibrant institution through the 1950s because of the perseverance and organizational skills of Wilhemina Blanks, Fern Gayden, Ida Mae Cress, Grace Thompson, Margaret Goss Burroughs, and many other women. Here, it is instructive to return to the FAP to determine whether it was actually a "godsend" to the SSCAC and to examine how the SSCAC remained a strong community institution. To be expected, there were conflicts between artists and the board of directors during the FAP's sponsorship, in part because artists were excluded from policymaking and in part because of the unequal division of labor. In Burroughs's estimation, it was the artists who kept the SSCAC afloat through their hard work. Another source of tension, according to artist Bernard Goss, was white director Pollack, who some artists found patronizing.[105]

There may also have been ideological differences between the FAP and the SSCAC. The FAP-sponsored centers were to nurture both the "fine arts" and the "socially useful arts," the latter referring to crafts and manual arts.[106] There is little evidence, though, that the SSCAC engaged in the latter, although there were good reasons for not doing so. First, there was a dire need for community art centers that showcased prominent black and African artists' work. Given the artistic and professional training of the women affiliated with the center, it was not surprising that they would direct their efforts accordingly. Second, given the historical connections between artisan work and slavery, the center may have chosen not to foster manual arts. This is not to suggest that black artists and writers did not collapse distinctions between "high" and "folk" art. As noted, one of the hallmarks of the Chicago Black Renaissance was its celebration of African motifs and traditions but not the legacy of slavery. Lastly, if art centers were to be grounded in the community, as the FAP insisted, then the SSCAC staff may have concluded the center, not a government agency, should decide what programs and activities best met community needs.

Notwithstanding these arguments, issues of representation probably confounded competing ideas of community. In the end, one must ask of any community institution: Who is the "community"? In the case of the SSCAC, there were at least three communities: patrons, artists, and viewers who promoted black American and African art; schoolchildren who enrolled in SSCAC classes and attended other activities; and the residents of public housing. The SSCAC staff realized that there were diverse needs within the black community and, as such, may not have collapsed "community" into one entity. Ideologically and pragmatically, the staff and its volunteers supported a multifaceted, activist approach through the promotion of "cultural democracy," through service to poorer residents, and through the cosponsorship of programs and activities with other black organizations.

Conclusion

There is no doubt that Chicago was one of black America's major cultural centers during the 1930s, 1940s, and 1950s. Many major black writers worked together on WPA projects, established writers' groups, and read and discussed their works before enthusiastic audiences at the Hall Library and other community institutions. Writers also published their writings in *Negro Story Magazine* and the *Chicago Sunday Bee,* and the *Chicago Defender* published reviews of their books. Similarly, Chicago had a strong little theater movement, although its cultural politics were often controversial. Nonetheless, Dunham, Lewis, and Graham promoted a pan-African consciousness, as well as an awareness of social problems that most blacks faced. There was also a formidable black museum, the SSCAC, which showcased both black American and African art.

As with any discussion of the arts, one must ask, for whom do the arts exist? Who patronized Black theater, art, and poetry in Chicago? Who supported the city's black cultural institutions? Were the expressive arts "democratic" and, if so, in what sense? Let us first look at the question of democracy at the national level. Certainly, the WPA gave black writers employment and opportunity for creative endeavors. But employment with the WPA was usually short-lived and unstable. Further, if we look at the FWP nationally, few blacks were employed: only 106 of 4,500 workers as of 1937.[107] One could hardly call this democratic. Nonetheless, many black writers and artists continued to fight for social justice during and after the war, following Wright's advice that writers should "attack" political and social problems.[108] Yet they, like other black citizens, faced discrimination in housing and access to mainstream social and health facilities.

But what took place within the Chicago black community? Were the institutions that supported literature and the arts democratic? In the ideological sense, certainly. Many black writers and artists presented a cultural front to promote a collective black identity. In practice, many black writers and artists drew from the southside community's multitudinous voices and perspectives. As such, they attempted to both present and represent the social strata and differences within the black and white communities. Indeed, many of their portrayals are veritable and evocative, if not "democratic."

If we look to the patronage of the expressive arts, however, we must question the extent to which a black collective participated. Instead, most of the persons who supported the cultural institutions were college-educated and professional. Regardless, they worked together to create opportunities for the community at large: art exhibits, authors' readings, and reading clubs. Accordingly, the SSCAC in particular created programs to improve the material and aesthetic conditions of public residents' lives. For example, Burroughs and the actors of "Destination Freedom" spoke at a radio listeners' coffee cooler held at the Wells Homes' community center in 1949, and many of the Wells Homes residents probably attended.[109] But did they attend the African art exhibit at the SSCAC or a theater production at the downtown Princess Theatre? Did they read Brooks's poetry or Wright's novels? If so, what would they have thought of Brooks's portrayals of Bronzeville women or of Wright's character Bigger? Would they have nodded and thought, this is what we have known? More likely than not, they had questioned, like the characters in Big White Fog, what they had lost and gained in their arrival to Chicago. But more likely than not, they had not seen the play.

4

Schools as Sites of Activism

Black Schools' Problems

Black schools on Chicago's southside experienced a number of problems from 1930 to 1960, among them segregation, overcrowding, half-day sessions, and dilapidated buildings. Certainly these problems were interrelated. Black migration after World War I resulted in segregated schools, which were so overcrowded by 1930 that black students could only attend schools for half-day sessions. Segregation also resulted in limited employment opportunities for black teachers, including restricted advancement to administrative positions, except in black schools. Black schoolteachers, clubwomen, and other activists addressed these issues through multiple organizations and strategies. The Chicago and Northern District Association of Colored Women (CNDA), the Chicago Urban League (CUL), the Chicago Council of Negro Organizations (CCNO), the PTAs, and various interracial organizations protested, petitioned, and boycotted to effect change within the schools. Teachers especially played a large role by creating meaningful curricula in black history, literature, and music, and they also devised human relations courses for teachers. One group of teachers started the first private, nonsectarian black school in the country, the Howalton School.

Protests by Black Organizations

Black migration, as well as limited construction of school buildings, resulted in overcrowding in many of Chicago's black schools from the 1930s through the 1950s. From 1929 to 1943, student enrollment in twenty-seven of the south-side schools had increased by 88 percent. Nearly one-third of the schools' new students had recently migrated from Mississippi and Arkansas. The increased enrollment meant that, as of 1941, classrooms had a high student-per-teacher ratio, an average of forty-one students per teacher.[1] James McCahey, then-president of the Chicago Board of Education, countered that black Chicago schools fared much better than those in the South. But he skirted the issue of overcrowding, referring instead to better-prepared teachers and a higher expenditure per black student in Chicago. What he did not compare were differences in expenditures between Chicago's white and black schools: those schools attended by mostly white students had budgets that were 12 percent larger than those of black schools.[2]

School administrators attempted to resolve overcrowding through double shifts, which meant that students attended school only for half days. Of the fifty-five elementary "double schools" in 1939, thirteen were in black communities and affected nearly 25,000 students.[3] The *Chicago Defender* protested the situation: "78% of the Negro children spend 40% less time in school than do children outside of the colored communities in Chicago." A. L. Foster, then-president of the CUL, echoed this concern: "My own boy, in the seventh grade, has never gone to school a full day."[4] The board of education considered redistricting so that black children could attend white schools in adjoining areas. But restrictive covenant associations blocked these initiatives.[5]

As overcrowding persisted through the 1940s, the black community continued to protest. In 1941, the CUL organized a tour of black schools to educate the community about overcrowding and its attendant problems. Concerned citizens visited Douglas Elementary School, which had a student body of 2,800, although it was built for only 1,800 students. They also went to Wendell Phillips High School, which enrolled 3,600 students, more than double its capacity. This was especially infuriating to black citizens since there were 20,000 empty seats in non-black schools. But, again, because of restrictive covenant associations, black children could not transfer to these schools.[6] Likewise, the CCNO joined in protesting double shifts, with Lillian Summers and Eva Wells heading these efforts. The Chicago Woman's Club, with mostly white members, coordinated a letter-writing campaign with the CCNO. The CNDA joined in as well, calling for an end to double shifts at a hearing on budgets at the board of education. The Wellstown Parents' Civic Organization of the Ida B. Wells Homes also collected three thousand signatures for a petition that requested additions to schools or black students' transfers to white schools.[7]

Concerned organizations also advocated for black representation on the school board. Irene Moore, chair of the CNDA's Schools Committee in 1937, circulated a petition to place a black member on the board. In the early 1940s, Dr. Midian Bousfield was appointed to the board; he was the husband of Maudelle Bousfield (the first black female school principal in the Chicago public schools). However, he did not represent the black community but instead sided with white board members.[8] When Gaines ran for the Illinois Senate in 1940, she advocated for a black school board member. Her platform included "a seat and a full school day for every child."[9] Although she did not win the election, she would later receive an endorsement from labor unions and also support for appointment to the school board from black and interracial organizations. Yet she would not be selected.[10]

Another problem that contributed to overcrowding was that black schools were generally older than white ones. But the term "white" demands qualification. As Diane Pinderhughes has noted, schools in some immigrant neighborhoods, especially Italian American and Polish American areas, were in more disrepair than black schools.[11] Similar to immigrant families in prior decades, many black migrant families had moved to older neighborhoods such as the Douglas neighborhood, which had dilapidated housing and school buildings. The school board tried to alleviate overcrowding by building new schools and portable structures. In 1931, construction of the new Wendell Phillips High School (renamed DuSable) started. But money was tight during the Depression, and the board of education ran out of money. Fortunately, the Public Works Administration loaned the board money to complete the building. However, right before the new school's dedication, a fire destroyed the gym, assembly hall, and lunchroom at the old Wendell Phillips High School. Because there was no money left for repairs, students had to use the Wabash YMCA for their physical education classes. In October 1936, black leaders organized a mass meeting to protest the older high school's condition and threatened to take legal action against the board of education. The board promised to make repairs, although it is not clear if it did.[12]

DuSable High School was the only school built for black students between 1934 and 1936, despite the black community's advocacy for others. During those years, only seven of the designated thirty-six school-building projects were in black neighborhoods. Of those, four were additions to older schools. Between 1935 and 1944, however, four new black schools other than DuSable were built: the Dunbar Vocational School and the Gillespie, Phillips, and Fuller elementary schools. Yet many black schools still remained overcrowded. The school board continued to use portable structures to alleviate these conditions. Some parents, though, preferred double sessions to the hot and unhealthy "portables."[13]

There were a number of black and interracial organizations that protested these problems. One of the more active groups, which drew from a cross section of teachers and concerned citizens, was the Citizens Save Our Schools Committee (CSC) (later known as the Citizens Schools Committee), organized in 1933. Composed of over a hundred groups, the CSC had little financial backing. Yet its members more than made up for that through volunteerism. Not surprisingly, many of its members also belonged to women's organizations, such as the CNDA, the Chicago Woman's Club, the Woman's City Club, and the Conference of Jewish Women. These women, along with liberal-minded teachers, analyzed each school board publication, questioning, for example, why so few schools had playgrounds or community centers. They also asked why so little money was spent on children's health. Beginning in 1935, they made sure that two or more representatives attended the board of education's budget hearings. As of 1939, they conducted annual surveys of schools in the black communities regarding overcrowded conditions, teacher loads, and social services available.[14]

The Chicago PTAs were also very involved, especially during the 1930s. From 1934 to 1935, many promoted school legislation, wrote letters to their congressmen, cooperated with the CSC, and studied local and state school problems. Yet some prominent black citizens did not think that black parents were as active as they should be in the PTAs. In 1939, clubwoman Maude Roberts George stated that no southside PTAs had more than 10 percent of parents involved.[15] The *Chicago Defender* agreed: "Today in two elementary schools with a combined population of 6,000 pupils, it is impossible to muster [up] 300 members for the parents teacher association."[16] But this was not true of some communities, such as the Ida B. Wells Homes or Lilydale.

Lilydale's PTA, along with other community groups, was active in promoting a new school in its community. School conditions in this working-class community in the far southside were so horrible that students "attended school" in portables. In 1931 the Women's Civic Welfare Club protested the continued use of portables, as did the North End Women's Division of the Nineteenth Ward. Lilydale residents organized a PTA in 1936 to demand that the board of education build a new school. The Citizens Committee of Lilydale, consisting of twenty representatives from neighborhood organizations, including the Women's Community Club, also joined this campaign. Headed by Juanita Grammar, a CNDA member and founder of the Women's

Community Club, and Arcola Philpott, Lilydale's columnist for the *Chicago Defender,* the Citizens Committee complained about the potential fire hazards of portables. Shortly thereafter, there was a fire, and the board of education received a letter threatening more arson if a new school was not built. Not surprisingly, there was another fire. Despite the fire damage, students still had to attend classes in these portables. Lilydale citizens then decided to picket and boycott the portables. Ten days later, the board agreed to build a new school.[17]

Another important focus for the black community was curricular development in black schools, including vocational curricula. In 1942, the building of Dunbar Vocational School was significant for the black community, especially with the concurrent boon in war-related employment for blacks. Dunbar had comprehensive curricula, with a 90 percent placement rate for students in industry. However, when Washburne Trade School relocated to Chicago's southside, Dunbar's future changed. As with the other southside schools, Dunbar and Washburne remained segregated. In fact, less than 1 percent of Washburne's students were black, in large part because of the school's connections to trade unions. Dunbar's budget was also smaller than Washburne's. More specifically, teacher salaries per student were 17 percent lower at Dunbar than at Washburne, and monies for textbooks and supplies at Dunbar were nearly half those at Washburne. Black alderman Dickerson protested that tax dollars should not be spent on Washburne, which practiced discrimination against blacks.[18] However, such practices persisted.

Like Dunbar, other black schools offered government-sponsored vocational classes during the war. For example, Willa Brown taught an aviation mechanics course at Wendell Phillips High School. But administrators at Wendell Phillips canceled her class and others late in 1941. They reasoned that since black students could not get jobs in those fields, there was no reason to offer these classes. Clearly there was a job ceiling for blacks. But as the CSC pointed out, schools did not have to reinforce existing prejudices. If anything, schools could promote economic mobility by providing training to black students.[19]

Conditions of segregation and overcrowding continued at Dunbar and other black schools during and after the war. The board of education's president, James B. McCahey, blamed the problem on black migrants, insisting that the board was not legally responsible for educating children who had "migrated from other states."[20] The black community was indignant. Gaines countered that even though segregation was illegal in Chicago, it remained entrenched. Horace Cayton responded that "the ragged schools of the cotton patches represent McCahey's notion of what the Negro really deserves, the implication being that what they are getting here, no matter what, is much too good for them."[21] Oscar Brown called the black schools in Chicago "a disgrace." Further, he concluded, "They [Chicago schools] are as much segregated as the schools in Savannah, Georgia, or Vicksburg, Mississippi."[22]

De facto school segregation in Chicago had been compounded by restrictive covenants, white flight, school district boundaries, and white students' transfers. As mentioned, most black students could not receive transfers to attend white schools outside of their district. Yet white students could. Even when Chicago public schools superintendent William S. Bogan canceled transfers for high-school students in 1933, white parents ignored him. But when black students were transferred, it was usually to other black schools, as was the case when black freshmen at the predominantly white Morgan Park High School were transferred to Shoop Elementary School in 1937. The CUL criticized the board for promoting segregation, and eventually the CUL succeeded in having the black students transferred back to Morgan Park High School, even though the school's white students went on strike.[23]

An alternative to student transfers was to redraw the boundaries of school districts so that schools would become more integrated. In Gaines's estimation, the board "arbitrarily changed school boundaries to exclude Negro children from so-called 'white' schools." Indeed, it was difficult to know the location of school boundaries, because district maps were not published, at least as of 1945. This left enrollment decisions to the discretion of principals. As such, when a principal at Parkman School (at 51st and Wells streets) told black parents that their children could not go to Parkman but had to transfer to Farren or Coleman schools because of school boundaries, parents had no way of appealing the decision.[24]

The board eventually concurred that redistricting was important to establish more equity in the schools. In the late 1940s, superintendent Herold Hunt worked with University of Chicago sociology professor Louis Wirth and the University of Chicago's Committee on Education, Training, and Research in Race Relations to establish a special technical advisory committee on intergroup relations in the Chicago public schools. This committee worked with parents and the schools from 1947 to 1949, advising them on the redistricting of elementary schools. Consequently, the board changed the boundaries of 102 elementary schools to relieve overcrowding in black elementary schools and to ensure that black children did not have to walk so far to school. Wirth had recommended a similar redistricting plan for Chicago's high schools, but Benjamin Willis, who succeeded Hunt in 1953, disagreed. Willis and the school board argued that since high-school districts were larger, and high-school students formed stronger allegiances to their schools than did elementary-school students, redrawing those boundaries was not feasible.[25]

Although redistricting may have led to less overcrowding in elementary schools, it did little to improve the advancement of black teachers and other black staff. As of 1940, there were only two black principals; only one, Maudelle Bousfield, was female. In 1930, black teacher Ruth Jackson had passed the principal's examination but still was not given an administrative job. This may have been because of "corrupt practices" related to the principals' examination, which the CSC uncovered. When Jackson did receive an appointment later, it was in a black elementary school. Similarly, the schools had few black employees, such as truant officers, playground supervisors, and clerks, even though many blacks had taken the civil service examination required for these positions. Of those blacks who were hired as of 1930, most worked in cleaning and repair; less than 3 percent were professionals.[26]

Certainly black teachers' opportunities were limited during the 1930s and 1940s. During the Depression, some lost their jobs, and others were reassigned to school projects on the southside, the west side, or in Chicago Heights. Still others taught classes in manual training, recreation, drama, and domestic science at social settlements, including the Abraham Lincoln Center (ALC), the Good Shepherd Community Center, and the Wabash YMCA.[27] The situation improved somewhat for black teachers during the 1940s, although Gaines emphasized that black teachers were usually rejected for jobs in white schools. Conversely, the majority of teachers in many predominantly black schools were white. Wendell Phillips High School, for one, had mostly white teachers. Of those white teachers hired at black schools, many were less experienced and took these jobs because they were the only ones available. Many of them would later request transfers to white schools.[28] Indeed, one researcher analyzed transfer applications of over 900 elementary teachers from 1948 to 1949, and the findings showed that most new teachers appointed to poor black schools sought transfers to "better" schools within a short time. When asked for their reasons for requesting transfers, many claimed that they had to travel too far to their jobs.[29]

There is little doubt that some of the white teachers were prejudiced. In one study of sixty white teachers, some spoke disparagingly about the black southside schools and their students. For example, one teacher spoke of the low expectations of black students: "Now in a school like the D—— you're just not expected to complete all that work." Another teacher agreed, "If you want to take it easy and not work too hard, you teach at a school like DuSable or Phillips. If you really are interested in teaching, then you work at one of these better schools." Similarly, "Down at DuSable they just try to keep the kids busy and out of trouble."[30] These attitudes, however, reflected not only racial prejudice but also social-class differences. Robert Hess, later a professor at the University of Chicago, conducted a study and noted the biases of middle-class white teachers toward their lower-class black students. As one teacher from his study stated, "They don't have the right kind of study habits. They can't seem to apply themselves as well. Of course, it's not their fault; they aren't brought up right. After all, the parents in a neighborhood like that aren't really interested."[31]

Most black teachers were keenly aware of the discrimination and other problems faced by black students. One of their solutions was to create meaningful curricula in black history, literature, and the arts. Some teachers, especially concerned that black children were disproportionately overrepresented in "special adjustment" rooms, started their own private elementary school. Other black teachers worked on a human relations curriculum in the 1950s to train teachers in Chicago's public schools to diminish their prejudices.

Black Teachers and School Activism

Perhaps some of the most innovative black curricula in urban schools were developed by a black Chicago elementary teacher, Madeline Morgan. So inspired was Morgan by the Chicago Negro Exposition of 1940 that she decided to create black history units for her students at Emerson Elementary School. The Exposition, though, was only one source for her ideas. Morgan was also active in the DuSable History Club, which was started by a history teacher, Samuel Stratton. Stratton had challenged black Chicagoans to ask why black history should be studied separately when they, too, had contributed to American history.[32] The club met at the George Cleveland Hall Library for lectures, discussions, and research projects. Members also read and discussed teaching materials published for teachers by the Association for the Study of Negro Life and History (ASNLH); some, such as Stratton, had published in the ASNLH's *Negro History Bulletin*.[33] An intercultural education movement was emerging in Chicago and nationally, and it challenged traditional concepts of race and promoted ideas of cultural pluralism, also creating a ripe milieu for Morgan's project.[34]

Morgan's curricula enlarged as she began to work with black teacher Bessie

King, as well as a larger committee of black and white teachers. For eighteen months, the group researched materials at the George Cleveland Hall Library and other Chicago public libraries, the University of Chicago, and the Chicago Art Institute. They submitted the curricula for review to Carter G. Woodson, Melville Herskovits, Mary McCleod Bethune, black historian Charles Wesley, along with black principals and schoolteachers Maudelle Bousfield, Ruth Jackson, Clara Anderson, Samuel Stratton, and Thelma Powell.[35] Bethune replied that the units were a "splendid piece of work."[36] Woodson was even more effusive in his praise: "I have received the units worked out by your committee in Chicago. It impresses me as being a creditable piece of work. It is evidence of a step in the right direction. I congratulate you and the Board of Education of the City of Chicago."[37] Indeed, the curricula reflected Woodson's belief that "the teacher must hold up before them the examples of their own people, who have done things worth while. Those who have no record of what their forebears have accomplished lose the inspiration which comes from the teaching of biography and history."[38]

With Samuel Stratton, Morgan piloted the materials in the Chicago public schools. The teaching units were designed for grades one through eight. The first grade's lessons focused on "community helpers," with a focus on the Pullman porters. In the second grade, students learned about famous blacks such as inventor George Washington Carver, musician Nathaniel Dett, and writer Langston Hughes. Third graders absorbed a more pan-African emphasis, as topics ranged from the Dahomey in West Africa to black life in Chicago. Grades four through six learned more about the history of black explorers, plantation life, and Jean Baptist Pointe DuSable. A focus on early history and contemporary leaders continued in the seventh grade, where students learned about black soldiers in the Revolutionary and Civil wars, as well as about contemporary black leaders W. E. B. Du Bois, Carter G. Woodson, Mary McCleod Bethune, and NAACP leader Weldon Johnson. The curricula culminated in the eighth grade with lessons about Chicago's black community institutions, including the South Side Community Art Center (SSCAC), the George Cleveland Hall Library, the Good Shepherd Community Center, Provident Hospital, and black insurance companies and newspapers. The teachers found that many black and white students were eager to learn about black history. Consequently, under the endorsement of superintendent William Johnson, the Chicago public schools adopted the curricula from 1942 to 1945 and, as such, was the only city to use such a citywide plan.[39]

Needless to say, the Chicago black community and schools were enthusiastic about the curricula. Sheil School offered Morgan's four-lecture series on "The History of the American Negro." The Felsenthal PTA, too, invited Morgan to discuss the "Intercultural Course of the Chicago School System." At a dinner sponsored by the CUL's women's division, Morgan spoke about her curricula. She also discussed intercultural exchanges at the South Parkway YWCA (SPY) for their women's week.[40]

But Morgan and her colleagues were not the only teachers to promote black knowledge and pride. For her history lessons, Roberta Bell made black dolls of famous black Americans George Washington Carver, Bethune, Harriet Tubman, Sojourner Truth, and Frederick Douglass. Similarly, Minnie York Rose, a graduate of Fisk, used her collection of African artifacts in classrooms to foster a pan-African consciousness. Margaret Goss Burroughs, too, taught African and Mexican art to her high-school students.[41]

The institution of Negro History Week, promoted by Woodson and the ASNLH, complemented Morgan's and other teachers' pan-African and black curricula. For example, DuSable High School held a mass meeting in 1946, with the themes of blacks' contributions to winning the war and the increased cooperation of white and black workers in working-class struggles for a living wage. Speakers included Gaines; Claude Lightfoot, president of the Southside Council of the Communist Party; and Sam Parks of the CIO United Packing House Workers. At Coleman Elementary School, the Mu chapter of the Phi Delta Kappa presented its annual Negro History Pageant, with the children reciting Langston Hughes's poems and performing dramas. At Wendell Phillips High School, Arthur Fauset spoke about plans for a black history museum in Chicago. Other speakers included Ismael Florey of the Communist Party, CNDA leader Lavonia Brown, and teacher Samuel Stratton.[42]

Black teachers not only created a new curriculum but also a new school. Howalton School started in the summer of 1946 when Doris Anderson, a black adjustment teacher at Forestville Elementary School, complained to Mayor Kelly about the horrible conditions in black schools but received no response. She and two other teachers—Jane Howe, an art instructor at Englewood High School, and Charlotte Stratton, a teacher at Douglas Elementary School—decided to open a summer school in the Michigan Boulevard Garden Apartments. This was not the first time that the "Rosenwald" Apartments had been selected as a site for an innovative school. During the 1930s, Rose Haas Auschuler, director of Chicago's WPA nurseries, had started a model nursery school for children there.[43] Because many professional blacks resided there, they could afford tuition for private schools and also volunteer in the classrooms.

All three founders had the professional experience and credentials necessary for such an endeavor. Anderson had been a teacher, assistant principal,
and acting principal with the Chicago public schools since 1929. She had
also received her master's degree from Northwestern University. Howe had
studied at the Art Institute. Stratton was an eighth-grade teacher with administrative skills. Howe approached Oneida Cockrell, supervisor of the
nursery school and kindergarten at the Rosenwald Apartments, and Cockrell
agreed to lease nursery space for the summer school, provided her kindergarten children were included. Howe next talked with Robert Taylor, then
manager of the Rosenwald Apartments, who agreed that they could use its
fieldhouse. Clearly the founders were dedicated to this project. They used
their own money to start the school and were later reimbursed from the
tuition. The also had to set up the school every morning because teenagers
used the fieldhouse the night before.[44]

The school opened July 1, 1946, with nineteen children. The following
summer, the school opened again. But the parents approached the founders
about keeping the school open year-round. So Stratton, Howe, and Anderson
decided to add one grade each year, provided each year was successful. In
1947, they started a first grade, with Stratton assuming responsibility as the
school's principal. The other two founders helped with teaching and fund-
raising. One of the student's mothers also volunteered to be the dietician.
The first year, schoolteacher Florence Miller taught French and ballet after
school.[45]

The primary goals of the school were consonant with the ideals of progressive educators: that teachers should nurture the growth and creativity of each
student and that the school should be an integral part of the community. In
fact, the founders often referenced their philosophical approaches by citing
John Dewey and other progressive educators. For one, the school's emphasis
was on the "whole" child, that is, his or her emotional and physical growth,
not just academic achievement. It was imperative that each child develop to
his or her "fullest capacity" through initiative and imagination. But this did
not mean that education was disconnected from everyday living.[46] Quite the
converse. The founders believed that "education [wa]s useful living in action."[47] In the spirit of Dewey's model of hypothesizing, students learned to
be open-minded and critical, evaluating evidence critically and basing arguments on facts. Such an attitude not only fostered critical thinking but also
respect and consideration for others, a requisite for a democratic society.[48]

Teachers, then, were a critical influence in their students' lives. And Howalton teachers took their responsibilities seriously. They met regularly to

discuss their pedagogy and curricula, as well as to attend in-service meetings. In the spirit of progressive education, they experimented with their teaching, eschewing traditional methods. For example, they decided after several years to not give out report cards but instead to issue an informal report on each child's efforts, application of knowledge, and accomplishments. They did not use phonics to teach beginning reading, but instead they used an "emergent literacy" pedagogy in which students learned through the contexts of their everyday environment. In their classrooms, they created learning centers, with an emphasis on the arts, music, and science. In disciplining their students, they focused on each child's personality and social needs. To further reduce student differences, Howalton experimented with an ungraded approach so that children of varying ages would learn together.[49]

Although the first students were from the Rosenwald Apartments, Howalton soon accepted black students from other neighborhoods. The founders were inclusive in other ways as well. Knowing that small classrooms were conducive for teaching gifted children, as well as those with learning problems, they accepted children of all abilities. Some students also had emotional problems, as in the case of one girl who had lived in foster homes most of her life. She attended Howalton until she was "well enough" to return to a public school. As such, Howalton teachers gave those students in need the individual attention and encouragement to succeed there and in their subsequent schooling.[50]

News about Howalton spread, so that soon there was a waiting list. By 1948, the Rosenwald facility had become overcrowded with thirty students, so Howalton moved to the Parkway Community House (PCH). Enrollment increased each year as the founders added successive grades. With forty students enrolled as of 1949, Howalton started a building fund so they could move to larger accommodations. By 1953, Howalton had six grades, and thus it held graduation ceremonies for five sixth-grade students, four of whom continued their schooling at the University of Chicago Laboratory School.[51]

Despite the school's expansion, the founders wanted to keep classrooms small so that teachers could still work with children individually. Further, the social projects and field trips to Chicago's community institutions and museums required that the classrooms remain fairly small. Social projects taught the children the black tradition of "social uplift." For example, they visited Provident Hospital to give toys that they had repaired to sick children. They sang songs for the elderly in a local nursing home. During one Christmas holiday, they helped with Christmas Seal mailings for tuberculosis prevention. Students sent clothing and other items to Ethel Payne, who was stationed in Tokyo as a Red Cross worker in 1952. These activities reflected the school's principle that "isolated learning [wa]s doubtful learning."[52] These projects also gave students a sense of social responsibility to the community. And they gave Howalton further visibility, as did the students' school publications. For example, younger students helped to write a booklet about their school; the older students issued their own publication, "Howalton News," with their own drawings, comics, and writings.[53]

Howalton students also participated in fund-raising projects. Fund-raising was, in fact, imperative since tuition covered only 90 percent of the school's expenses. Although the parents' council and fathers' club were largely responsible for organizing the fund-raising events of annual teas and benefit performances, students assisted. They put together flyers for each fund-raising event and also performed in musical and dance performances and skits. Fund-raising was also imperative, since parents wanted Howalton to add seventh and eighth grades.[54] Again, the founders added one grade at a time, and they also moved to a larger facility, the Blackstone Building, which was owned by John Johnson of *Ebony Magazine.* In 1955, the first eighth-grade class of Howalton graduated.[55]

By 1957, ten years after its founding, Howalton had much to be proud of. Its total school enrollment was 160, which meant that classes still remained small. Students' reading and math scores were higher than those of students in the Chicago public schools, and they were on a par with children attending the University of Chicago Laboratory School. Howalton students engaged in creative and intellectual learning as well as meaningful community projects. In terms of finances, the school was self-supporting through tuition and fund-raisers. Because the school rented facilities, it did not have to pay for building repairs and overhead.[56] In fact, Howalton and its students would thrive until 1986, when the school closed because of the deteriorating neighborhood and partial loss of their funds.

Although Howalton was a success story, the same could not be said for many southside public schools. Through the 1950s many black schools still remained segregated and overcrowded. As such, "intercultural" and "human relations" education became the passwords for school change for some school staff, including Annabel Carey Prescott, a black teacher and principal who would become the Chicago public schools' director for the Bureau of Human Relations from 1956 to 1959. Indeed, since the end of World War II, intercultural education had been one of the primary movements for reducing racial prejudices and tensions. As early as 1945, the University of Chicago, in conjunction with the American Council of Education, had sponsored an intergroup education workshop with a renowned intercultural educator, Hilda Taba. School board members, teachers, librarians, group workers, and other professionals from four cities, including Chicago, had worked on curricular materials, student activities, in-service teacher training, and community projects. Charlemae Rollins, for one, participated in the literature discussion group.[57]

University of Chicago faculty from the Schools of Sociology, Anthropology, and Education assisted in the intergroup education workshops. Black professor Allison Davis lectured, as did Philip Hauser and sociologists Saul Alinsky and Clifford Shaw. Davis in particular emphasized how most schools promoted middle-class values, often at the expense of poorer children. Similarly, he argued, IQ tests were culturally biased. Therefore, poor black children suffered from double discrimination due to racial caste and social class. He elaborated on social-class differences within the black community that likewise affected student learning. Middle-class black children, he argued, used education to fight racism and become race leaders, whereas for poorer black children, aggressive behavior, even violence, gave them prestige. These latter behaviors led to teachers' low expectations of poorer black children. One consequence of teachers' low expectations was that the poorer students' academic performance remained low. Accordingly, Davis recommended that teachers learn more about their students' families and home conditions to reach them academically and socially.[58]

Black school principals and teachers also led discussions at these workshops. Madeline Stratton talked about black history; Maude Stubbings of Lawson Elementary spoke about the educational and social adjustment of the "Negro Boy from the Deep South." Nancy Winfield of Corliss Elementary discussed a study of the Altgeld Gardens Homes, an all-black public housing project on the far southside. Clearly much of the focus of the workshops was on black children. As such, the reading recommendations for the group were apt: *Black Metropolis,* as well as literature by Arna Bontemps, Bucklin Moon, Richard Wright, and Charlemae Rollins.[59]

Although superintendent Hunt believed that intercultural education was important in the public schools for "democratic living," he also advocated for more systemic changes. He believed that the school board should also reflect democratic principles through hiring practices, by redrawing school-district boundaries, and by lowering the teacher-student ratios in overcrowded schools.[60] True to his word, Hunt was instrumental in changing the boundaries for 102 elementary-school districts in 1949. Steadfast in his ideas about "democratic living," he invited community organizations to play a role in decisions relating to redrawing school districts' boundaries and instituting human relations curricula. He also realized that teachers, especially white teachers, needed to be retrained so that they could better reach black students. A key component of retraining would be a human relations curriculum so that teachers could learn new pedagogies and knowledge and, in turn, teach their students about diversity. Accordingly, Hunt asked University of Chicago faculty to work with teachers, community organizations, and other key professionals on these reforms.[61]

The university agreed and formed the Committee on Education, Training, and Research in Race Relations. The committee was composed of faculty members who had been devoted to racial justice, such as Allison Davis, sociologist Louis Wirth, anthropologist Robert Redfield (who had testified at the *Brown vs. Topeka* court case), and education professor Robert Havighurst. One of their first projects was an intercultural relations "inventory" of school programs as of 1950. Indeed, some schools had implemented successful programs; for example, one Chicago school broadcast a radio program that included music, stories, and drama on intercultural topics. There were also student associations, councils, and clubs that "promoted" democracy. School assembly programs likewise focused on intercultural relations, as did some school libraries and athletic departments. Some schools celebrated Brotherhood Week (February 20 to 27), which was organized by the National Conference of Christians and Jews in 1950.[62] Through formal curricula and extracurricular programs, students discussed the critical concepts of race, racism, and democracy.

But when some schools revised their twelfth-grade social science curricula in 1950 to include the topics of urban housing and international relations, some Chicagoans called the material "communistic."[63] One reason was the inclusion of George Counts's publication, "I Want to Be Like Stalin," in which he talked about the falsehoods told to Russians about America. Another reason was that urban housing at the time was an especially sensitive topic to many white Chicagoans because of urban renewal, the integration of public housing, and the exclusionary practices of restrictive covenant associations. To further complicate matters, there were published reports that Chicago was a "hotbed" for communist teachers. In fact, some Chicago public schoolteachers, including black teachers, had been asked to sign loyalty oaths.[64]

Nonetheless, Hunt and the University of Chicago faculty realized that the Chicago schools needed someone to coordinate the schools' intercultural education curricula, as well as to present to the public a rationale for their materials. Hunt asked the Committee on Education, Training, and Research in Race Relations to help establish qualifications necessary for such a position. Committee members met with diverse community organizations, such as the Anti-Defamation League, the YMCA, and the Chicago branch of the National Council of Negro Women. All involved decided that the coordinator should have experience with social service agencies, should understand school-community relationships, and should have teaching and administrative experiences.[65]

In 1950, Herold Hunt appointed a white teacher and political activist, Mary Herrick, as the schools' director of human relations. Herrick was a good choice. A teacher at Wendell Phillips High School since 1928, she had been concerned about the conditions of black schools and its staff. This prompted her to write a master's thesis in 1931 on black employees in the Chicago public schools. Two years later, Herrick helped to found the CSC; she also helped to organize a rally of 27,000 teachers, parents, and citizens at the Chicago stadium to protest reductions in school funds. During the 1940s, she taught at DuSable High School and also continued her activism with the CSC. In 1944, when the CSC held a mass meeting to protest the poll tax at Canaan Baptist Church, Herrick was one of the key speakers. Even while she was director of human relations, she continued to teach and, in fact, coordinated exchanges between DuSable and white schools. In 1956, she retired from the Chicago public schools to work with a national teacher organization.[66]

Right in the middle of Herrick's directorship, superintendent Hunt was accused of being a communist. The *Chicago Tribune* highlighted his education at Columbia University, then considered a hotbed of radicalism. But his integrationist stand probably made him unpopular with whites as well. He was ousted in 1953 and replaced by Benjamin Willis. That year, Prescott began her doctoral studies at Columbia, where she participated in intercultural programs and wrote a dissertation based upon her intercultural experiences while assistant principal at Cregier High School. She returned to Chicago in 1956, and Willis appointed her director of the bureau of human relations for the Chicago public schools.[67]

Since the onset of Willis's superintendency, conditions in black schools had worsened. Black and white activists alike accused Willis and the school board of intentionally enforcing segregation, resulting in continued overcrowding. Willis attempted to reduce overcrowding by installing portables. The black community was indignant and organized a sit-in to protest these "Willis wagons."[68] The Chicago NAACP and other Chicago civil rights groups especially pressed Willis about Bright School, near Trumbull Park Homes. Was it going to be integrated, they asked? And if so, how would he ensure the fair treatment of black students there? In this case, Willis was conciliatory. Black students were admitted the following year and teachers participated in training sessions.[69]

Clearly, there was a need for someone other than Willis to take a leadership role in the Chicago public schools. That person was Prescott, a respected activist and professional. She had come from a prominent black family: her father, Archibald Carey, was an A.M.E. bishop; her brother, Archibald Carey Jr., was a prominent lawyer who served on Chicago's city council. Prescott, too, was known by the black community and interracial organizations for her work in the schools. She had been a teacher at Doolittle Elementary School and Wendell Phillips High School, as well as an assistant principal at DuSable High School, Medill High School, and at the Cregier branch of Crane Technical High School in 1948. At Cregier, a west-side school known for its interethnic conflicts, she had successfully integrated black, Mexican, and Italian students through intercultural curricula. Working with the Committee on Education, Training, and Research in Race Relations and superintendent Hunt, she had also organized intercultural community and teacher workshops, as well as worked on a human relations handbook for Chicago public schools staff.[70]

But there may have been another reason, other than Prescott's qualifications, that Willis, an accused segregationist, hired her. He may have done so to head off the intense pressure from Chicago civil rights organizations. Many of these groups had been involved in the institution of human relations programs under superintendent Hunt and wanted these programs to continue. More than likely, these groups recommended Prescott, given her outstanding record and credentials. Although Willis may have thought of Prescott's position as token, she clearly did not. Prescott realized that teacher training was necessary to successfully "integrate" black and white students in the classroom. She also wanted to halt the practice of white teachers transferring out of black schools. She had, in fact, recommended that white teachers be given credit for taking jobs in "high transiency" schools.[71] Accordingly, under Prescott's direction the Chicago public schools developed a four-semester human relations training course for teachers, offered in cooperation with the Chicago Teachers College. In 1957, 138 teachers participated; the following year, 200 did. Teachers were not given textbook assignments but instead were asked to go out into the neighborhoods where their students lived. There they conducted surveys of housing, recreational facilities, and other community institutions. Teachers interviewed their students' parents as well as the staff at social settlements and recreational facilities. Teachers then returned to the classroom for the second section of the course, "Psychological Insights." There, they discussed their findings, with attention to specific problems faced by their black students.[72]

Next, the teachers taught one another. Prescott encouraged those teachers and principals who had implemented successful human relations projects in their classrooms and schools to share their experiences with other teachers. Indeed, there were innovative projects in some schools, where white and black high-school classes met to discuss racial issues. One suburban school visited a school on the near west side, attended by mostly Mexican and Puerto Rican children. Prescott praised these projects, which she thought led to intergroup understanding. Further, she emphasized, children from less privileged areas were given opportunities to "test" their ideas against others and to discover that they were "not inferior." Teachers, too, learned that the material conditions of many black students' lives were quite different from their own.[73]

Clearly, Prescott was not an administrator who remained in her office and shuffled papers. Adamant that a human relations approach led to democracy, she worked directly with teachers to effect change in and out of the classrooms. She admonished that "the interest and energy of the classroom teacher must be awakened and enlisted in the cause of human relations."[74] The end result, she hoped, was that teachers would understand and communicate with their students and see them not just as students but as human beings.

Although Prescott believed that schools could be sites of democracy, she was only able to achieve so much. Like Hunt, Prescott was pushed out of her position in 1959, although she continued to work with community organizations on human relations and social justice issues. In the meantime, most Chicago black schools remained overcrowded and segregated. To appease the black community, the mayor appointed Loraine Green (wife of Judge Wendell Green) to the school board, at that time the only black member. The Chicago NAACP and the CUL disapproved strongly of her appointment because she had voted against a referendum that would have made it mandatory for high schools to redraw their boundaries.[75] The *Chicago Defender*'s editor was even more scathing in his attack when Green was reappointed to the school board several years later: "Mrs. Green's attitude leaves no alternative to the distasteful belief that people on the bottom rungs of the economic and social ladder have a monopoly on Uncle Tomism."[76]

By the early 1960s, the conditions of Chicago's black schools had so worsened that several black parents filed a lawsuit against the Chicago board of education, claiming that segregated schools violated the Fourteenth Amendment. Community activism stepped up, and Willis was eventually ousted. Some scholars have viewed these 1960s school protests as the high tide of activism in Chicago. Concurrently, others have dismissed the previous decades as conservative.[77] Michael Homel, for one, has concluded that black activism had "failed" during the 1930s because blacks had not taken a hard stand on integration but were more interested in improving existing conditions.[78] Similarly, Diane Pinderhughes has argued that the black community was successful with school issues only when they were in agreement with Chicago politicians and the school board.[79] What she did not include in her analysis were the initiatives of Morgan, the Howalton school founders, and Prescott. However, both observers are correct on one very critical point: Chicago's powerful political machinery, along with a recalcitrant school board and influential white segregationists, kept many black schools' conditions inferior. Nonetheless, many black teachers—with support from community and interracial organizations—instituted curricular and pedagogical changes that reflected black intellectuality and pride.

Irene McCoy Gaines with Eleanor Roosevelt, Chicago, Ill., 1930s. Reprinted by
permission of the Chicago Historical Society (ICHi-37508).

National guests at the Mary Church Terrell Luncheon, the Headquarters Open House, and the Frederick Douglass Committee, 1952. Irene McCoy Gaines is third from the left, first row. Reprinted by permission of the Chicago Historical Society (ICHi-37509).

Girls sewing at the South Parkway YWCA, 1932. Reprinted with permission from the YWCA of Metropolitan Chicago (YWCA neg. 58), Special Collections, University Library, University of Illinois at Chicago.

Children playing at the Abraham Lincoln Center's nursery, late 1930s. Reprinted with permission from the Rose Auschuler Papers (RA photo B154), Special Collections, University Library, University of Illinois at Chicago.

Negro History Week, c. 1944. Vivian Harsh is standing on the left; Charlemae
Rollins is sitting on the right. From the George Cleveland Hall Branch Library
Archives, neg. 72. Reprinted by permission of the Vivian G. Harsh Center
for the Study of Afro-American History and Literature, Chicago Public Library.

Opening day at the George Cleveland Hall Library, the Children's Room, January 22, 1932. From the George Cleveland Hall Branch Library Archives, neg. 79. Reprinted by permission of the Vivian G. Harsh Center for the Study of Afro-American History and Literature, the Carter G. Woodson Regional Library, Chicago.

The women's reading group at the George Cleveland Hall Library, 1940; Vivian Harsh is on the left, Charlemae Rollins on the right. From the George Cleveland Hall Branch Library Archives, neg. 033. Reprinted by permission of the Vivian G. Harsh Center for the Study of Afro-American History and Literature, the Carter G. Woodson Regional Library, Chicago.

Poet Margaret Walker, member of the Southside Writers Group in Chicago and winner of the Yale Younger Poets Award for her book, *For My People,* c. 1942. From the George Cleveland Hall Branch Library Archives, neg. 121. Reprinted by permission of the Vivian G. Harsh Center for the Study of Afro-American History and Literature, the Carter G. Woodson Regional Library, Chicago.

Poets Gwendolyn Brooks and Langston Hughes. From the George Cleveland Hall Branch Library Archives, neg. 101. Reprinted by permission of the Vivian G. Harsh Center for the Study of Afro-American History and Literature, the Carter G. Woodson Regional Library, Chicago.

The Association for the Study of Negro Life and History Committee, 1936. Carter G. Woodson, eminent historian and founder of the organization, is seated at the far left, first row; Vivian Harsh is seated third from the left, first row. Claude Barnett, editor of the Negro Associated Press, is seated on the far right, first row. Maude Roberts George, known musician and club woman, is standing in the second row. From the George Cleveland Hall Branch Library Archives, neg. 109. Reprinted by permission of the Vivian G. Harsh Center for the Study of Afro-American History and Literature, the Carter G. Woodson Regional Library, Chicago.

Partial Board of Directors of Howalton School, n.d., from the Howalton School
Papers, neg. 016. Reprinted by permission of the Vivian G. Harsh Center for the Study
of Afro-American History and Literature, the Carter G. Woodson Regional Library,
Chicago.

Group photograph of educators involved in the writing and promotion of a black-centered curriculum in the Chicago Public Schools, 1942–45. *Left to right:* Elinor McCullom, principal; Madeline Morgan, teacher; Dr. William Johnson, superintendent of the Chicago Public Schools; and Bessie King, teacher. From the Madeline Stratton Morris Papers, neg. 043. Reprinted by permission of the Vivian G. Harsh Center for the Study of Afro-American History and Literature, the Carter G. Woodson Regional Library, Chicago.

Olive Diggs, editor of the *Chicago Sunday Bee* and Links member, 1950s. From the Links, Inc., Chicago Chapter Papers, neg. 652. Reprinted by permission of the Vivian G. Harsh Center for the Study of Afro-American History and Literature, the Carter G. Woodson Regional Library, Chicago.

The Chicago chapter of the Links, founders photo, 1950. From the Links, Inc., Chicago Chapter Papers, neg. 001. Reprinted by permission of the Vivian G. Harsh Center for the Study of Afro-American History and Literature, the Carter G. Woodson Regional Library, Chicago.

Francis Reese Johnson, director of Parkway Community House's nursery, 1945 (*sitting*), and Ida Mae Duncan, nursery teacher (*leaning*). From the Horace Cayton/Parkway Community House 2 Collection. Reprinted by permission of the Vivian G. Harsh Center for the Study of Afro-American History and Literature, the Carter G. Woodson Regional Library, Chicago.

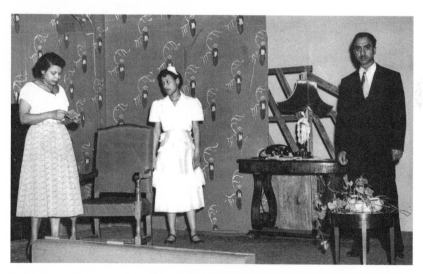

From the performance of Craig's Wife performed by the Skyloft Players of Parkway Community House, 1945, with Louise Jenkins, Miki Grant, and Lestor Chung (*left to right*). From the Horace Cayton/Parkway Community House 2 Collection. Reprinted by permission of the Vivian G. Harsh Center for the Study of Afro-American History and Literature, the Carter G. Woodson Regional Library, Chicago.

Horace Cayton, director of Parkway Community House preparing for Charles Sebree's art exhibit, 1946; identity of two women unknown. From the Horace Cayton Collection, neg. 039. Reprinted by permission of the Vivian G. Harsh Center for the Study of Afro-American History and Literature, the Carter G. Woodson Regional Library, Chicago.

5

Black Women's Clubs

Club Memberships

Most scholars of women's clubs have focused on the Progressive Era and for good reason. Certainly there was momentum then, as white and black women fought for and achieved suffrage, among other reforms. But women's political involvement did not cease after the 1920s. Rather, as Estelle Freedman has emphasized, women participated as delegates at political party conventions, worked professionally in government agencies, and continued to advocate for women's advancement.[1] While it is true that membership in the National Association of Colored Women (NACW) declined during the 1920s, it was not the case for the Chicago and Northern District Association of Colored Women's Clubs (CNDA). Under Nannie Reed's presidency in 1928, the CNDA had a membership of 2,800 women in sixty-seven clubs. That year alone, the association raised nearly $12,000 to support community institutions, including the Phyllis Wheatley Home for Working Girls, Provident Hospital, and the Home for the Aged and Infirm (also known as the "Old Folks' Home").[2]

Indeed, many of the CNDA women's clubs established at the turn of the century continued to flourish through the 1930s and even later. For example, the Ida B. Wells Club, founded in 1893, celebrated its fortieth anniversary in 1933; the North Side Women's Club, also founded by Wells, marked its thirty-fourth anniversary in 1935. Similarly, at least twenty CNDA-affiliated clubs—including the Chicago Union Charity Club, the American Rose Art Club, the Cornell Charity Club, the East Side Woman's Club, the Gaudeamus

Club, the Volunteer Workers Club, and the West Side Woman's Club—continued fundraising for community institutions and advocating for political reform from the 1930s through the 1950s.[3] There were, of course, some Chicago black women's clubs that chose not to belong to the CNDA, such as the Women's Community Club in Lilydale. Nonetheless, the Lilydale club's goals closely resembled those established by the CNDA and the NACW at the turn of the century: "to standardize the Negro home, to safeguard the interest of the same, to encourage the proper environment for the children."[4] Although I estimate that there were eighty black women's clubs in Chicago from 1930 to 1960 (including clubs that were not affiliated with the CNDA), there were probably more. Additionally, there were twenty-five clubs for young girls. (See Appendix B.)

The CNDA clubs were made up of primarily middle-class women, many of whom were active in the Chicago chapters of the NAACP and the Urban League (CUL). Their church memberships were mostly Presbyterian, A.M.E., and Baptist, reflecting their middle-class status. Nannie Reed, for one, divided her time between Bethel A.M.E. Church, the CUL, the Chicago NAACP, the South Parkway YWCA (SPY), and various women's clubs. Maude Smith, another president of the CNDA and of the Illinois State Association of Colored Women's Clubs, founded the Maude E. Smith Children's Home, later renamed the Federated Home for Dependent Children. At the same time, she participated in Quinn Church's auxiliaries, the Lady Elliott Circle, and the Order of Eastern Star. Ada McKinley, a prominent member of the Phyllis Wheatley Club, was president of the Citizens Community Center during the Progressive Era, and through the CUL she had volunteered as a hostess for black soldiers during World War I. In 1924, McKinley founded the South Side Settlement House (SSSH), later renamed the Ada McKinley Community House.[5] As will be discussed further in chapter 6, the SSSH, unlike other community houses and social settlements, worked with residents of one of Chicago's poorest public housing projects, the Ida B. Wells Homes.

Irene McCoy Gaines is another exemplary clubwoman who remained active in many community institutions. Indeed, Gaines followed in the footsteps of her mother, Mamie Ellis Kelly, who moved to Chicago in 1898. A member of Bethel A.M.E. Church and the Old Settlers' Club (an elite group containing the first black men and women of Chicago), Kelly had joined the CUL and the first black Chicago YWCA.[6] By the 1920s, her daughter had been president of the Colored Women's Republican Clubs of Illinois, as well as a theosophical society and the American Rose Art and Charity Club. A member of the Bethel A.M.E. Church, Gaines had also served as chair for their annual youth essay contests. From 1939 to 1953, she was president of the Chicago Council of Negro Organizations (CCNO), chair of the hostesses of the American Negro Exposition of 1940, and a social worker with SPY. Gaines also became active in partisan politics as president of the Colored Women's Republican Clubs of Illinois, as delegate to the National Republican Nominating Convention in 1948, and as candidate for the Chicago Board of County Commissioners in 1950. In fact, her staunch Republican support gave her visibility nationally: she was a member of President Hoover's Housing Investigation Committee and of the Woman's Executive Committee of President Eisenhower's White House Conference on Highway Safety.[7]

There were other notable first-generation clubwomen, whose enduring community work should be acknowledged. Among them was Annie Oliver, founder and president of the National Du Saible Memorial Society for thirty-three years. Violette Neatley Anderson had been president of the Elite Social Charity Club and secretary for the Alba Rose Club in the early 1900s. She was also the first African American lawyer to be hired as an assistant state attorney. During the 1930s, she supervised the Friendly Big Sisters League and was a member of the Special Shelters Committee of the CUL, while continuing her work as a lawyer. Genevieve Coleman, president of the Samaritan Club and the Cornell Charity Club during the 1910s, continued as director of the Old Folks' Home during the Depression.[8]

But what of the younger generation of black women? Did they join the CNDA clubs? The CNDA recognized the need to recruit the next generation and so organized girls' clubs. But the CNDA did not fulfill its goal of "a junior club for every senior club."[9] Perhaps one of the most prominent young clubwomen was Bertha Moseley Lewis, daughter of Chicago lawyer and colonel B. F. Moseley. Even as a teenager, her literary pursuits as president of the Grace Presbyterian Church's Youth Lyceum were noteworthy. After completing her master's degree from the University of Chicago at the age of twenty-two, she worked as a schoolteacher and recreation director. Despite these professional commitments, she sustained her love of theater. As discussed in chapter 3, she founded several community theaters, worked with the Federal Theatre Project (FTP), and directed CNDA theater productions during the 1930s.[10]

By and large, though, younger black women did not join the CNDA clubs from the 1930s through the 1950s. As teachers, social and welfare workers, journalists, dramatists, and artists, many were employed by the public schools, the court system, city agencies, and community institutions such as Parkway Community House (PCH), SPY, and the SSSH. Many also engaged in volunteer work as chaperones, teachers, and fundraisers for institutions such as the South Side Community Art Center (SSCAC). Rather than join the CNDA, then, many preferred their own networks of sororities, college clubs, and professional organizations. Some also joined the National Council of Negro Women (NCNW), not the CNDA, such as *Chicago Bee* editor Olive Diggs, lawyer Edith Sampson, and aviation instructor Willa Brown.[11]

However, NACW and NCNW memberships were not mutually exclusive, especially since the NACW was an organizational member of the NCNW. In fact, NACW officials had been involved in the NCNW's founding in 1938, even though some NACW leaders such as Mary Church Terrell had been skeptical of the need for another black women's organization. In Chicago, the NCNW presence was strong since Chicagoan Marjorie Stewart Joyner, a well-known cosmetologist and head of the *Chicago Defender*'s Charities, had cofounded the NCNW with Mary McCleod Bethune. Perhaps because of Joyner, some older clubwomen had also joined the Chicago chapter. Annie Oliver, for one, remained a CNDA member, while serving as treasurer and second vice-president of the Chicago NCNW chapter. Similarly, CNDA members Lavonia Brown, Jessie Mae Davis, Mayme Mason Higgins, Georgia Ellis Jones, Jeanette Jones, Rebecca Stiles Taylor, and Mayme Williams—to name only a few—had joined the Chicago chapter of the NCNW.[12] (See Appendix A for further information about these clubwomen.)

Perhaps one reason younger professional women did not join the CNDA was because they perceived the CNDA to be social rather than political. Despite the poverty of many blacks during the Depression, some Chicago women's clubs still continued their social balls, dances, and card playing. For example, the Ladies of Entre Nous Club held an extravagant dancing party, with the following coverage: "To the strains of 'pennies from heaven' the women marched to the center of the ballroom floor and took their places under the rainbow" (which had a pot of gold at each end).[13] Even into the 1940s, the CNDA's "extravagant" club events, as well as their clubhouse, were targets of one NCNW member's criticism. In a 1946 *Chicago Bee*'s "Windy City Sophisticates" column, editor Olive Diggs took the CNDA and its president, Gaines, to task. Referring to Gaines as a "self-styled leader," she criticized Gaines for her remarks about black congressman William Dawson's inattention to the Tennessee riot. After setting Dawson's record straight, she directed her attention to the CNDA, making light of the group's decision to sell or keep its clubhouse. As Diggs made clear, the younger generation had "more important matters" to discuss. Aligning herself with the NCNW, she concluded: "WINDY predicts that type of 'old-fashioned' leadership will bring about the same upheaval which made First Lady Mary Bethune's organization."[14]

Exactly what "important matters" did the younger generation have to discuss? Interestingly, there seemed to be little difference between the activism of the CNDA and the NCNW, at least in Chicago. Both groups were committed to protesting housing problems, as well as improving interracial relations.[15] At the national and international levels, however, the NCNW was more visible. In 1938, NCNW leaders had organized a White House conference to focus on black women's exclusion in upper-level government positions. In 1940, the NCNW held a conference with black Cuban women to draw attention to their political struggles. And during World War II, the NCNW helped to desegregate black women in the WACs.[16] To be discussed later in this chapter, the NACW, under Gaines's presidency, would rival the NCNW in the national and international arenas during the 1950s.

Despite generational and organizational differences, one point remains clear: the CNDA clubs engaged in multiple kinds of community activism. To be sure, much of their work was focused on issues of child and youth welfare, but they did not neglect political and economic issues. Their social uplift, cultural contributions, and political activism during the three decades of the Chicago Black Renaissance was extraordinary.

The Links was another organization that young, professional women joined after World War II. Members of the Chicago chapter included Pauline Kligh Reed, one of the founders of the SSCAC; Olive Diggs, editor of the *Bee;* Edith Sampson, a lawyer; Roberta Bell, known for her handmade black dolls; Oneida Cockrell, a preschool principal; Madeline Stratton, an elementary teacher who created a black history curriculum; and Thelma Jackson, an elementary school principal and president of the Links. Founded in 1946, the Chicago chapter's activities reflected postwar concerns for social justice and civil rights. For example, the group became a lifetime member of the NAACP and supported its litigation efforts. Likewise, the Links sponsored debates and speeches on issues such as "gradualism" and segregation. But it was especially active in outreach to underprivileged black children. The Links raised funds for the South Side Boys' Club and SPY and also donated black history books for children to the George Cleveland Hall Library.[17]

The CNDA and Social Uplift

During the 1930s, CNDA-affiliated clubs devoted their efforts to the maintenance of longstanding black community institutions, especially the Old Folks' Home, the Phyllis Wheatley Home, Provident Hospital, and the Federated Home for Dependent Children. Since its founding in 1898, the Old Folks'

Home had been sustained through the clubwomen's fundraising, in-kind gifts, parties and holiday celebrations, and regular visits to the elderly. Clubwomen continued these activities through the Depression. Some of the older clubs—the Dorcas Art and Charity Club, the Gaudeamus Woman's Club, and the Cornell Charity Club—held their meetings there, thereby giving the women further opportunities to visit the elderly and to sponsor programs of interest. Likewise, clubwomen such as Genevieve Coleman, former president of the Cornell Charity and Samaritan clubs, served on the Home's board of directors.[18]

Clubwomen also volunteered for Provident Hospital so that its medical services could be expanded to serve Chicago's growing black population. Through the financial assistance of the Julius Rosenwald Fund and various black women's groups, a new child's clinic opened at the hospital in 1930. Bertha Hensley, former president of the Gaudeamus Club and an officer for the Phyllis Wheatley Club and Home, was capably assisted by Pauline Jackson, Shirley Green, and Grace Wells. All three women were experienced in fundraising and social welfare activities. Jackson had been a YWCA president in Philadelphia and Birmingham; Green, a member of the CUL's Junior Woman's Auxiliary, had completed her sociology degree at Loyola University. And Wells, a native Georgian, had founded the Dorcas Art and Charity Club. Wells not only became the CNDA's president during the 1940s but also would continue to recruit women to volunteer at Provident and Oak Forest hospitals during the 1950s.[19]

One example of a successful fundraising event organized by the clubwomen for Provident Hospital was the "Royalties Bal de Tete," which took place in the 1950s. In the spirit of publicizing the "grand" balls at the turn of the century, the *Chicago Defender* listed the celebrities in attendance (such as Marva Spaulding, former wife of boxer Joe Louis) and described how they were dressed. As Langston Hughes described the opulence, "Next to the Mardi Gras in New Orleans, I've seen nothing like it."[20] There were, of course, less fashionable fundraisers from the 1930s through the 1950s, such as annual picnics and teas, bathing beauty contests, fashion shows, and popularity contests organized by the Provident Guild and Provident Hospital's Women's Auxiliary Board.[21]

The CNDA, however, directed most of its attention during the 1930s to the Federated Children's Home, which cared for orphaned and dependent children. Previously two community institutions, the Amanda Smith Industrial Home in Harvey, Illinois, and the Louise Juvenile Home and Industrial School in Chicago, had taken in girls and boys, respectively. But both facilities closed before 1920, leaving few facilities in Chicago that accepted black children.[22] One organization, the Illinois Children's Home and Aid Society, had assisted in placing orphaned and dependent black children, but the clubwomen concluded that foster care was not a viable solution. Some situations required expediency, which led to the founding of the Federated Children's Home in 1927. When the staff at a white hospital realized that an infant was black, the administration ordered the child's "immediate removal."[23] The clubwomen took in him and other rejected infants and cared for them. Within a short time, the number of children accepted at the Home exceeded its capacity of twenty. Accordingly, the Home moved to a larger facility in 1934, hired a social worker and a superintendent, and organized an intake committee.[24]

It is not clear how much per diem monies the Home received from the Chicago juvenile court, as court records were available only until 1928. Regardless, earlier per diem allotments per child for such institutions were meager, forcing many institutions to rely upon philanthropic support and women's volunteerism. The Home's records indicated that most of the Home's support during the 1930s came from CNDA fundraisers, such as baby shows, calendar sales, lawn parties, bazaars, tag days, teas, rummage sales, indoor picnics, and anniversary celebrations.[25] These traditional fund-raisers also supported the Home's improvements, including a new roof and a refurbished basement. Individual clubs, such as the Gaudeamus Club, furnished and decorated the girls' dormitory. Clubs also donated hundreds of pounds of food during their "food showers." The Young Matron's Culture Club, for example, participated in an annual shower of milk cans at the Home, providing at least sixty cans of milk; they also sponsored a canned goods shower and contributed forty pounds of corn.[26]

During the Depression, the CNDA and the Chicago clubs also expanded their social welfare work beyond the community facilities discussed above. Many black families were hit hard during those years, as evidenced by one WPA interviewee's 1931 recollection: "One night, the investigator for the Welfare Committee found more than 200 unescorted women of good character sleeping in the city's park. Some of them had young children tied-up [sic] like bundles of newspapers against the cold. There were whole families too which managed to stick together in spite of hunger and homelessness."[27] Although it is not clear how the clubwomen responded to this particular incident, they did provide relief and services to black families in need. For example, the CNDA, under the presidency of Belle Fountain, started a Family Relief Committee in 1931 that opened a relief station and health clinic in the heart of Bronzeville. As in earlier years, the committee relied upon the goodwill and volunteerism of clubwomen and other community members. A real estate agent "donated" the building; a furniture company provided furniture. One junior club member volunteered her time as a stenographer, and other clubwomen investigated homes and worked with the United Charities.[28]

Additionally, doctors Anna Cooper, Lucille Miller, and L. Eudora Ashburn—all members of the Mary B. Talbert Club—volunteered their medical expertise, with the assistance of nurse Gertrude Webb, so that poorer blacks could receive free medical treatment. Although little is known of Drs. Miller and Ashburn, Dr. Cooper had originally arrived in Chicago in 1898, after completing course work at Wilberforce University and the University of Medicine and Surgery in Cleveland. She soon became the president of the board of the Paul Dunbar Tuberculosis Sanitarium, as well as a member of the Phyllis Wheatley Club. At some point, she left Chicago but returned again in 1929. She not only worked at the clinic but also became chair of the CNDA's Health and Hygiene Committee.[29] There is also scant information about nurse Gertrude Webb. But it is quite possible that she was a relative of Elizabeth Webb Hill, a doctor at the Community Hospital in Evanston. Both may have been daughters of Rhoygnette Webb, one of the first graduates of Provident's nursing school, who became head nurse at a sanitarium in Evanston.[30] Regardless, all four volunteers for the health clinic took care of eighty-three patients in 1932 alone. The CNDA had also planned to organize a birth control clinic under Dr. Mary Waring's initiative, as well as establish classes for blacks at the Hull House. Unfortunately, there is no information about such activities. Waring, then vice-president of the NACW, probably had her hands full.[31]

The Family Relief Committee also opened a shop where they "made over" old garments and sewed new ones. The women involved in these projects included not only Dr. Cooper and Gertrude Webb but prominent clubwomen Ida B. Wells, Carrie Horton, and Eva T. Wells.[32] To many readers, Wells needs little introduction. She was nationally and internationally known for her anti-lynching campaigns and her protest against the absence of black American representation at the 1893 Chicago Exposition. She was also active as a club organizer, a founder of a social settlement (the Negro Fellowship League), and a suffragist.[33] Carrie Horton, too, had been extremely active in the women's clubs. She had been president of the longstanding Cornell Charity Club, as well as board member for the Chicago Metropolitan YWCA and member of the CUL's Special Shelters Committee. Eva Wells was involved in the Chicago Recreation Commission, chaired the CNDA's Schools Department, and helped to introduce black history into the Chicago public schools. Together, these women coordinated the efforts of women's clubs in distributing food baskets, money, and clothing to needy families. To raise money, the women organized cultural events, such as the production of a play written by club-woman Ruth J. Steele.[34]

The CNDA started two other social uplift initiatives in the early 1930s: the Club Home Association for Working Mothers with Children, and the Sunshine Home for single women and mothers. Little information is available about either home, so I suspect that they were short-lived. The Club Home Association's officers, though, were prominent CNDA clubwomen. One officer, Bertha Hensley, had been involved in the Phyllis Wheatley Club and Home, and she was also president and theater director of the Elite Social Charity Club that fund-raised for the Home. She was also secretary of the Elite Social Charity Club and a member of the board of directors for the Home. Other officers for the Home were Mrs. Robert Abbott, wife of the *Chicago Defender*'s founder; Mrs. George Hall, a prominent clubwoman who had helped to found the first black YWCA in Chicago; and Helen Sayre and Irene McCoy Gaines, both experienced social workers and club organizers.[35] There is even less information about the Sunshine Home and its officers. But in 1932 alone, the Home purportedly assisted 614 families and 970 children, in part through donations by famous performers such as Bo Jangles.[36]

These prodigious efforts were especially remarkable during the Depression. But what of social uplift activities during the 1940s and 1950s? Curiously, there were few records for this time period. Clubwomen did, however, continue to assist the needy with Christmas baskets and other contributions. The Fleur Delis Club, Giles Charity Club, Jeanette Smith Educational and Social Club, Dorcas Art and Charity Club, CNDA, Irene McCoy Gaines Educational and Civic Club, and Jolly Twelve Social Club were especially noted for their charity work. And at least until 1944, the clubwomen remained involved in the Old Folks' Home. Significantly, the Federated Home for Dependent Children relocated during the 1950s, perhaps to take in even more children, and it cared for both white and black children.[37] Additionally, clubwomen turned their attention to cultural activities.

The CNDA and Cultural Work

In addition to social uplift, black clubwomen participated in literature readings, music and theater performances, and discussions of black history. As in earlier decades, the clubwomen's study of literature, the arts, and history was both a means of self-cultivation and a venue for fund-raising. Similar to the earlier lyceums, the clubs also continued their outreach to youth, especially through essay contests. As before, there were women who contributed their writing talents to club efforts, such as Geraldine Glover, described by other clubwomen as a "real doer." A published poet who also exhibited her art work locally, Glover was chair of the CNDA's Business Department.[38] There was also Ruth Steele, whose plays were often performed at CNDA fund-raisers. As previously noted, Bertha Moseley Lewis, chair of the CNDA's Department of Fine Arts, both produced and wrote plays for the clubs' fundraising benefits.[39]

Various clubs sponsored cultural events for both self-cultivation and fund-raising. For example, the clubwomen in Morgan Park sponsored a concert and literary program in 1930 for the benefit of the Woman's Welfare Club, which was devoted to developing a civic spirit in Morgan Park. The Gaudeamus Woman's Club presented a joint recital at the Blackwell A.M.E. Zion Church with dramatic readings and voice solos. Hoping to establish a community library in the church, the Finer Arts Guild of Pilgrim Baptist Church sponsored a "twilight hour," with musical numbers and a talk, "Between the Book Ends."[40] Fashion shows, often sponsored by the women's clubs, assumed their own form of theatricality during the 1930s and 1940s. One fashion show, arranged by Bertha Moseley Lewis, included dance and music recitals at the Savoy Ballroom. Sometimes renowned persons participated, ensuring large audiences. The acclaimed singer Etta Moten, who had just completed a tour of *Porgy and Bess,* served as a style commentator for one fashion show. Marva Louis, too, participated in fashion shows, and also made her singing debut at a benefit party for Provident Hospital. A CNDA fashion show featured music by Johnie Long's Orchestra, along with vignettes of the history of famous black women's lives, interspersed with dance and song numbers.[41]

The clubwomen had a longstanding interest in history that dated from the turn of the century. At that time, the Frederick Douglass Center had invited Carter G. Woodson to speak about his book, *The Negro Prior to 1861.* At a meeting of the Center's women's club, Fannie Barrier Williams had organized a Frederick Douglass Program, where she shared her own memories of Douglass. Irene McCoy Gaines's presentation of African history and authors in one essay contest was described as "a revelation."[42] It is thus not surprising that in one of her later articles, in which she retold the history of black women's achievements, she began with Sheba and Cleopatra and ended with the suffrage movement. But Gaines's interest was never purely historical or literary. Instead, she urged that other black clubwomen also learn more about politics.[43]

As in the past, the study of literature and history reflected race pride and progress. The clubwomen not only celebrated renowned black authors and intellectuals but also were considered noteworthy in their own right for their presentations. For example, when Gaines gave a talk to the Gaudeamus Club in 1930s about eminent blacks, including sociologist Monroe Work and novelist Charles Chestnutt, her talk was described as that "which was highly intellectual from beginning to end and its brilliancy will linger in the minds for many years of those who had the extreme pleasure of listening."[44] Inflated rhetoric aside, Gaines's presentation vividly demonstrated how literature was invariably conjoined to politics.

Clubwomen also recognized the history of their own activism and honored those clubwomen who had preceded them. At one Gaudeamus Club meeting in 1939, Joanna Snowden spoke of the Old Settlers' Club, a club founded in the 1880s by the first members of the black elite of Chicago. Nine years later, the clubwomen commemorated her as the founder of the Northwestern Federation of Colored Women and also as one of the first black probation officers in the Chicago juvenile court.[45] At another meeting, clubwomen listened to Mrs. George Cleveland Hall recalling the "past glories" of Chicago. Hall had been a founder of the Frederick Douglass Center and the first black YWCA in Chicago.[46]

As noted in chapter 4, the clubs' study of history was crucial to their advocacy of a black history curriculum, especially in the Chicago public schools. So important was this issue that the CNDA established a black history department in the 1930s to coordinate efforts of the women's clubs and schools. Accordingly, many clubs studied black history, literature, and the arts. For example, one club celebrated Negro History Week with a series of dramatic tableaux. Leading clubwoman Elizabeth Lindsay Davis was represented in the tableaux and was also a guest speaker.[47] Perhaps the clubwomen used the resources of the George Cleveland Hall branch library, whose repository of black literature and history was already impressive. Clubwomen also sponsored ongoing events so that children and youth could learn about black history. Similar to the turn-of-the-century black church lyceums, the Willing Workers and Strangers Club organized a program where over thirty-five children shared their knowledge of black history through dramatic recitations and recitals. Similarly, the CNDA sponsored an annual essay contest for high school students and CNDA junior clubs, including the Sophisticated Debs Club, the Clara Jesamine Gay Teenettes, the Phyllis Wheatley Junior Club, and the Illinois Association of Colored Girls. The 1946 topic for these groups was "The Contribution of Ten Negro Women to American Life and Culture."[48]

Perhaps one of the most significant cultural achievements of the CNDA was its participation in the 1940 American Negro Exposition. This was not the first time that clubwomen were involved in organizing an exposition. The CNDA and other groups had sponsored "The Negro in Art Week" in 1927, which included exhibits of African art and presentations of literature, music, painting, and sculpture. The clubwomen also invited Alain Locke and James Weldon Johnson to lecture.[49] But the 1940 exposition was more ambitious in its presentation of black history, achievements, and artistry. Langston Hughes and Arna Bontemps traced black theater and music from minstrelsy to jazz. Works from the WPA Writers' Program were displayed through the assistance of Claude Barnett of the Associated Negro Press, Parkway Community House director Horace Cayton, historian Dorothy Porter, and librarian Vivian Harsh. There were displays of black accomplishments in labor and the National Youth Administration (NYA), as well as a social science exhibit, based upon E. Franklin Frazier's sociological theories. There were also twenty dioramas of historical achievements, and there was also a display of a map of Chicago that featured the Ida B. Wells Homes and the George Cleveland Hall Library. These dioramas surrounded a replica of President Lincoln's tomb.[50]

As president of the CNDA, Gaines played four critical roles, supported by a number of prominent clubwomen, in the 1940 Exposition. First, Gaines served on the board of directors of the Exposition, along with clubwomen Nannie Williams and Freda Cross. Second, Gaines was in charge of the Registration Committee for the hostesses at the Exposition. Third, with the assistance of six black sororities, Gaines organized a "Woman's Day" at the Exposition, which featured portraits of prominent black females Marian Anderson, Mary McCleod Bethune, and Jessie Fauset.[51] And fourth, Gaines, Bertha Moseley Lewis, and Mary Morgan of the SSCAC assisted in organizing the Exposition's art exhibit, which featured paintings and sculptures by Federal Art Projects (FAP) artists, as well as several works by SSCAC artists. They also organized a series of prominent speakers, including Melville Herskovits, who lectured on "primitive race art," and Dr. Metz T. P. Lochard of the Abraham Lincoln Center, who spoke on "Democracy in Art."[52] Unfortunately, neither Gaines nor the other women received much public recognition for their work on the art exhibits.

More often than not, the clubwomen's literary and artistic contributions reflected the cultural politics of black identity. But the women were also conscious of a strong black *female* identity, expressed, for example, through the theme of Cleopatra, dramatic tableaux about black women, the Exposition's Woman's Day, or the honoring of older clubwomen. Despite the clubwomen's awareness of their own contributions to black history, they were not always publicly acknowledged. Nonetheless, they continued their activism, joining social and cultural work to politics.

The CNDA and Political Work

As in the first decades of the century, the clubwomen remained active in city, as well as national, politics. When Ruth Hanna McCormick ran for Congress in 1928 and again for reelection in 1930, the NACW and the Chicago black women's clubs worked for her campaign. However, tensions developed among clubwomen when the NACW selected Mary Church Terrell, a black clubwoman from Washington, D.C., to assist in McCormick's campaign. Ida B. Wells, who had longstanding differences with Terrell, led a protest, pointing out that it was a "slight" to the black women of Illinois to hire an "outsider." Gaines agreed, pointing out that black women in Illinois deserved credit for their enduring work with the Republican Party. As she emphasized: "We dislike the idea of always 'importing' colored women from other states during national and other campaigns to direct our political activities."[53] As president of the Colored Women's Republican Clubs of Illinois, Gaines had recruited seventeen new clubs into the organization during the first year of her term.[54]

In 1932 Gaines wrote to Roscoe Simmons, Chicago's black representative at the Republican National Convention, to request the representation of Chicago's black women at the presidential conventions, comparable to the representation of black women from Ohio and Missouri. Gaines's work with the McCormick election apparently gave her additional leverage with which to further Illinois black women's involvement in politics. Two months later, she wrote Simmons again, recommending that Chicago's black women be placed in the party's national headquarters.[55] The outcome of this request is not clear, although that same year Gaines was appointed as a member of the Committee on Negro Housing of Hoover's Conference on Home Building and Home Ownership.[56]

Despite this national recognition, Gaines remained politically active in Chicago. Indeed, as early as 1930 she encouraged other clubwomen to join her in becoming more involved with labor concerns. Speaking under the auspices of the Brotherhood of Sleeping Car Porters, Gaines stated, "The Negro worker gives to the clubwoman more than all the problems implied in this situation that others give, plus some additional features that arise out of the very fact that the worker is a Negro."[57] Clubwomen, she advised, should approach labor problems seriously, rather than work based on a "more social pretension." As such, they should encourage "the promotion of an honest mental attitude" and also provide workers with useful information.[58] Apparently, the CNDA did become more involved in employment issues and conducted an employment survey in 1933, concluding that employment conditions were "almost tragic." Later, in 1939, the CNDA encouraged Illinois Bell Telephone to hire more black women.[59]

When Gaines became the CNDA's president from 1937 to 1939, the clubwomen stepped up their political advocacy. They supported the legislative committee of the Chicago NAACP, the CCNO, and the CUL to fight against restrictive covenants and to promote better housing for blacks. Similarly, they participated in the South Side Chamber of Commerce's parade to protest substandard housing and other southside problems.[60] Along with the Citizens Schools Committee (CSC), of which Gaines was a member, the clubwomen protested old and overcrowded schools, and they continued to protest explicit cases of segregation and discrimination. For example, they refused to hold their meetings at Chicago hotels that maintained separate entrances for blacks or refused to even admit blacks. They also wrote protest letters to the *Chicago Tribune* for using derogatory language, such as "Hot Ziggety," or using dialect such as "Chicawgo Folks i on de go agin!" In response, the newspaper editor issued an apology.[61]

The CNDA also worked with federal agencies, such as the NYA, to increase employment opportunities for youth. When NYA director Mary McCleod Bethune visited the local WPA office in Chicago, she met with Gaines and prominent black women. Bethune's message was clear: she wanted more black youth involved with the WPA. One result was that the CNDA's Federated Club House and the Phyllis Wheatley Home did hire several black youths, with salaries provided by the NYA. The Phyllis Wheatley Home, too, offered NYA-sponsored classes in dressmaking, drafting patterns, remaking old garments, knitting, and handicrafts.[62] In 1943, when Senator Everett Dirksen (R-IL) suggested that the NYA be abolished, the CNDA wrote black congressman William Dawson, informing him that the NYA remained "a matter of great interest to the Negro women of Illinois."[63] Nonetheless, the NYA was discontinued five months later.

In addition to local advocacy, CNDA members supported national causes, including the Scottsboro boys' case. In fact, Robert Taylor, chair of the Scottsboro *Defender* Committee, had invited Gaines to come to a meeting and meet two of the Scottsboro boys. Shortly thereafter, the CNDA sponsored a mass meeting on their behalf.[64] The CNDA's civics department, under the guidance of chair Eva Wells, also sent letters to Congress, encouraging them to endorse the anti-lynching bill, an issue that persisted through the 1950s.[65]

International interests of the CNDA reflected an emerging pan-Africanism as well as concerns about the Spanish Civil War and the Italian invasion of Ethiopia. At one 1938 meeting, Thyra Edwards, journalist and consultant for the CNDA's industrial department, and Alice Belester, executive secretary of the United Consumers Association, spoke about high black unemployment and the cost of living. Wedding global to local concerns, Belester urged members to form consumer organizations and to boycott Japanese goods and also to advocate for lower rents for poor people. One year later, after her visit to Europe, Edwards spoke to the CNDA again, this time about Danish democracy. She directly compared former estates there to southern plantations.[66] Club discussions continued about Spain, Ethiopia, and northern Africa. For example, the Douglas League of Women Voters held a meeting at the Metropolitan Church to hear a talk on "the fighting French in Africa." *Chicago Defender* journalist and CNDA member Rebecca Stiles Taylor kept the clubwomen informed about the occupancy of northern Africa, as well as General Smut and South Africa.[67]

During World War II, Chicago clubwomen also demonstrated their patriotism by selling war bonds and stamps, most notably Fannie B. Obanion, who alone sold over $35,000 worth of bonds and stamps. The women also sponsored an annual tea to honor war mothers.[68] Following the war, they voiced their concerns about the marginalization of black women and the indignities they continued to face. Clearly, they were aware that, despite blacks' involvement in the war, victory at home had not been achieved. Stiles Taylor, for one, connected the exploitation of black Americans to sexism, especially in the South, where some signs said, "No women and no colored people allowed."[69] Gaines's vision connected black American women's plight to the worldwide exploitation of black women. Speaking before the United Nations in 1947, Gaines exhorted: "The colored women in America are as much concerned about the subjugation and exploitation of women by the colonial powers as we are about our own status in the United States."[70]

During and after the war, some CNDA members also became members of citywide commissions that purportedly promoted race relations and "unity." Other black leaders, most notably Horace Cayton, were skeptical of these commissions. Cayton pointed out that they did not improve race relations or decrease unemployment. Once a committee or commission was formed, he noted, the community felt it had accomplished its end. But most committees and commissions had no power to create or enforce legislation. At best, he concluded, these groups could sensitize citizens; at worst, they could "dead-end" activism.[71] In 1944, Mayor Kelley had invited Gaines to a series of conferences on city planning in race relations. We should, however, question the mayor's motives. At that time, plans were underway to raze a large part of the southside black neighborhoods for urban renewal. More than likely, the mayor did not want to lose black political support. The next year, he invited members of the black women's clubs to the "Home Front Unity" Conference.[72] But what kind of postwar "unity" could there be when black soldiers were denied adequate housing for their families or viable employment? In 1948, Gaines and other clubwomen also became delegates to the Chicago Crime Commission. The women complained about one local theater that was poorly lit and "unsanitary," thereby encouraging youth to smoke "reevers." When one fifteen-year-old girl was raped there and another shot, the women became even more outraged. Here, results were probably more achievable, although none were reported.[73]

Arguably, Gaines became more visible through her participation in these commissions. Perhaps because of this, she won the election for county commissioner in 1950, thereby becoming the first black woman to be endorsed by both political parties in Chicago. She attributed her election to a number of constituencies. Knowing how influential ministers were with their congregations, she wrote them letters and sought their endorsements.[74] She also appealed to various groups by invoking the traditional image of municipal housekeeper: "I'm a good housekeeper as well. I think I'm qualified to be a good county commissioner."[75]

Even though Gaines held a political office, she did not withdraw from civil rights protests in the city. In 1953, she joined the interracial Trumbull Park Committee, at a time when Trumbull Park and other public housing projects were being desegregated. Following the 1954 landmark Supreme Court case of *Brown vs. Topeka,* Gaines spoke before a crowd of 3,000 persons at Olivet Church, urging Congress to pass more civil rights legislation. And in 1959, Gaines and Coretta King spoke on "Woman's Day" before the Monumental Baptist Church congregation.[76] During most of the 1950s, she was also politically active as NACW president.

Gaines and the NACW Presidency

In 1952, Gaines became NACW president, an office she would hold for three terms. Her last term, to say the least, was contentious. Nonetheless, she accomplished a great deal during her tenure. She established the Mary Church Terrell Fund to fight discrimination and also secured tax-exempt status for the NACW. She helped to finalize a settlement for Sallie Stewart's estate of $50,000, as well as resolving legal issues relating to the stewardship of the Frederick Douglass Home. She also appointed an NACW representative to observe at the United Nations. Last, through her careful negotiations, the NACW was awarded a $50,000 grant from the Sears Roebuck Company to conduct a pilot neighborhood improvement contest.[77]

At the national level, Gaines continued to advocate for black women's employment. Speaking on behalf of the NACW, purportedly 100,000 strong in 1954, she endorsed President Eisenhower's efforts to ensure equal opportunity in federal employment by speaking before a senate subcommittee through the President's Committee on Government Employment Policy. In turn, the commission invited two NACW representatives to one of their conferences, through the arrangements of Gaines's Chicago friend and commission member Archibald Carey, Jr.[78] Even though Gaines openly supported Eisenhower, she continued to express her concerns about employment for black women, who worked longer hours and for lower wages than most other women. Using the United Nations as leverage, she claimed that when the UN found out that black Americans were still denied equal opportunities in employment, the UN would be skeptical about the United States. This, in turn, would affect American markets. As she advised, "Americans [can]not afford this sort of menace to our social, civic, political and economic good health."[79] In all likelihood, Gaines's argument was not persuasive since government officials knew that UN officials had no jurisdiction over any country's internal problems.

However, Eisenhower knew he needed the black vote for reelection and so he courted black Chicagoans, amongst them Carey and Gaines. In turn, Gaines learned to "work the system" by garnering Eisenhower's support for the NACW. In late 1954, she praised him for his efforts toward racial equality and his appointments of blacks to federal government positions. She referred particularly to the appointment of Chicagoan J. Ernest Wilkins as assistant secretary of labor that year.[80] The following year, Eisenhower invited fourteen women from various organizations to breakfast, including the NACW. Gaines followed up by thanking Eisenhower for the "lovely" breakfast, then asked him to give the NACW more recognition to "recapture the large number of our membership which deflected during the previous (Democrat) administration."[81] What did Gaines mean? She wanted the NACW to be included in delegations to other countries, as were members of the General Federation of Women's Clubs. As Gaines suggested, NACW members would be "wonderful" representatives of America for "colored women of the world."[82] She also asked that NACW officers be hired in federal positions, in part to defray transportation costs to and from the Capitol. Here, Gaines was thinking particularly of herself, for she had asked Senator Dirksen and Max Rabb, White House advisor on minority problems, to help her secure such an appointment so she could be at the NACW headquarters each month. When they could not help her, she contacted Carey, who responded that he would try his best.[83]

Gaines also used her federal connections to pressure officials to respond to violations of civil rights, especially in the South. In 1955, concerned about the murder of Emmett Till, she sent a telegram to the chief of the civil rights section and assistant attorney general of the criminal division of the U.S. Department of Justice. She may well have attended Till's open casket funeral in Chicago and seen his brutally beaten body. She urged the federal government to protect the rights and lives of blacks in Mississippi. Because the murder involved violations of state, not federal, laws, the department claimed that it had no jurisdiction. They were, however, conducting "extensive" investigations regarding civil rights violations in the state, including violations of the right to vote.[84]

At the same time, Gaines acknowledged the civil rights activism of southern blacks, especially women. She praised Rosa Parks for following in the footsteps of Harriet Tubman and Sojourner Truth. Again, she noted, a black woman took the first stand. In recognition of her achievements, the NACW awarded Parks a lifelong NACW honorary membership.[85] Following the Montgomery bus boycott in 1956, the NACW wrote to the National City Lines Bus Company in Chicago, protesting discrimination in their services. Gaines urged NACW women, too, to write their congressmen, asking them to investigate all acts of discrimination against blacks in the South.[86] The NACW also contributed financially to assist southern black activists. In 1956, they sent a check to Dr. Martin Luther King and the Improvement Association of Montgomery. The president of the Alabama Association of Black Women's Clubs thanked Gaines, stating, "The club women from all over the state have aided in this struggle for freedom and first class citizenship."[87] In 1957, the NACW gave financial help to black students attending Little Rock's Central High School, and it also assisted efforts by the Student Nonviolent Coordinating Committee (SNCC) and the NAACP by providing monetary donations and volunteers for voter registration.[88] At a NAACP rally of 25,000 in Washington, D.C. in 1957, Gaines represented the NACW.[89]

Under Gaines, the NACW expanded its role not only nationally but also internationally. Scholars have noted American women's involvement in postwar and Cold War international activities, which often promoted Americanism at the expense of internationalism. But Gaines's position was different. At one UN session, she spoke out against black women's exploitation throughout the world, not just in America.[90] Instead, she advocated for more visibility of black American women in international politics. For example, Gaines called Dirksen to request a "wider recognition" for "Negro womanhood" and he agreed. But Gaines was thinking specifically about the NACW. She wrote Archibald Carey, Jr. again, asking that the NACW women be included on the "People to People" trips to Europe, Asia, and Africa. At that time, Vivian Carter Mason, then president of the NCNW, had been sent by the State Department on such a trip for a week. Further, Gaines noted emphatically to Carey, she was a Democrat. Carey responded that he would try his best to help her.[91]

Gaines' insistence that the NACW be accorded the same opportunities as the NCNW was not unreasonable. In all fairness to Gaines, the competition between the two organizations was triggered by other situations. For one, Jane Morrow Spaulding, appointed director of the NACW's Sears Project in 1956, also contributed to tensions between the two organizations. Spaulding had been active in both organizations since the 1940s, as president of the West Virginia Federation of Colored Women's Clubs, while also an assistant for a statewide drive for an NCNW-sponsored worldwide conference.[92] As such, she was certainly qualified to oversee the Sears project, which consisted of competitive $4,000 grants to NACW chapters in five states, including Illinois, to be used for neighborhood beautification, rehabilitation, and information centers.[93] From the beginning, though, Gaines and Spaulding had their disagreements. When Gaines did not give Spaulding a requested salary raise, Spaulding went to the NCNW and offered to assist them in securing a project like Sears, at a 25 percent commission. Gaines was furious when she found out and demanded Spaulding's resignation. But Spaulding retained a lawyer and joined with other NACW members in declaring that Gaines's NACW presidential election of 1956 was unconstitutional.[94]

Gaines may also have been angry at Spaulding for other reasons. Before their involvement on the Sears project, Gaines had "pulled strings" to help Spaulding get a federal job transfer, when her job as assistant to Oveta Culp Hobby, secretary of Health, Education, and Welfare, was suddenly eliminated in 1954. Apparently, Spaulding had disagreed with Hobby's decision to "slow down" the desegregation of twenty-one military schools in 1954 and instead sided with the NAACP.[95] Gaines was sympathetic to Spaulding and wrote to Harold Stassen, the newly hired special assistant to Eisenhower on disarmament. She asked him to help Spaulding and he did so.[96] Gaines may have felt that Spaulding should stand by her, and not against her, because of this favor.

But Gaines's relationship with Stassen had its own interesting history. In 1953, he had refused to speak before an NACW session because of one NACW officer's suspected affiliation with a "blacklisted" group. That officer may have been Bertha Lomax, who was then being investigated by the FBI. Concerned about the NACW's reputation, Gaines asked that Lomax's name be left off an NACW Anniversary Souvenir Program.[97] Shortly thereafter, the NACW passed the resolution, "that the NACW vigorously opposes any individual or group that conspires by word or deed to overthrow the United States Government."[98] However, Gaines, too, had been accused of communist ties, perhaps because of postwar talks with a Communist Party member, Claude Lightfoot. In 1955, she asked that she be allowed to testify before the House Committee on Un-American Activities (HUAC) to clear her name of any connections to "communistic" or "front" organizations. Gaines admitted that she had "associated" with three or four organizations considered communistic during the war but withdrew when she learned about their affiliations. Stassen may not have been thinking of those organizations as much as her involvement with the Trumbull Park Committee, which he called "communistic."[99]

Gaines and Spaulding's disagreements may also have been aggravated by Spaulding's membership on the Frederick Douglass Home's Memorial and Historical Association. Indeed, one of the NACW's most difficult tasks was the stewardship of the Frederick Douglass Home. Since 1916, the NACW had assumed responsibility for its upkeep, in part through fund-raising and also through the association, which contained only NACW members. Unfortunately, the Douglass Home was in desperate need of repairs by the 1950s, which the NACW could not afford. To complicate matters, the association's accounting was so "muddled" that Gaines froze its monies until an audit was conducted. Gaines was then accused of being autocratic by some members of the association and the NACW, and the NACW retaliated by challenging Gaines's third term as NACW president.[100]

Indeed, Gaines's third election was rife with irregularities, ranging from denying members their voting privileges to hiring her husband to legally represent her.[101] Still, Gaines fought fiercely for this term because there were so many issues she wanted to resolve, including the financial problems of the Douglass Home and the building of the new NACW headquarters. She also wanted see the Sears Project through to its completion. If these pilot projects were successful, Sears had promised that the competition would extend to all, not just five, states. Further, Gaines and Chicago black leaders had hoped that Chicago organizations would receive a Sears grant, which they did.[102] But Gaines's allegiances to the Republican Party complicated her NACW presidency, a matter that did not go unnoticed by some NACW members and the press. At the fiftieth CNDA anniversary dinner in 1956 (at which Democrats were lambasted for their lack of a civil rights agenda), a *Defender* reporter wrote, "Gaines sat looking blissfully on at the crowded room of solid clubwomen clucking indignantly at the implications of the speaker's remarks."[103] The columnist concluded that the NACW was part of a Republican agenda.

This was unfortunately true to some extent. Two months after the anniversary dinner, Gaines had asked an NACW member to revise her speech for the 1956 NACW convention so that the Republican Party, not Mary Church Terrell, would be given credit for desegregating restaurants in Washington, D.C. Terrell led a three-year protest against restaurants in Washington, resulting in her victory in the court case, *District of Columbia v. John Thompson.* Her victory was nationally known and celebrated by blacks. Yet various organizations had credited Eisenhower with desegregating the Capitol's restaurants since he had vowed to do so in his State of the Union Address. In actuality, he had done very little.[104] Gaines had also asked the NACW speaker to credit the Republican Party with school desegregation, rather than the NAACP. Again, this was contrary to the widely known fact that the lawyers for *Brown vs. Topeka* had worked closely with the NAACP. Eisenhower, in fact, had distanced himself from the Supreme Court in 1954 so as not to alienate his southern white constituency.[105]

Conclusion

What do we make of Gaines and her "ascendancy" from Chicago to national politics? And what can we learn from her? Certainly her activism demonstrated how one black woman gained access to federal politicians and leveraged those connections to advocate for black women and civil rights. Although her strategies were sometimes questionable, she acted in part because of her high expectations for the NACW. To be sure, Gaines did achieve many of her NACW goals: the appointment of an NACW representative to the UN; NACW participation and influence in federal policy; advocacy of black civil rights; the establishment of the Mary Church Terrell Fund to fight discrimination; the building of a new NACW headquarters; securing tax-exempt status for the NACW; legal settlements of the Frederick Douglass Home and the Sallie Stewart Estate; and the NACW's unique Sears Project.

At the same time, we cannot dismiss the difficulties of her third term as NACW president. Her determination to straighten out legal and financial problems that had historically plagued the NACW was interpreted by other members as willful. Factionalism resulted, further aggravated when Gaines demanded absolute allegiance from clubwomen she had appointed as officers.[106] But perhaps the most grievous actions on her part were those which "muddied" her affiliations with the NACW and the Republican Party. That Gaines would deny Terrell and the NAACP their fair share in civil rights victories shows an abuse of power.

Gaines's legacy is also instructive because she left a documented trail of her activism of over fifty years. As such, one can detect specific strategies she used at the local, state, and federal levels. For one, she fostered coalitions. Her leadership in the CSC, the CCNO, and the Colored Women's Republican Clubs of Illinois reflected her ability to create a collective vision with diverse groups. Likewise, in her own political campaigns, she drew from various constituencies: labor unions, church groups, white and black women's clubs, and civil rights organizations. Her participation in the Chicago mayoral committees and commissions also taught her the symbolic, as well as pragmatic, value of working across ethnicities. Second, Gaines "worked" all levels of the government. For example, she understood how important the black Chicago vote was to state and national politicians. She also understood the critical role that Chicago blacks played in civil rights organizations. In short, Gaines was politically savvy, knew it, and acted upon it.

Third, although Gaines presented a public face, she spent a great deal of time behind the scenes. In some cases, she was not acknowledged, as with the 1940 Exposition. Similarly, the hours she devoted to judging youth essay contests or chaperoning teen dances were not ones that gave her high visibility. Clearly, Gaines was a hard worker and an indefatigable activist. Lastly, Gaines did not waver in her commitments. One always knew where Gaines stood on any issue, whether it was overcrowded schools, substandard housing, black women's lack of employment opportunities, or black women's worldwide exploitation. Regardless of her political aspirations, she never compromised her beliefs.

However, Gaines did not stand alone in her achievements. In her early years, she had the collective support and activism of the black women's clubs, who sewed clothes, provided medical care for needy families during the Depression, and donated food and other necessities to the Old Folks' Home and

Federated Home for Dependent Children. She also had the collective support of the CNDA, an organization that continued to support Chicago's black community institutions while also engaging in political advocacy. Indeed, because the CNDA was such a visible NACW district, it helped to propel Gaines into national leadership.

Although black women's clubs in Chicago were an enduring tradition, women in Chicago's public housing projects had also established their own mothers' clubs and social uplift activities in the early 1940s. The next chapter examines the women of the Ida B. Wells and Altgeld Gardens projects, who organized successful nurseries, kindergartens, and youth and adult programs.

6

Women's Activism in Public Housing

History of Chicago Public Housing

As noted in earlier chapters, one response to Chicago's housing shortage, especially in black communities, was public housing. During the late 1930s, the Public Works Administration built four low-rent projects: the Jane Addams, Julia Lathrop, Trumbull Park, and Ida B. Wells Homes, although the last project was not completed until 1941. Thereafter, the responsibility for building and operating public housing rested with the Chicago Housing Authority (CHA), consisting of five members appointed by the mayor.[1] Clearly city hall had a great deal at stake in the housing situation, both politically and economically. Concerned about race relations, the CHA followed what it called "community patterns" in public housing projects.[2] This meant that the racial composition of a particular project was to mirror that of the surrounding community. Initially, then, the southside Wells and Trumbull Park Homes were all black and all white, respectively. Conversely, the northside Addams and Lathrop Homes were multiethnic, although that did not necessarily mean that there were amicable social relations among the tenants.

Given the immense need for housing for blacks, how did the CHA select tenants for its projects? The first criterion was the income of potential residents. Initially, the CHA did not generally accept families whose incomes were five times over the cost of rent. During the war years, however, the CHA did raise the income level of public housing residents to accommodate more wartime factory workers. The second criterion was that residents be families with children; in most cases, nuclear families were preferred. The third criterion pertained to the housing conditions under which families currently lived. The CHA favored those families who lived in the most substandard housing, determined through a score sheet that assessed overcrowded kitchenettes, lack of kitchen and toilet facilities, and structural defects. As would be expected, there were more families who qualified for public housing units than units available. In fact, a 1939 study of 6,000 families rejected for public housing showed that many were living in substandard conditions.[3]

Most residents of public housing from the 1930s through the 1950s were not on public relief or assistance but were gainfully employed. In the late 1930s, for example, in all of Chicago's housing projects only 20 percent of families were on relief. The only exception was the Ida B. Wells Homes, because the CHA changed its eligibility requirements to accept more single mothers, including those on relief and assistance. Nonetheless, when the Wells Homes opened in 1941, at least half of the Wells residents worked, although many held menial jobs.[4] Even as late as 1950, 61 percent of all public housing residents worked, many in meatpacking and steel industries; only 27 percent of families had their rent paid through public assistance.[5] Overall, then, there was a strong working-class presence in Chicago public housing, at least until the mid-1950s.

Despite construction of more public housing during the war years, the CHA could not keep up with the housing demand. Using patriotic rhetoric, city officials declared that decent housing for workers was essential to the war effort. Accordingly, from 1942 to 1945 the CHA built an additional 3,200 units for war industry workers, based on projections of an estimated 110,000 new war jobs by 1943. At Altgeld Gardens alone, a project built for black wartime workers near the far southside industries, the CHA initially accepted only 1,500 families, even though CHA executive secretary Elizabeth Wood envisioned up to 8,000 units there.[6]

The demand for public housing did not abate after the war. In 1946, the CHA installed 3,400 temporary housing units at twenty-one sites, including parks and forest preserves. Again, demand exceeded supply: over 168,000 veterans applied. Consequently, the CHA converted five housing developments into low-rent housing for returning veterans. As a consequence, 53 percent of all new residents in public housing were veterans and other servicemen as of 1946. To accommodate them, the CHA lowered residents' income maximum to $1,500 annually.[7] In the process, some longtime residents of public homes were evicted. As the 1947 CHA annual report observed, "That a $1,500–a-year family would go to higher court to fight to remain in decent low-rent housing indicated need for housing in Chicago for lower and middle-income groups."[8]

Another reason for the great demand for public housing was that it was touted as modern, decent, and safe, at least until the mid-1950s. According to one CHA annual report, the following scenario awaited any visitor: "Visit a CHA community and you will see neat lawns, immaculate curtains at the windows, groups of adequately, even jauntily dressed children. You will get an immediate and strong sense of general good housekeeping, of plain but certainly respectable living."[9] Often these descriptions contrasted with conditions in adjacent impoverished neighborhoods: "Instead of dangerous streets, children who live in publicly owned homes play in safe, open spaces of their own. When evening comes, families work creatively together and have no need of getting as far away from home as they can. They get together and discuss many things."[10] Although the rhetoric may seem inflated now, at the time these descriptions matched the hopes of many CHA applicants. The prospects of a two-bedroom apartment—with running water, indoor toilets, separate bedrooms for parents and children, and flower and vegetable gardens—were what many parents, regardless of race or class, wanted for their families. Nearby parks, recreation areas, and schools gave families a further sense of security, safety, and community. The overwhelming number of applications to the Lathrop, Addams, and Trumbull Homes—280,000 for only 2,414 housing units—demonstrated how many people wanted to live in public housing.[11]

As such, most residents were eager to participate in public housing's community programs. Accordingly, the first public housing tenants organized credit unions, job placement offices, newspapers, craft shops, scout troops, nurseries, kindergartens, drama groups, social and mothers' clubs, PTAs, branch libraries, junior municipality governments, and athletic teams. For youth, there were dance clubs, such as the Silver Star Nite Club and the "Tropical Tut," with jukeboxes, floor shows, and coke bars. During the war, tenants planted victory gardens; in the summer of 1942 alone, public housing residents grew a total of 570,000 pounds of vegetables.[12] It was the first time, said the CHA, that many public housing residents had the chance "to handle damp earth, to see tiny green shoots poking up through the ground, to smell growing things."[13]

For its model of community development, the CHA drew in part upon the Michigan Boulevard Garden Apartments, a private housing complex for blacks built in 1929 through the philanthropy of Julius Rosenwald, founder of Sears Roebuck. Located within an entire city block of Bronzeville, the complex contained 421 modern apartments with gardens and courts. Most residents held professional and clerical jobs, and in fact they had been screened for "good character" and their ability to pay. These tenants developed a "neighborly spirit" by electing a representative from each unit who was then appointed to the board of advisers to help establish community improvements and activities. This board was instrumental in starting a nursery and mothers' and parents' clubs as well as in planning social activities.[14]

To be sure, the black residents of public homes considered themselves fortunate, compared to those in their surrounding neighborhoods, especially in the late 1940s and 1950s. By 1949, housing conditions for blacks had become even more desperate. One black elementary schoolteacher, who interviewed 162 children at her southside school, found that most lived in horrible conditions: only 28 percent had a private bath or toilet in their homes; nearly 60 percent used toilets in the hallways.[15] During the 1950s, the city demolished 10,000 of these "homes" on Chicago's southside. Yet the CHA found it difficult to procure the land for public housing, because those areas were purportedly zoned for industrial use, then later approved for private development by the city council. Of the 10,000 families displaced for slum clearance and private development, 9,000 were black. Ironically, 70 percent of them were ineligible for public housing because their income levels were too high.[16] As CHA social worker Mary Bolton Wirth explained the situation: "There is no real answer to the problem as long as public housing is a slum clearance program only, as not only do we tend to take the worst problems from the slums but we are running into slum dwellers in demolition areas who must be relocated and who have been denied public housing several times previously in other areas now demolished, as well as families whose leases were terminated by public housing as 'undesirable' families."[17]

To assist more blacks in securing public housing units, the CHA lowered residents' income requirements in the 1950s, accepting those whose incomes were in the city's lowest tenth. Further, the CHA accepted more single parents, poor parents, or elderly families without dependents, contrary to its original priority to accept mostly nuclear families with young children. Indeed, Wirth's prediction that more tenants would be on public relief and welfare came true.[18] Concurrently, the CHA expressed concern about the changing population by employing outdated sociological language that referred to "broken" and "disorganized" families, corroborated by reports of increased incidents of vandalism, antisocial behavior, and lack of involvement in community events.[19] One CHA solution to these purported problems was the formation of advisory committees, whose elected members addressed tenants' specific problems. For example, Altgeld Gardens' advisory committee tackled the lack of medical facilities and doctors in the community. Another project's committee advised that tenants be more carefully screened, resulting in the denial of applications from single mothers and alcoholic parents.[20]

Public housing became not only poorer in the 1950s but also increasingly black. By 1956, blacks lived in 76 percent of Chicago's 14,205 public housing units. In fact, seventeen of Chicago's twenty-seven public housing sites were made up entirely of black residents.[21] When the city council in 1956 approved six sites along State Street to build high-rise projects in the poorest black neighborhoods, it was one more sign that public housing was intended for only poor blacks. The CHA and Welfare Council of Metropolitan Chicago (WCMC) administrators were adamantly opposed to high-rises, which they claimed would result in further isolation and segregation of black residents. The WCMC was especially concerned about the segregated character of public housing. The council recommended a "quota" system so that housing projects could be integrated. Another recommendation was the use of scattered housing, that is, building public housing sites throughout the city so that blacks were not confined to one area. The WCMC also proposed that income limits be raised so that a "better" element of blacks and whites would live together in public housing.[22] Despite these recommendations, a "second ghetto" was created in Chicago.[23]

Perhaps because of the effects of increased isolation and segregation for blacks in public housing, the CHA had emphasized a neighborhood spirit and participatory governance structure as early as 1939. Accordingly, public housing units were divided into blocks, each with its own neighborhood council and captain, to facilitate participation. The CHA also encouraged tenants to develop certain forms of "appropriate" social behavior, for example, taking care of their own and CHA's property, cooperating with one another, and practicing "good citizenship."[24] In assuming that these skills needed to be cultivated, the CHA clearly worked from a deficit model.

In the early 1940s, the CHA, city officials, and funding agencies praised the all-black Wells Homes and the Altgeld Gardens Homes as model public housing projects. Women's clubs, university students, and schoolchildren from around the city toured them to witness the process of "bootstrap" community building. During the 1950s, however, differences in social class, nativity, family structure, and income levels created tensions among tenants. How these differences affected women's activism is examined in the next two sections.

The Ida B. Wells Homes

The site for the Wells Homes had been selected as early as 1934, following the "neighborhood composition rule"—that is, that public housing should not change the racial character of a neighborhood. Certainly, overcrowded conditions were exacerbated by demolishing existing tenements and kitchenettes in the predominantly black Douglas neighborhood to make way for the new Wells Homes. The siting of public housing in the neighborhood also aggravated nearby restrictive covenant associations, who protested that their real estate values would be affected. In fact, racial tensions were so great that some residents worried there would be race riots similar to those of 1919.[25] Although the project was completed in 1938, lawsuits delayed occupancy until 1941. Black organizations—including the Chicago Urban League (CUL), the Chicago Council of Negro Organizations (CCNO), and the Chicago and Northern District Association of Colored Women's Clubs (CNDA)—protested the delay, especially since over 1,200 families had been dislocated from their homes in order to build the Wells Homes. Black social worker Fern Gayden further emphasized that many families were on relief and so could not afford alternative housing.[26]

The naming of the project also stirred debate. The president of the CUL, A. L. Foster, suggested Ida B. Wells as the name; others put forward the names of once-prominent black clubwomen Joanna Snowden and Elizabeth Lindsay Davis. The members of the longstanding Ida B. Wells Club campaigned to have the project named after Wells and were successful. They were also active at the Wells Homes' dedication ceremony, placing Wells's biography, portrait, and diary excerpts in the project's cornerstone. Members of the Citizens Advisory Committee for the Wells Homes included Ida K. Brown, president of the Ida B. Wells Club; Nannie Williams, president of the CNDA; and prominent black women Dorothy Bushnell Cole, Irene McCoy Gaines, Loraine Green, Lula Lawson, and Mrs. Sewall Wright.[27]

When the Wells Homes opened in 1941, it was the largest housing project in Chicago, with forty-seven acres and a population of 6,900. But again, demand far exceeded availability: there were 18,000 applications for the first 1,600 units.[28] This situation may have been due to the fact that the CHA at the time was accepting tenants with the lowest income levels for all four projects. In 1941, half of the residents who were employed earned low wages, evident in the fact that nearly 95 percent of the tenants' annual income was less than $1,000 (the average family income was $775).[29] Not surprisingly, 24 percent of the Wells Homes' tenants in 1941 depended upon the WPA, 17 percent depended upon relief or charity, and 9 percent depended upon a combination of sources.[30] Further, half of the Wells Homes' tenants were so poor that they had none of their own furniture for their new homes. Oscar Brown, manager of the Ida B. Wells Homes (and later president of the Chicago chapter of the NAACP), wrote to various civic-minded groups, requesting their assistance. Ever-mindful of the need to "maintain the self-respect of the tenants," Brown suggested that the tenants pay a small fee for used furniture, which they could then repair in the Homes' wood and craft shop. One of the groups that donated furniture was the Women's Joint Committee on Adequate Housing (WJCAH), discussed in chapter 1.[31]

The Wells Tenant Council, similar to those in other public homes, was organized through the tenants' initiative. As such, they established their own programs infused with the spirit of family and neighborhood: nurseries, kindergartens, mothers' and youth clubs, victory gardens, clubs for home and lawn beautification, health facilities, and classes. Because city officials wanted the Wells Homes and other public housing projects to be success stories, the city and other funding agencies provided monetary and advisory assistance for community activities. For example, local schools and branch libraries worked with the Wells Homes' PTA, nurseries, and kindergartens.[32] The Elizabeth McCormick Fund provided nutrition education; the Infant Welfare branches assisted with the nursery. Through 1950, the American Red Cross provided courses on home nursing and surgical dressing. The Chicago Department of Health set up prenatal and preschool clinics, dental clinics, and milk stations; it also provided venereal disease and tuberculosis screenings. (At least thirty-one persons in the Wells and Brooks Homes died of tuberculosis from 1944 to 1946.) Compared to poorer black residents in nearby neighborhoods, the Wells Homes' tenants had greater access to health services and thus enjoyed improved health. Studies by the CHA in 1947 and 1948 showed, for example, that infants had a much better chance of survival if they lived in housing projects, compared to the "slum" areas nearby.[33]

In order for their programs to be successful, the Wells Homes' tenants had to engage in some degree of fund-raising. At a celebration of the first anniversary of the Wells Tenant Council, the parents decided on which playground equipment to purchase for their children, and subsequently organized fund-raising activities. Realizing the importance of a dental clinic on location, the Wells Homes' residents raised money for its equipment as well. The funding amounts may have been compromised, however, by tenants' low incomes. To counter that problem, the Wells Homes' tenants organized a program called "Get Off and Keep Off the WPA and Relief," whereby they secured job listings for several hundred jobs.[34] Whether this initiative actually led to tenants' employment was not clear. Regardless, these "bootstrap" activities supported the CHA's motto regarding the "self-respectability of poverty and what it can accomplish."[35]

Both fathers and mothers joined the Wells Tenant Council, although much of the programs' organization and development rested on women's shoulders. There were several reasons for this. First, more men than women were employed at the Wells' Homes and so they had less time to devote to council activities. Unlike some women at Altgeld Garden Homes who worked in war-related factories, mothers at the Wells Homes did not work as much outside the home.[36] Second, child- and home-related matters were conceived as traditional female issues. I have already discussed how black female activists historically circumscribed their work around issues of family and home. By necessity and tradition, the black women at the Wells Homes also wedded these concerns to community issues through the creation of institutions that cared for children, youth, and mothers.[37]

Appropriately, then, women at the Wells Homes organized a number of programs in 1945 for children and youth. One was a children's club, the Wee Wisdom Club, with a membership of eighty or more children. Headed by a tenant leader, Mrs. Callie Murphy, the club's goals were to cultivate the children's love of music, art, and drama and to better their understanding of racial and national groups worldwide. Murphy organized "travel parties," which included tours of Chicago's museums of art and natural history and attending theaters. The children also learned their own lessons in social uplift: they sent their old clothes to poor children in other countries.[38] The Wells Homes' women also established a nursery, with a sliding scale of fees that could accommodate mothers with lower incomes. The mothers supervised the playschool and took turns as leaders. Without this nursery, some mothers at the Wells Homes would not have been able to afford child care, as some of the nearby nurseries' fees were prohibitive.[39] Finally, the Wells Homes' women helped to organize a student government, the Wellstown Junior Municipality, which had a mayor and twelve alderpersons elected by young people in the project and the neighboring community. In turn, this group learned organizational skills by establishing a youth canteen and their own social events. This intergenerational model supports Patricia Hill Collins's elaboration of how black women, as "other mothers," collectively raised children and youth in their communities.[40]

Following the war, there was no decrease in activities at the Wells Homes: the craft shop opened to repair furniture and electrical equipment and to construct new pieces; the Boy Scouts used the shop to work toward their merit badges; garden clubs organized programs throughout the development; and the music and dramatic department's performance of children's plays provided monies for musical instruments for children who wished to study music at the Wells Community Center. In addition, there were leadership training courses at the community center for female tenants and classes in charm, cooking, drama, ballet and modern dancing, arts and crafts, piano, and sewing. The tenant health service committee promoted programs in prenatal and infant care and funded a dental clinic. Further, the Wells Homes now accepted older tenants, who organized their own club for recreation activities such as horseshoes, croquet, and shuffleboard.[41]

It is difficult to know how differences in the tenants' income levels and family structures (nuclear or female-headed) affected participation in the councils, committees, and women's clubs at the Wells Homes. Were single and married mothers as active in the mothers' and women's clubs? Were officers and program leaders elected from both groups of mothers? Unfortunately, there is little or no documentation on these matters. As would be expected, the CHA annual reports and monthly bulletins were largely celebratory, listing only the tenants' accomplishments. However, since the CHA screened applicants to ensure the success of public housing, at least through the late 1940s, those chosen probably demonstrated a great deal of motivation to participate in community development. Undoubtedly, the tenants enjoyed their new housing with modern amenities, which were a far cry from their previous residences, and they also appreciated opportunities to build better futures for their children. Lastly, architectural structures such as row houses and garden apartments, as well as the centrally located community center, encouraged social exchanges and participation among the tenants.

Scholars have noted the present isolation and containment of public housing tenants. But how did this historically occur? The Wells Homes had functioned from the beginning as a community in and of itself, with its own community center and facilities. To the extent that the CHA encouraged community building within public housing, it may have inadvertently discouraged connections with the larger black community. The Wells Homes, situated near the Bronzeville neighborhood, was within one mile of Parkway Community House (PCH), the South Side Community Art Center (SSCAC), the Wabash YMCA, and the South Parkway YWCA (SPY).[42] The black YWCA and YMCA did collaborate with Wells Homes' tenants in sponsoring programs for children, youth, and mothers in the 1950s. For example, the YMCA offered a variety of classes in art, languages, sewing, dancing, drama, and millinery along with recreational services for children of tenants of the Wells Homes as well as other neighborhood children. The women of the Wells Homes also used SPY's services. Mothers brought their babies to the SPY, then went swimming, had lunch, took a class, or just had a day of relaxation called "Homemaker's Holiday." Similarly, the SPY had been active at other public housing sites, mostly notably the Victor Olander Homes, the first high-rise project built in 1953. There, the SPY staff, with a group of tenant mothers, supervised a preschool program and helped to form a Y-Wives Club to supplement tenants' knowledge about child development.[43]

Women at the Wells Homes probably did not use the PCH's nursery and after-school programs because they had organized their own. But did they attend the PCH's evening forums, where concerned black citizens listened to political speakers and discussed community issues? Perhaps, but Wells Homes residents had formed their own committee in 1946 to sponsor guest speakers and group discussions.[44] In fact, there was a duplication of services at the PCH and the Wells Homes, including a tuberculosis clinic, a library, a nursery, an after-school program, and a speaker series.

In terms of financial support, the city gave more financial assistance to the Wells Homes' tenants than it did to other black community institutions. There were several reasons for this. First, the resources of the black community's institutions were already overtaxed by providing much-needed services to poor blacks. They competed with other black institutions for philanthropic monies. Second, since the mayor appointed CHA members, he had a direct interest in the public homes' success. That success relied largely upon tenants' volunteerism and social commitment, which were lauded by CHA reports. However, the mayor and the city council had contradictory goals; they wanted exemplary public housing but not at the expense of preventing private development. Although the city continued to provide health and recreational services to public housing residents through the 1950s, the success of those programs mattered less than accommodating large numbers of blacks in high-rise public housing and in privately developed apartments, such as Lake Meadows, located just north of the Wells Homes.

Interestingly, there are no records of women's clubs at the Wells Homes joining the CNDA. Perhaps some of the women at the Wells Homes did become members of CNDA-affiliated clubs, but it is more than likely that many did not. For one thing, women at the Wells Homes formed their own mothers' clubs and corresponding activities. Second, the women's involvement in tenant committees and councils probably limited their time and commitment to their own immediate community. Third, social-class differences were probably significant enough so that the Wells Homes' women would not have been recruited by clubwomen. As noted in the previous chapter, many clubwomen were middle-class professionals who were married to prominent black lawyers, doctors, and businessmen. The mothers' club at the Wells Homes did participate in health-education sessions at nearby Poro College in 1947 and 1948, along with the Douglas League of Women Voters, PTA members, CNDA-affiliated clubs, and black sororities. But such an inclusive event tells us little about specific social interactions or interclub relations.[45]

There was one interracial group of women, however, who were quite active at the Wells Homes. The Women's Joint Committee on Adequate Housing (WJCAH), discussed in chapter 1, had conducted two protests at the Wells Homes in the early 1940s. In the first case, the group seemed to be less interested in female tenants themselves than in soliciting information from tenants about the substandard conditions of their previous housing. The WJCAH planned to present this information to the city's department of health. The second occasion involved hearings related to a case in which two black women burned to death because of a neighborhood house fire. The WJCAH members drafted a petition protesting the inconsistent evidence presented by health, building, and fire department officials. Almost 650 women from various clubs and organizations signed the petition at the Wells Homes, which was then presented to the city council.[46] Most likely, the women at the Wells Homes also signed the petition.

In addition to the WJCAH, other groups visited the Wells Homes for purported activist causes. In 1941, the National Council of Jewish Women organized a tour of the housing project. They sent invitations to various "important" women's groups. Perhaps it was educative for those women, but what purpose did it serve for residents of the Wells Homes? During the war, University of Chicago nursing students also toured the Wells Homes, most likely to gain a fuller understanding of health problems and services at the project.[47] But the students did not volunteer their time. White schoolchildren, too, toured the housing projects and nearby "slum" areas. The Public Housing Association wanted to give these children firsthand information for a roundtable discussion on housing, which was to be presented to the northside district's principals and superintendents. As such, more privileged children learned about how the poor lived. As one youth observed, "We saw how people had to live, with rats running around their feet all the time." Another said, "Kids, just our age, had to share a bath tub with as many as 15 kids from four or five other families."[48] But, again, what political purpose did these children's discussions serve? If anything, these activities bordered on a kind of sanctioned voyeurism.

To be discussed more fully in the next chapter, the SPY moved to the Wells Homes' community center building in 1953. According to their agreement with the CHA, the SPY's mission was broadly defined to consider the social needs of the Wells Homes' community. Accordingly, the SPY staff was to develop educational and recreational programs for the residents; in turn, the residents would pay reduced YWCA membership fees. But because the Wells Homes' community center was already used a great deal by the residents, there was tension when the Y moved there.[49] Why, some residents may have asked, should they pay fees for programs in their own community center?

Nonetheless, the SPY's staff of four directors, four clerks, eleven teachers, one aide, and thirty-five volunteers developed a series of programs for Wells Homes residents, especially for mothers, youth, and children. There were workshops in sewing, millinery, knitting, leather crafts, and typing; offerings of over twenty classes in art, crafts, dramatics, book discussions, and singing; and even a class on "World Politics" cosponsored by the University of Chicago. Classes were apparently popular, as over 1,750 persons attended them. (Here the SPY probably tallied persons enrolled in each class.) A monthly forum series featured prominent politicians and policymakers such as black alderman Archibald Carey and University of Chicago professor Robert Merriam. One prominent speaker was lawyer William Ming, Jr., who spoke about the recent Supreme Court's decision on school desegregation and its implications for the Chicago public schools. Admission to the talks was free and dinner was optional.[50]

Additionally, the SPY staff tried to enlarge the residents' sense of community beyond the Wells Homes. They organized trips to Chinatown, the Hull House, the International House at the University of Chicago, and the Chicago Art Institute. There was a tour of the nearby Michael Reese Hospital so that Wells Homes residents would learn about medical research. But there may have been another reason for touring the hospital. The SPY staff wanted Wells Homes residents to learn how the hospital was connected to community development. At that time, deliberations for slum clearance were underway; but along with the Institute of Industrial Technology and the South Side Planning Board, Michael Reese Hospital planned to develop seven square miles for interracial living. Regardless, Mayor Kennelly and the Chicago aldermen found out about the plan and opposed it.[51]

But by and large, many of the SPY's programs were for youth, who were eager for their own clubs and activities. Indeed, as the CHA administration noted, "The YWCA has made a place for itself at Wells, especially with the young people, but has been disappointed in the failure of adult tenants and community leaders to respond to its program."[52] The teenagers published their own newsletter and organized their own speaker series. One guest speaker, black journalist Era Bell Thompson, talked about her recent trip to Africa; following her presentation, members of a percussion club practiced Afro-Cuban music and a Haitian dance. (Era Bell Thompson had, in fact, contributed monies to help pay for the instruments.)[53] There were other youth clubs: the Trenta-ettes (for girls) and the Y-Teen Club, a coeducational club joined by purportedly over 200 teens. However, there were no clubs organized only for boys, who more than likely participated in the nearby YMCA programs.[54] The SPY staff also cooperated with Planned Parenthood to extend programs to teen girls at the Wells Homes. But they were not sure how to proceed since Planned Parenthood had programs for married women only. One suggestion was to educate parents in hopes that they, in turn, would teach their daughters about sexual matters. As SPY director Regina Saxton put it, "We felt that since our community is an unsophisticated one, unused to verbalization about sex—that we proceed with caution."[55]

As noted in chapter 2, the SPY and the PCH cosponsored teen dances at the Wells Homes, which were popular with neighborhood youth. By 1957, the Coca-Cola Company agreed to underwrite summer dances at the Wells Homes and hired radio personalities to play teens' favorite records. The company also interviewed some of the teens and played these interviews on a local Sunday radio program. But Coca-Cola's motivations were not philanthropic. Company representatives noted that blacks drank more of their soda, and so they used this opportunity to expand their market. The SPY staff, though, was intent on other matters. As noted earlier, they sought to cultivate appropriate teen behavior, as evidenced by the dress codes. They were also worried that there was too little adult supervision for the numbers of teens who wanted to attend the dances.[56] Rival gang members sometimes tried to attend these dances, prompting the SPY staff to call the police. Apparently, some of the male youth who helped to plan the dances were members of the Nobles, a gang at the Wells Homes.[57]

At the same time, the SPY staff was struggling to define its own mission, specifically asking what communities it should serve. To be more fully explored in the next chapter, the SPY's move to the Wells Homes may have resolved some financial problems but it also created new ones. Further, the SPY staff found it difficult to recruit volunteers at the Wells Homes, in part because of gang-related problems and social-class differences. The staff's interest in expanding participation by Wells Homes residents in the larger community spoke to the SPY's own interest in becoming more involved in the larger community of Bronzeville. In fact, many working- and middle-class residents of Bronzeville had asked the SPY staff to expand its programs so they could be included. As such, the SPY began considering alternative locations. By the late 1950s, however, the SPY remained at the Wells Homes' community center. As the SPY's reports indicated, they were less successful than they had hoped, as they found that female residents at the Wells Homes and other nearby housing projects were increasingly disinterested in the SPY's programs.[58] This may have been because the SPY staff had its own model of middle-class leadership and so disregarded the forms of community building prevalent among poorer female tenants. Perhaps the staff did not work *with* the women at the Wells Homes as much as for them.

The Altgeld Gardens Homes

When the CHA built the Altgeld Gardens Homes in 1944, close to the iron and steel mills, its intent was to accommodate black wartime workers. Unlike the Wells Homes, Altgeld was physically remote and isolated, located twenty-six miles from downtown Chicago. The nearest community, Roseland, was eight miles away; Morgan Park, one of the oldest and wealthier black communities, was ten miles away. Significantly, Altgeld Gardens was also built on a dump site that had been used since 1940. Despite the isolation and potential environmental hazards, the CHA praised Altgeld Gardens for its spaciousness. As of 1947, there were only nine families per acre, compared to twenty-two at Trumbull Park, thirty-three at Cabrini Green, and fifty at Jane Addams. For these reasons, some Altgeld residents called their new home the "suburbs."[59] One high-school student wrote idyllically about her new residence there: "Away from the city's foul vapid breath / Out from the slums [*sic*] slow insidious death / Where God's clean air and pure breezes blow / Stands a small city state that's really aglow."[60]

But Altgeld Gardens' isolation would prove to be a disadvantage. For one, the nearby white communities of South Deering and Roseland were often hostile, refusing Altgeld residents access to hospitals, shopping centers, and other facilities. Second, Altgeld Gardens did not have access to the usual public services, such as public transportation, because of its distance. This would exacerbate residents' isolation so much that social worker Mary Wirth would later compare Altgeld Gardens to an Indian reservation.[61] Third, Altgeld Gardens' social services, especially the nursery, would founder because it was difficult to keep professional staff, given the great distance they had to travel.

Many of the first Altgeld Gardens residents were working- and lower-middle-class blacks, employed as factory workers, teachers, mailmen, and semiprofessionals. Among its first residents were eleven mothers who worked in war-related factories. As noted, to accommodate war workers, the CHA had raised public housing residents' income levels to $1,500. But at Altgeld Gardens, there was never a limit. As such, there were few residents initially who were unemployed or on relief. However, by 1952, 73 percent of Altgeld Gardens residents would receive public assistance. Further, more social problems would be reported, including fighting, theft, gambling, drugs, and alcoholism.[62] What caused these changes at Altgeld Gardens? In large part, they can be attributed to the CHA's shifting eligibility requirements, as well as Altgeld Gardens' physical isolation.

Like the Wells Homes, Altgeld Gardens had its own community center, nursery, kindergarten, and health clinic as well as coordinating councils, committees, and block captains to develop recreational and social programs. Each block had two rooms to use for game rooms, teenage canteens, or classes and meetings. Similar to the community spirit at the Wells Homes during the 1940s, the Altgeld Gardens Cooperative organized activities for all residents, including an annual festival with a parade and guests of honor.[63] But because of Altgeld Gardens' isolation, the CHA had to build an infrastructure beyond other public housing projects. There were plans for a shopping and amusement center located in the project, replete with privately operated food stores, a bakery, a drugstore, a restaurant, a beauty shop, laundry facilities, and a motion picture theatre with a 1,000-seat capacity.[64] Schools had to be built at and near Altgeld Gardens, as 61 percent of its population in 1947 were youth and children, that is, 1,000 preschoolers, 2,000 elementary children, and 1,000 high schoolers.[65] Although these facilities were essential, they would again reinforce Altgeld Gardens' isolation.

The Altgeld Gardens tenants were also active in various associations, at least until the mid-1950s. Many joined the PTA, even though its members were later perceived as "uppity" by poorer residents. The most active community group, though, was the Tenants League, which recommended civic improvements. Another group, the Bureau of Commerce, comprised of men only, advocated for cheaper transportation, more housing units in Altgeld, a new sewer system, and raising income eligibility for Altgeld Gardens, especially during the 1950s. The group also wanted to oust Ninth Ward alderman Reginald Du Bois, whom they considered a segregationist, and for good reason. In response to the desegregation of the Fernwood Housing Project in the late 1940s, Du Bois had insisted that blacks were being agitated to move into white communities.[66]

As with the Wells Homes, many of the health, educational, and social facilities were for children and youth. Described by CHA administrator Wood as a "model project," Altgeld Gardens had the largest children's building in all of Chicago's public housing, with a health center, nursery, auditorium, branch library, kitchen, and meeting rooms.[67] The Chicago Department of Health underwrote the cost for baby and prenatal care, preschools, and dental clinics, as well as for dentists, part-time doctors, and a full-time nurse. The Municipal Tuberculosis Sanitarium and the Tuberculosis Institute of Chicago tested children and adults for tuberculosis. Altgeld Gardens residents could receive Red Cross certification for first aid courses, especially important since there was no available hospital nearby.[68]

Other than its isolation, there was another reason that the city provided health services to Altgeld Gardens residents. The closest hospital in Roseland refused to accept Altgeld Gardens residents, forcing them to drive thirteen miles to Provident Hospital, a black southside hospital, or twenty miles to Cook County Hospital. Altgeld Gardens residents worked closely with the Community Fund of Chicago in the early 1950s to seek alternatives. For example, Altgeld Gardens residents asked Roseland Hospital to set aside two beds for its residents in emergency situations, for which the Community Fund would pay.[69] The hospital refused, prompting Altgeld's doctor, Louise Coggs, to declare: "Roseland Community Hospital is one of the most prejudiced hospitals in the Metropolitan Area of Chicago."[70] It was not until 1954 that the matter would be resolved, when the Community Fund funded an emergency ambulance service to Provident Hospital near Hyde Park and an emergency clinic with two part-time doctors at Altgeld Gardens. These services were usually critical for women in labor and children who needed emergency care. Since most doctors refused to travel to Altgeld Gardens and the police usually arrived too late, some women had their babies in cars before they arrived at Provident Hospital. Children, too, sometimes died because of delayed care.[71]

Because of Altgeld Gardens' isolation, there would be later problems for its nursery as well. But when it opened in 1945 as one of twenty all-day Chicago nurseries made possible through the Lanham Act, the nursery was the pride of the community. Considered "undoubtedly the best nursery plant in and around Chicago," its facilities surpassed other nurseries. It had six large playgrounds (one fenced for the youngest children), office space, a kitchen, laundry and bathing facilities, and "isolation" quarters. It could accommodate up to 200 preschool and kindergarten children, but with existing staff it could accept only eighty children. Children of all races were accepted, but since Altgeld was an all-black project, so was its nursery.[72] The all-female staff—including a director, two teachers, four aides, a nurse, a counselor, a cook, and a housekeeper—was exemplary as well. The director, Dorothy Jones, was a black woman with a graduate degree in nursery education from the University of Chicago. The Community Fund, which supported the nursery, called her "one of the most progressive and able directors."[73] Her teaching staff was also competent. One had graduate training; the other had three years of undergraduate training in kindergarten and nursery education. The four aides, too, had some college training, as well as nursery experience. A registered nurse gave physical examinations weekly and checkups periodically. A counselor from the Chicago Orphan Asylum came weekly for intake studies and to advise parents on home activities for children. The director noted that the mothers' knowledge of child development markedly improved because of the counselor and her experiences with the nursery school staff.[74]

The nursery programs were varied and creative in play. The staff divided the children into play groups by age and individual differences. Additionally, there was individualized treatment for some children who needed speech therapy or more quiet activities. The programs were considered so successful that parents from a nearby black neighborhood, West Chesterfield, asked if their children could enroll. The Altgeld Parents' Council agreed to accept these children, as it meant more monies to sustain the nursery. Ironically, the nursery was forced to accept outside children, even though the council estimated that there were nearly 200 children within Altgeld Gardens who needed nursery care. But some Altgeld Gardens parents could not afford nursery fees, even though fees were only three dollars weekly, less than other nurseries.[75]

A parents' council oversaw the operations of the nursery and playschools. Although all parents of nursery children were eligible for council membership, mostly women became involved in the budget, membership, programs, and publicity committees. Following the withdrawal of federal funds, the council worked with the Illinois Parents' Council on drafting a bill that would provide public funds for nurseries. Unfortunately, they did not succeed.[76] They then directed their efforts towards fund-raising, although they had little experience. Regardless of budgetary concerns, Altgeld's nursery received a positive evaluation from the WCMC in 1946 because of its strong staff, interested parents, and excellent programs. Yet, the WCMC noted, the nursery did not have a board of health permit nor were its fees scaled to match parents' ability to pay. Similar to the PCH's nursery, Altgeld's had to rely upon philanthropic support. In order to qualify for Community Fund monies, the nursery was asked to charge a minimum fee for those who could not otherwise afford childcare. Since tuition fees accounted for 43 percent of its income, this would represent a significant loss for the nursery. To compensate, the council organized fund-raisers. They purchased a movie concession and hoped to make $75 a week showing films. But if some parents could not afford nursery fees, how could they afford weekly movies? The council also tried to interest outside groups and individuals in contributing but were not successful, given Altgeld Gardens' distant location. In the WCMC's words, the nursery had been living a "hand-to-mouth" existence since 1946.[77]

During the late 1940s and 1950s, the nursery's budget fell increasingly in the red. Tuition fees, fund-raising activities, and outside funding were insufficient to meet the costs. As of 1955, the nursery still relied on the Community Fund, although it also received some monies from school fees, the Joint Negro Appeal (a southside black organization), and proceeds from a thrift shop opened by a parent-teacher group. Although the parents were active in fund-raising activities and seeking outside monies, the Community Fund considered them inexperienced and erratic. In all fairness, some of the parents' monetary resources were already tight. By the 1950s, most residents were low-income tenants. The situation became even more serious when later, in 1959, some parents were laid off because of the steel strikes.[78] Given Altgeld Gardens' physical isolation, it was difficult for tenants to seek other jobs or to attract blacks outside of Altgeld Gardens to their fund-raising events. Further, some families were on relief and so could not contribute. To add to their difficulties, there was turnover in the nursery staff because of low salaries and Altgeld Gardens' distance. Even the director, Dorothy Jones, resigned in 1955.[79]

Still, the nursery council remained active through the late 1950s in parent education programs, mostly through parent-teacher conferences and parent lunches with speakers from the library, the Infant Welfare station, and the Chicago Park District. Two trained social workers also tried to encourage poorer Altgeld Garden parents to use the nursery.[80] But a demographic shift had occurred at Altgeld Gardens, beginning in the early 1950s. According to the nursery's application to the Community Fund, the "more stable and intelligent" families had moved from Altgeld Gardens because they had better jobs and so had exceeded the CHA's income levels. In turn, new residents from a "less desirable class" moved there.[81] Many were, in fact, migrants who had lived in the slum areas slated for private development. Once again, the nursery application described the new households in the sociological jargon of "broken homes." The nursery staff complained that the parents not only had little money to pay for nursery care but also were not interested. Prefiguring the Head Start rhetoric, the nursery staff noted that by 1960 there were more than 1,000 preschoolers in Altgeld Gardens who needed to learn school-readiness skills.[82]

The language here is telling, because it reveals the perceptions of a largely middle-class professional staff. Although one could argue that their descriptions served a pragmatic purpose—to convince the Community Fund that the Altgeld Gardens nursery needed more money to expand its services, especially its staff of social workers—I do not believe that tells the full story. Paradoxically, the Community Fund insisted that the community organizations it funded provide most of the financial support (through fund-raising, tuition fees, donations, and so forth), yet the Community Fund did not consider how the physical isolation of Altgeld Gardens affected the nursery's ability to generate monies.

On the other hand, the staff now faced a different clientele: incoming families who were mostly unemployed or on public assistance. One black researcher, also a teacher at Altgeld Gardens, argued that reduced income limits compromised the quality of tenants and isolated poorer blacks from working-class models. As he observed, many families were headed by unmarried women who purportedly had more children to draw more public aid. Teenage girls, he noted, also became pregnant, thereby "perpetuating this pattern."[83] As one older resident complained, "The Housing started letting any and everybody move out there. Practically all of them just came up from the South. They have ruined this place. All they do is drink, fight, make babies, and stay on ADC."[84] Certainly the number of single-headed households had increased at Altgeld Gardens and other public housing projects. As such, these perceptions spoke especially to class differences and tensions among officials, funding agencies, and tenants.

Researchers and social workers had also noticed a decrease in associational involvement during the 1950s at Altgeld Gardens, as well as at other public housing sites.[85] However, they too, along with philanthropies and city agencies, privileged certain kinds of community involvement, as well as middle-class models of leadership. More than likely, poorer tenants' associational life was more informal and less subject to CHA supervision. For example, in 1954, the purportedly "communistic" Temple of Islam visited Altgeld Gardens to recruit members. Little is known about them and their activities, except that they were anti-white and anti-CHA.[86] However, at one of the Altgeld meetings, Brother Minister Malcolm spoke to a group, admonishing them about "the Negro's language, his flag, and where we come from."[87] That minister was none other than Malcolm X. This group and Malcolm X's involvement raise intriguing questions about poorer tenants' associational life that have not yet been documented. Did many tenants join the group? Might this group have contributed to some tenants' reluctance to participate in CHA-led activities? We should not assume that some poorer tenant women did not take on informal leadership roles within their blocks or units. Perhaps the CHA and other agencies underestimated the degree to which poorer residents resisted their rules, regulations, and recommendations. For example, when social workers at Altgeld Gardens "tipped off" the management about unwed mothers' sexual activities, we should not be surprised that there was animosity and resistance.[88] Unfortunately, we have only the official records of city and funding agencies, not the perspectives of the poorer tenants themselves.

Conclusion

Clearly, many similarities can be drawn between the Wells Homes and Altgeld Gardens. During the 1940s, most residents, especially female tenants, were active in establishing programs and activities at the two projects, especially for mothers, youth, and children. Although this created a sense of community within the projects, it had the effect of isolating the residents from the larger community. In the case of Altgeld Gardens, its residents became the most isolated. Both housing projects began to change in the postwar years and especially in the mid-1950s, when the CHA lowered tenants' income requirements and also began to assume more of a social worker-client relationship with the tenants. The CHA did so most often through their own staff, as well as through collaboration with other social institutions, such as the SPY. What becomes clear, although unacknowledged by the CHA or the SPY, is that their expectations for residents' behavior were based upon middle-class versions of leadership and lifestyles. There is little evidence that they worked with and respected female tenants' ways of organizing. Their sometimes derogatory summations of the women's disinterest in their children's welfare and CHA-sanctioned activities may well have masked these tenants' own initiatives and resistance to the CHA's and the SPY's programs.

7

The Chicago YWCAs

Introduction

The history of the YWCAs (Ys) of Chicago demonstrates how female activism occurred on multiple levels: among administrators and board members of the citywide Ys; among the professional staff of the black Ys; and among the black and white Y residents and club members who conducted protests to integrate the Y's facilities and programs. Not surprisingly, there were sometimes class-based and racial tensions as Y administrators and staff sought to provide services within their designated neighborhoods, while also extending those services so that their facilities would become more interracial. To be expected, black and white administrators sometimes held different ideas about integration.

While white administrators usually recommended a gradualist approach toward integration, the all-black staff at the South Parkway Y (SPY) insisted that their facility was intended primarily to serve the black community. Because the SPY's budget was minimal, however, it limited its outreach and fund-raising efforts to the black community. Further, its attempts to negotiate autonomy, as well as its interdependence with other Chicago Ys, revealed how fragile its influence and monetary base were. Forced to sell its Bronzeville property in 1953, the SPY relocated to the Wells Homes' community center, where the staff faced new challenges in developing programs for low-income residents.

Conversely, the West Side Y (WSY), largely through its residents and club members, was successful in establishing interracial clubs and in desegregating its residence and swimming pool. Its history reveals how the direct action of black and white working-class women and girls helped to change the Chicago Metropolitan Y's separatist policies and segregated facilities.

Desegregating the Chicago Ys

In 1934, members of the Gloom Chaser Dance Group, a WSY white club, expressed interest in race problems. They decided to invite black speakers to their meetings so that they could interpret black literature and spirituals.[1] The group was also interested in changing the Y's segregated pool policy, as was a group of black and white girls who had become friends at Camp Sagawau, the Y's summer camp. Indeed, Camp Sagawau was the Y's most successful multiracial program, with Mexican American, Asian American, American Indian, black, and white girls.[2] When the white girls at the camp realized that their black friends could not swim with them at the WSY, they boycotted the swimming pool. They then formed their own interracial club, the Jolly Go Getters Club. Like the Gloom Chaser Dance Group, they read black literature and discussed race issues. But the Jolly Go Getters were more politically active, perhaps because of the club's black membership. At an American Youth Congress meeting, they listened to Angelo Herndon speak about his experiences in organizing sharecroppers in Georgia and being sentenced to a chain gang. The girls sent letters of protest to free Herndon, as well as to free the Scottsboro boys, unfairly accused of raping a white woman in Arkansas. They also circulated a petition supporting a federal anti-lynching bill. Lastly, they continued to demand that black girls be able to use the WSY's swimming pool.[3]

The girls' clubs were not the only groups to protest the Y's segregated pool policy, however. In the 1930s, when a black girl tried to attend a swimming class at the WSY sponsored by the International Ladies Garments Workers Union, she was told that she could use the gym but not the swimming pool. The union immediately protested, prompting the WSY to establish a special committee on the matter. The committee later recommended that the WSY be allowed "to experiment" and let black girls use the pool. The Metropolitan Board agreed, although it stipulated that white and black girls use the pool separately.[4]

Until the early 1940s, all of the Chicago Y residences were also segregated, in large part because of neighborhood locations. Additionally, the Chicago Y policy explicitly stated that black women could not live in the whites' residences, unless they were "transients," that is, guests with a two-week limit.[5] In such situations, they were still segregated and made to feel so unwelcome that few black women sought such arrangements. Yet the crowded conditions and substandard housing of most Chicago black neighborhoods, as well as the influx of black wartime workers in the early 1940s, severely limited young black female workers' housing choices. The first black transient resident of a white Chicago Y was Mildred Slaughter, a wartime worker, in 1942. The white residents befriended her and decided to petition for her to stay as a long-term resident. But the staff disagreed and sent Slaughter to the downtown Y.[6] Later that year, staff members from the three mostly white Ys, including the WSY, recommended that their residences be desegregated. But they cautioned that this be done gradually. Further, they advised, black applicants had to "fit" with the residence, probably referring to issues of respectability and Christian behavior. Further, they could stay for only one night, with the staff assisting them with subsequent housing.[7] The Y's central administration considered their 1942 recommendation progressive, stating that "the last stronghold of segregation, discrimination against Negroes in the residences should be abolished."[8]

The integration of residencies occurred slowly, although the Metropolitan Board aimed for a policy of integration by the end of 1944. Again, however, their idea of integration was limited to black women as "transients" at the white Ys. Some white staff members thought that more time and experimentation were necessary to avoid potential conflicts. One residence director cautioned that there was a difference between "taking in" a person and a group. Another director noted that even the SPY, the black Y, did not accept all black girls but only those who met certain criteria, such as providing three references.[9]

However, the issue was not limited to black women only. In 1943, the Y's board of directors had "endorsed" the Japanese American evacuees as part of their war service committee program. The Chicago Metropolitan Y organized an orientation committee for Japanese American women at which the staff and volunteers invited Japanese American women to the Y and provided them with information about other recreational facilities and churches.[10] Yet not all Japanese American women who applied to the Y residences were accepted. At the McGill Y, only eight of its ninety residents were Japanese American. (Three were black.) The WSY had also decided to accept a few black and Japanese American women, along with several American Indian and East Indian women.[11] Still, all of these nonwhite women could only live there as "transients."

Yet some clubs and programs did become more integrated. Members of the WSY's Industrial League continued their involvement in race issues, including efforts to abolish the poll tax and to create a permanent FEPC. Several black girls also became members of the league's executive committee. Club memberships became more diverse as well. By 1944, the Waller Club was two-thirds black and one-third white; the Hi-Flicka Club, a previously all-white club, had accepted two black members. The staff, too, became more diverse. By 1944, some of the WSY's advisers were black and Japanese American.[12]

That same year, the Chicago Ys distributed a questionnaire to better understand the effects of their interracial efforts. Black girls responded that they thought the white girls had gained a better understanding of blacks' difficulties, especially with housing. For most white girls, the interracial committees and clubs had been new experiences and their first opportunities to meet black college girls "of culture and education." In response to a question about race relations, one white girl replied, "Many circumstances have hindered race relations in Chicago. I can think of none that have bettered it. Job opportunities have increased only because of the emergency of the war effort. Many opportunities are still denied."[13]

Yet not all Chicago Ys were so successful in integrating their programs. The SPY's advisers and committees were all black; their clubs, too, were mostly black, with only a few Chinese American women.[14] This was not surprising, given their location in the center of Bronzeville. As such, the SPY staff did not see themselves as a Y branch as much as a "center located in the heart of the Negro community."[15] Promoting outreach to the immediate neighborhood was more important to them; as such, they were not as interested in integration. The Evanston Y's clubs and staff were also segregated, although for different reasons. The exclusivity of this wealthy suburb was not conducive to integration in general. For example, even though a number of black students attended Northwestern University, they could not live in its dormitories. Some of Evanston's newspapers had policies that dated back to the 1930s preventing group pictures of blacks and whites.[16] When a photographer of the Evanston Community Chest took such group pictures in 1931, the Chest cut out sections of them, stating that they could not display pictures in Evanston "which showed the two races together."[17]

To bolster the interracial efforts of all Chicago Ys, the Chicago Metropolitan Y formed an interracial practices committee in 1945. Its central concern was recruiting volunteers who would promote their interracial programs. One way to recruit volunteers, they decided, was to "softpedal" intercultural programs so that the volunteers would experience "feelings of togetherness."[18] Discussion groups, teas, and parties were suggested activities. The white Ys also invited black women "of some significance" as speakers.[19] Although the report listed no names, invitees probably included the SPY staff and prominent black clubwomen.

As a result of these activities, the Chicago Metropolitan Y's 1946 report was largely congratulatory about its integration efforts. To be sure, the Ys had made some progress so that their policies were more in agreement with Christian principles. The Chicago Metropolitan Y staff had become even more diverse when Mary Smith of the SPY became the Chicago Metropolitan Y's first black vice-president.[20] Likewise, there were many interracial clubs and programs, especially at the WSY. Camp Sagawau continued to be described as a place where "different races lived and played together in perfect harmony."[21] As early as 1944, 25 percent of the camp's girls were black, and six other ethnic groups were represented there as well. Admittedly, the integration of the residences was still a problem, although admitting black and Japanese American women as "transients" was considered a gesture in the right direction. Within a short time, the McGill Y would accept black female students from the nearby George Williams College as "permanent" residents. Because of their educational level, these black women more than likely "fit" the Y's criteria for long-term residents. There was no indication, though, that black working-class women were accepted, except as "transients."[22]

The SPY and Black Activism

The SPY provided a very different portrait in terms of outreach and interracial activities. During the 1930s and 1940s, it had promoted programs that fostered pride in black literature, drama, and music, as well as an awareness of black political and economic issues. Because of its location in the heart of Bronzeville, the staff worked directly with neighborhood institutions and poorer residents. When it relocated to the Wells Homes in 1953, the SPY became one of the few organizations to work directly with public housing residents of the Olander and Wells Homes projects. To be expected, there were sometimes ideological and class differences as the SPY staff negotiated how it worked with the projects' residents.

The SPY's staff consisted of mostly middle-class, educated black women, deeply involved in other Bronzeville community organizations. Social worker Mary Smith, a graduate of Fisk University and the University of Chicago, had worked with the Chicago Urban League's (CUL's) Special Shelters Committee and as a vocational guidance teacher at DuSable High School during the 1930s. As head of the SPY's membership drive, she was assisted by staff member Ruth Moore Smith, a board member and fund-raiser for the PCH, as well as other clubwomen such as Mrs. Louis B. Anderson and Ella Moseberry. Mattie Waters, director of the SPY fund-raising campaign, had been active in many black women's clubs. Maude R. George, chair of the SPY branch committee of management, had been president of the Douglas League of Women Voters, the Chicago and Northern District Association of Colored Women's Clubs (CNDA), and the Illinois State Association of Colored Women's Clubs.[23] Indeed, most prominent black women activists of the Chicago Black Renaissance were involved in the Y at some time.

The SPY staff organized a number of programs for young working women and neighborhood residents. They offered classes and clubs on race history, world problems, and current events, as well as arts and crafts, sewing, cooking, dancing, drawing, and painting. As early as 1933, industrial secretary Thelma McWorter (later Wheaton) taught female workers about labor laws, especially unemployment, minimum wage, and child labor.[24] In addition to these educational opportunities, the facility had social rooms for members and a residence that could accommodate forty-eight girls.[25]

The SPY's residents not only participated in Y activities but were directly influenced by the larger community, since many community organizations met there. In 1937, the girls started a business program, sparked by a CUL conference that noted that most black women did not obtain jobs through employment agencies but through social contacts. This prompted discussion about how southside white businesses hired only white women and whether even the other Chicago Ys would hire black women.[26] Likewise, when the Chicago branch of the Association for the Study of Negro Life and History (ASNLH) celebrated its anniversary at the SPY, the girls had an opportunity to meet the association founder, Carter G. Woodson. They also heard Adah Waters, former supervisor of the Amanda Smith Industrial School, and prominent clubwoman Georgia Faulkner give short histories of the Chicago ASNLH branch's founding. The South Side Forum also presented a speaker series, including talks by Pauline Redmond, the CUL's director of social relations, and Neota McCurdy, the *Defender*'s music editor who spoke on blacks' contributions to American music.[27]

Despite the SPY's location, it was still successful in establishing some interracial programs. As early as 1932, staff members had held a race relations tea and invited other Y branch club members. At this tea, two black and three white women formed the Equal Rights Committee of the League of Industrial

Girls. The committee grew to ten members who started a rental library of books by and about blacks, so that they and others could learn more about blacks' contributions. They also published an anthology of black poetry, *The Rhythm of Color,* which sold 250 copies. (Unfortunately, I have not been able to locate a copy of this anthology.) They studied the anti-lynching bill, endorsed it, and wrote their congressional representatives. They also invited a representative from the Y's civil liberties committee to discuss "equal rights" from both a racial and an economic point of view.[28] Given the SPY's geographical isolation, such interracial activities were remarkable, especially during the early 1930s.

Before and during the war years, the SPY's staff focused mostly on race problems, especially black employment and the housing shortage. The SPY formed a special committee to encourage black residents to open their doors to black female workers in need of accommodations. As Ella Moseberry, head of the committee, stated, "In times like this, the offering of a home to a war worker isn't just a business proposition—it's a patriotic service."[29] Likewise, the SPY staff promoted other events related to work and politics. For example, a black union leader spoke to several of the SPY's clubs, and members discussed the goals of the Brotherhood of Sleeping Car Porters. The SPY's staff promoted the members' and residents' interests in such events, asking them in a questionnaire to indicate their interests in international relations, minority issues, the anti-lynching bill, birth control, and labor standards.[30] Their efforts paid off. During the war years, there were over eighty black members in the business and professional program, many of whom were college educated and who sought employment commensurate with their education. The largest memberships, however, were in the Industrial Program, with 211 members, and the Girls Reserve Program, with 368 members.[31]

Given Bronzeville's need for health and recreation facilities, the SPY designed a comprehensive health program for women from 1944 to 1949. This service provided complete medical exams, which included gynecological exams and chest X-rays to test for tuberculosis. There were classes in nutrition, reproductive issues, venereal disease, and health legislation. The staff initiated a special program, the "Ladies Day Out Program," to encourage mothers and their children to participate in the health programs. Mothers listened to lectures on child development, followed by lunch, an exercise class, and a medical exam for themselves and their children. For many of the women, this was a new experience for they had never had a complete physical examination before. The SPY staff also encouraged the women to use its recreational facilities in tennis, archery, swimming, bowling, dancing, fencing, and rhythmic gym, as well as the neighborhood bowling alley and roller-skating rink. During the program's first two years, from 1944 to 1945, over 7,385 women took advantage of these services, an indication of how sorely such medical and recreational services were needed in the community.[32]

In 1944, the SPY also established another critical program, the employment counseling service. This was in response to some factory employers' complaints of "maladjusted" black female workers' "inappropriate behaviors and attitudes."[33] Clearly, these vague remarks tell us little about the social dynamics or relations between blacks and whites in workplaces. To be sure, industry was rife with incidents of discrimination, especially during the war years. Yet the Chicago Council of Social Agencies (CCSA), who funded the project, framed the problem as one of blacks' social disorganization, saying it was due to "the influx into the community of Negroes unaccustomed to city life and unacquainted with Chicago."[34] The SPY staff tried to get to the bottom of the issue, sending letters to over seventy-five companies that had hired large numbers of black women. But only three replied. The SPY counseling staff then met with those company officials who stated that such problems were generally handled through their personnel departments.[35] It was not clear whether the staff was ever successful in arranging a meeting with the personnel staff.

Regardless, from the very beginning there were conflicts about what the employment counseling service should provide. The CCSA wanted the program to provide information on various types of work, with an emphasis on black women's "adjustment" to their present jobs. The SPY staff, though, realized how tenuous black women's employment was. They wanted counseling that would help black women prepare for the possibility of postwar unemployment, as well as maintain the gains that black women had already made in employment. The black female workers themselves wanted vocational testing and counseling so that they could find better jobs. This was especially true for the college-educated women.[36] The SPY was in a difficult position. Keenly aware that black women would be laid off after the war, they wondered whether the best strategy was to assist workers in keeping their present positions. Although not stated, they may have realized that employment opportunities were further limited for those black migrants who had limited schooling in the South.

Nonetheless, the SPY staff adopted several strategies. From 1944 to 1945, the program staff counseled at least sixty girls "toward better job adjustment."

These sessions were to teach black women how to adjust to the frustrations of their jobs. Realizing the limitations of this program, the staff cooperated with other agencies in providing over 100 girls with group counseling. Significantly, the SPY staff held at least seventy meetings with factory and union personnel, government agencies, and community agencies on the problems of black female employment.[37] In their words, their objective soon became not only to help women keep their present positions but also "to work for secure, unrestricted employment for Negro women."[38] This entailed further vocational counseling and testing. As such, the program counselor worked with the U.S. Employment Service and the Metropolitan Service Department of the YWCA. From 1944 to 1946, they interviewed 339 women, administered 269 vocational tests, and counseled 183 girls. The SPY staff hoped to help girls further improve their skills so employers would "be impressed with their indispensability."[39] Nonetheless, many employers did not want to hire any women, much less black women, after the war.

During the postwar years, the SPY had its own problems as well. There were budget deficits, staff turnover, and difficulties in soliciting volunteers. Like other black institutions, the SPY could not serve the needs of all residents of Bronzeville, which was becoming even more crowded and impoverished. As such, the SPY continued to be pushed in different directions. Public housing projects were a part of Bronzeville, and their residents also needed help. Because of the Chicago Metropolitan Y's goal of inclusive membership, the SPY was thought to be an ideal Y branch to work with the CHA homes. When the SPY hired a new assistant residence director, she was excited by this prospect. A graduate of the Atlanta School of Social Work, Jennie Buckner was well prepared to work with public housing residents, as were the other credentialed SPY directors.[40]

Shortly thereafter, the SPY moved to the Wells Home in 1953. One specific goal of the SPY staff was to enlarge the concept of neighborhood for residents of the Wells Homes so that the residents would participate in activities of other organizations. The staff had also hoped to expand their services beyond the Wells Homes. Given their present location, however, this proved somewhat difficult. Within a short time, the staff discussed moving to another location, one that would be more "inclusive."[41] This word, though, was contentious on several grounds. For one, the SPY staff now wanted their programs and membership to become more interracial, similar to those at the other Chicago Ys. During the 1950s, the human relations approach had added momentum to the Y's existing interracial activities, and so the SPY staff may have felt even more pressured to integrate their center. Some SPY staff pointed out how the Woodlawn Y, another black Y, had moved to a mixed neighborhood of white, black, and Puerto Rican residents. The staff there had been able to establish interracial programs and membership, in part through a cadre of black and white female volunteers.[42]

Second, the SPY staff acknowledged that they had difficulty in recruiting volunteers from outside the Wells Homes. Potential volunteers may have feared gang activity at the Wells Homes or were concerned that the SPY did not serve the larger community. Third, the SPY staff knew that, despite the increased poverty of Bronzeville, there were social-class differences among black residents. Some staff members questioned whether the middle-class residents living in the private development of Lake Meadows could "relate to" Wells Homes residents.[43] At one point in 1959, when an administrator of the Welfare Council of Metropolitan Chicago (WCMC) stated that there was no stable black southside community to be integrated, a SPY staff member, Olive Diggs, vehemently disagreed. She found that the black southside was remarkably diverse in terms of culture, economics, religion, and social class. To her, the word "integrated" meant more than just "interracial."[44] Fourth, some persons asked whether services could be made available to middle-income groups, not only the poor. If so, perhaps another location would better serve all. In short, the SPY staff needed to decide which people it would serve and where.

Lastly, the SPY had been forced to relocate to the Wells Homes because of its large debt. When the SPY had purchased the property at South Parkway in 1927, the women had raised only $22,000 toward the payment. The staff voted to use the $100,000 in a reserve fund, a gift from white publisher Victor Lawson, to purchase the property. They later returned only a small amount of the money they had taken from the reserve. When they sold the SPY building in 1953, that money went back into the reserve, not for a new facility.[45] Given the SPY's debt, the staff had little choice except to relocate to the Wells Homes, which charged them a token $1 to use their community center.

The SPY had not been the only social agency to locate at the Wells Homes' community center. In 1952, the South Side Settlement House (SSSH), which had occupied the center since the late 1940s, had vacated the building for a new facility farther south in Bronzeville. Most tragically, its director, Ada McKinley, had died the same evening that the cornerstone of the new building was laid. One of the most prominent among black clubwomen and a social welfare activist in Chicago and the state of Illinois, McKinley was well known for her community accomplishments.[46] Under her able directorship, the SSSH staff had assisted Wells Homes and other public housing residents, including the elderly at Prairie Avenue Courts. Additionally, they assisted Bronzeville residents in finding new housing during the slum clearance of the 1950s. One could argue that McKinley and her staff had provided a formidable model for the SPY's staff in how to conduct outreach with public housing residents and the larger community of Bronzeville. But the SSSA had the advantage of being an indigenous and enduring community institution, not a branch of a large metropolitan organization.

Given the SPY's debts, the staff resorted to fund-raising. They had a brilliant idea, but it would become controversial with the Metropolitan Y's administrators. In 1957, they proposed to invite Daisy Bates, chair of the Little Rock NAACP, which had been critical of the desegregation of the Little Rock schools. In addition to a speech by Bates, the SPY staff planned a fashion show and a film. Even though Bates was a controversial speaker, the Metropolitan Y officials didn't know who she was and so gave their approval. When they found out more about her, they became concerned that a talk on integration would not be appropriate for Chicago, which was having its own problems in school desegregation. In the end, Bates canceled the talk, worried that she would have to "soft pedal" her message. However, the SPY staff and volunteers had already sent out invitations and posted publicity, so they had egg on their faces. They had hoped that the speech would give their Y greater prestige and help to recruit more volunteers. The Metropolitan Y saw it differently. They worried that if the SPY sponsored the event, it would look as if only the SPY, not the Chicago Metropolitan Y, favored integration.[47] Further, they did not want to ruffle Chicago politicians' feathers.

Needless to say, the SPY remained at the Wells Homes, where it continued its outreach efforts, along with outreach at the Victor Olander Homes. In fact, the same year that the SPY had moved to the Wells Homes, it had also started programs at the Olander Homes. Significantly, the Olander Homes was a fifteen-story high-rise, then the tallest public housing building in Chicago. Unlike the Wells Homes, the Olander Homes was initially interracial.[48] Yet its architecture must have presented challenges to the SPY staff and the tenants in terms of how to build community and consensus. Additionally, the block units of the CHA's governance structure may have reinforced the physical isolation of tenants of the Olander Homes. It is not clear whether tenants segregated themselves according to race, but at the very least the SPY staff had an opportunity to promote interracial programs.

The SPY staff informed the Olander Homes' residents about their programs, and a group of tenant mothers took the initiative in starting a nursery with their assistance. The tenant women also volunteered their time supervising the children five mornings a week. They quickly decided that they needed to learn more about child development. Accordingly, the SPY staff organized a Y-Wives Club, which sponsored movies about children's behavior and speakers from the Association for Family Living.[49] Initially forty-five women enrolled, but attendance significantly decreased over time. The SPY staff claimed this was because of the women's different interests and their personality conflicts. Certainly, there were varying interests, as some club members had younger children and others had grown children. Some women also claimed that a small group of women made all of the decisions. Although it is difficult to reconstruct the clubs' social dynamics, perhaps the younger mothers were more involved in the club, since it offered the most to them in terms of learning about their children's development. Moreover, because their interests in learning about children's health and social growth aligned with the SPY and other agencies, the SPY staff may have given more time and resources to their activities. Significantly, the SPY staff did not mention race, although this does not rule out the possibility of racial tensions. Despite the fall in attendance, a small group of women persuaded the SPY staff to continue working with the club. Consequently, the club sponsored a successful fund-raising party with sixty tenants and sent a Y-teen to summer camp.

The following year, the SPY staff conducted an evaluation of the preschool and the Y-Wives Club. In their estimation, there were three problems. First, the staff found it necessary to constantly interpret to the mothers their responsibilities as volunteers. Apparently, the mothers did not always send the required nursery fees and did not always come for their assigned volunteer time. The second problem was more subtle. The SPY staff reported that the tenant women had a difficult time understanding that they were to take responsibility for the development of the nursery program. The staff noted that a small group of female tenants was interested, those they described as the "articulate, interested, intelligent, aggressive women, tenants themselves."[50] Again, because the women's interest agreed with the SPY's, the report complimented them. Regardless, most tenant women had less knowledge than the SPY staff of social agencies and speakers to invite, and so perhaps they had to rely upon the staff.

Third, the tenants council and the Y-Wives Club had developed concurrently, and some women were active in both groups. The staff noted that it was difficult to get the women involved in both groups to understand that their roles as tenants and as volunteers were distinct.[51] It is quite possible, however, that these roles conflicted. Allegiances to the Olander Homes' collective and to a women's club perhaps carried different obligations. More than likely, the tenant women were better able to develop their "homegrown" leadership skills in the tenants council, rather than under the SPY's supervision. One might well question why the SPY did not work more closely with the tenants council. Nonetheless, on the basis of their evaluation, the SPY decided that more staff and time were necessary to maintain the preschool, even though the Y-Wives kept the playschool open for a short while longer.[52]

A second scenario at the Olander Homes provides another glimpse into the differences between the SPY staff and the residents. Within a short time, there was a second wave of tenants, most of whom were black, so that black residents outnumbered white ones. In the fall of 1955, the CHA staff told the SPY that the female tenants had again expressed an interest in discussing what services might be available to them through the SPY. A graduate student from a nearby university and an employee of the SPY worked with those women interested in developing their homemaking and mothering skills. But the student had other ideas and thought that an open house for the new tenants would be a suitable project and a way for the tenant women to develop leadership skills. The group was eager but also reluctant to give up their sewing project. Nonetheless, group members found out the names of the new tenants, baked cakes and made coffee, and personally invited the new tenants to an open house. They also organized a card party and a square dance for the new tenants, which were more popular than the demonstration apartment that they had furnished. Yet the evaluation noted problems similar to the first scenario: many of the women were reluctant to assume formal leadership responsibilities. According to the report, when the student showed the tenants what each person could do, the women assumed more responsibility for deciding what they wanted.[53]

Further, the report stated, "Many [we]re afraid that in a group they may make comments which would be used against them with CHA or neighbors."[54] This statement indicated concern about possible adversarial relationships between the CHA and tenants. As noted in chapter 6, CHA officials and social workers had increasingly become critical of public housing tenants during the 1950s. Their assessments of low-income and single-parent households spoke of "disorganized" and "unstable" family life.[55] The SPY staff, too, presented its own version of middle-class leadership and activities, perhaps alienating some tenant women. If anything, these episodes raise critical questions about who should have decided which community activities were most important to a community and whether the intervention of the SPY created further divisions within the Olander Homes.

The SPY was somewhat more successful with its Olander youth programs. Again, tenant women took the initiative and asked the SPY staff to help them establish programs for teen girls. A SPY staff member surveyed the teens as to their interests, with the assistance of a tenant mother who was a girl scout leader. The girls expressed an interest in sewing and cooking, and so the SPY staff and parents decided to divide the girls by age groups. Not surprisingly, the older girls also wanted to plan dances. Within several months, the SPY staff worker found there were too many problems with coeducational activities, and so they focused on developing activities for girls only. Consequently, the Olander girls cooperated and set up their own projects, including a ballet film, modern dance instruction, skating and volleyball, and a bake sale. Yet, again, the group remained small.[56] (Still, as of 1959, there were five boys' clubs, eight girls' clubs, and three coeducational clubs.)[57] The problems of budget and shortages of staff and volunteers, as well as the SPY's leadership models, may have limited programmatic activities for the girls.

Conclusion

How do we appraise the Chicago Y's activism during these three decades? To be expected, there were successes and failures, dependent upon the bureaucracy of a large organization, the geographic location of Y branches, and the larger race problems of Chicago. Nonetheless, some of the Y branches did successfully integrate, albeit gradually. Although the neighborhood boundaries did not become permeable, at least some Ys did expand their boundaries.

The SPY was perhaps in the most difficult situation. Yet with its small staff, group of volunteers, and budget, it accomplished a great deal. It provided a residence for black women, cosponsored programs that fostered black pride and political activism, and established programs with the women and youth of public housing. To be sure, there were social-class differences between the staff and their public housing clients, which compromised the staff's interactions with the tenant mothers. But their assistance to the girls at Olander was more welcome and successful.

Conclusion

AS DOCUMENTED throughout this book, black women participated as activists on all fronts of the Chicago Black Renaissance: as ministers, clubwomen, schoolteachers, fund-raisers, members of black sororities, artists and writers, politicians, and founders and board members of leading black cultural and social institutions. Likewise, many women at two central public-housing sites were also activists, although they did not usually belong to Chicago's leading black female organizations. As such, their activism has not been thoroughly documented, in part because scholars have continued to "fragment" activism from mothering.[1] However, as this book has shown, black women of all social classes conjoined children's welfare issues to political and social change. In the case of clubwomen, especially Irene McCoy Gaines, they made these connections explicit.

It behooves scholars of women's history to rethink how black clubwomen of later generations drew from the early-twentieth-century club movement. Further, the enduring commitments of Chicago's black clubwomen to those social institutions founded by earlier clubwomen suggests that the periodization of the club movement from 1890 to 1920 may be an artifact of our own scholarship. If anything, the clubwomen themselves invoked a sense of history. For example, when a black woman was finally chosen as American mother of the year in 1947, the clubwomen claimed that they had finally been vindicated of the aspersions cast upon their moral character in the 1890s.[2] If the clubwomen themselves saw this chain of events as historical, why don't we as scholars recognize it?

While writing this book I observed history in the making and unmaking. I am thinking of the demolition of many highrise public-housing units. Sadly and ironically, their fate had been foretold by social worker Mary Bolton Wirth, who decried their sense of isolation and the subsequent loss of community. Scattered housing, now touted as the remedy for public-housing residents, was recommended by her as early as the 1950s.[3] Despite some public perceptions today of public-housing tenants as passive welfare mothers, we should think otherwise. Nancy Naples and other scholars have documented the activism of tenants and of women especially. Again, women's involvement in the tenant associations and other public-housing groups need to be historicized, for indeed, since the inception of Chicago's public housing, its female tenants were proactive.

On a larger scale, I hope that scholars will continue to expand the histories of civil rights, especially in northern cities. As Kenneth Goings and Raymond Mohl have emphasized, there were many civil rights movements, not just one.[4] Many histories have focused on the South, but without considering how northern organizations assisted in the movement through financial contributions, the promotion of legislatures, protests, and so forth. Similarly, we need to reconsider how civil rights in major northern cities, such as Chicago, were shaped by migrants who settled there. Lastly, when we think of civil rights' activism, we might think more broadly about what "politics" means. Just as marches and protests played a significant part in civil rights, so too did art, literature, and drama. To be sure, one could not write about the Chicago Black Renaissance without considering cultural politics— remarkable artists and writers and the major black community institutions that patronized them.

Many Chicagoans think that civil rights started in their city with the arrival of Martin Luther King, Jr. But as this book has shown, that was not true. In fact, I would argue that the activism of the Chicago Black Renaissance paved the way for King and, interestingly, for black nationalist groups in Chicago. To be sure, the Nation of Islam brought its own pan-African ideology to Altgeld Gardens, which was eschewed by many other black Chicagoans. But during the 1960s, their movement became stronger.[5] It would be wise, therefore, to revisit the 1960s in Chicago with our thoughts turned back to the earlier decades.

As I completed this book, I realized how much more work needs to be done on the Chicago Black Renaissance generally and women's roles specifically. In attempting to balance scope with depth, I often put aside topics that beg for book-length studies. Black journalism, social work, theater, art, women's involvement in state and national politics, and the collaborations of interracial organizations are only a few ideas for dissertations and other studies. Some black sororities, such as the Alpha Kappa Alpha, were active in the sponsorship of arts. Their role needs to be examined, as does the active Chicago chapter of the National Council of Negro Women. There should also be a collection of oral histories that honors those persons central to the Chicago Black Renaissance.[6] Unfortunately, in the years I have been working on this project, a number of key female activists of the Renaissance have passed on. I have had the fortunate opportunity to talk to some of the activists and artists informally. Their perspectives are critical to our understanding of this complex time period.

Finally, as I completed this book, events on Chicago's southside, which is still predominantly black, gave me hope as well as concern. The good news first. There is now black gentrification in the poorer black neighborhoods, including Bronzeville. The black middle class is returning and revitalizing these communities. Second, some of the institutions of the Chicago Black Renaissance still exist and, in some cases, thrive. The South Side Community Art Center, for one, still holds art classes, exhibits, and fund-raisers. The Parkway Community House, although now a part of the Hull House Association, still houses a theater that performs regularly. But it is discouraging to me and others to see that so many of the magnificent institutions of the Chicago Black Renaissance are in disrepair or have been demolished. All too often I have shown a friend a vacant lot and said, "This is where the Parkway Community House or where the South Parkway YWCA once stood." Bronzeville residents are proud of their history and want to revitalize their community. I hope that such plans include the restoration of those cultural and social institutions that still stand.

In conclusion, the women of the Chicago Black Renaissance proved to be astonishing research subjects. I learned so much from their generosity and their unflagging commitment to culture and politics. While writing this book, the list of female community activists and professionals in Appendix A kept growing. And I suspect that my list does not include all of the women whose contributions should be acknowledged. Together, these women created a movement that spanned the Depression years, World War II, and the demolition of many of their neighborhoods during the 1950s. The women of Chicago's Black Renaissance movement deserve greater recognition for their prodigious civil rights activism.

Appendix A

Black Female Community Activists, Artists, and Professionals in Chicago, 1930–60

Abbott, Mrs. Robert: vice-president of a home (name unknown) for black working mothers, founded in 1930

Abernathy, Ina: probation officer in the Mother's Pension Department of the Cook County Juvenile Court; social worker for United Charities

Alexander, Frances: director, Good Shepherd Community Center nursery, 1941

Anderson, Doris B. Allen: cofounder of Howalton School, a private black elementary school; adjustment teacher, Forestville Elementary School

Anderson, Violette Neatley: assistant state attorney; first vice-president of the Cook County Bar Association; president of the Friendly Big Sisters League; member of the Special Shelters Committee, Chicago Urban League (CUL)

Ashburn, L. Eudora: doctor who volunteered her services for a free medical clinic during the Depression

Austin, Lovie: musician at the Joyland Theater and at Jimmy Payne's Dancing School

Austin, Roberta Martin: composer of gospel songs

Bailey, Mrs. Silas: social worker; former committee member of South Parkway YWCA (SPY)

Barnett, Brunetta Mouzon: actress with the Skyloft Players of Parkway Community House (PCH)

Bell, Roberta: YWCA administrator and counselor; made black dolls for teaching elementary children black history

---

This list does not purport to be comprehensive. Information is from the *Chicago Defender,* the *Chicago Sunday Bee,* and materials found in archives and bibliographic sources.

Blackwell, Olive: dance teacher who worked with dormitory residents at PCH; directed recreational clubs for soldiers through the Red Cross

Boaz, Sophia: lawyer, social worker, and probation officer, Cook County Juvenile Court

Bond, Margaret Allison: musician, composer, and concert artist who attended Julliard School of Music, Chicago Musical College, and Coleridge Taylor School of Music; wrote scores for the Federal Theatre and Goodman Theatre in Chicago

Bonner Occomy, Marita: writer of short stories who lived in Chicago during the late 1920s and early 1930s

Bousfield, Maudelle: principal of Douglas Elementary School, 1931–1939; principal of Wendell Phillips High School, 1939–1950; conducted research on black children's reading and IQ scores; the only black member of the women's advisory committee of the War Manpower Commission (during World War II); active in the Mayor's Commission on Juvenile Delinquency; member, board of trustees, Provident Hospital; helped to found St. Edmund's Parochial School and was a chair of its school board from 1949 to 1959; member of the CUL's Women's Auxiliary

Bowles, Wilhelmena: medical doctor

Boylan, Frankie: director of community service, Kenwood-Ellis Center

Brooks, Gwendolyn: Pulitzer-prize poet; member of South Side Community Art Center's (SSCAC) writers group

Brown, Ida K.: president, Ida B. Wells Club

Brown, Lavonia: member, Women's Army for National Defense; assisted PCH with its dormitories; secretary of the *Defender* charities; member of board of directors, PCH, 1955

Brown, Mrs. Oscar: member of the CUL's executive committee; president of Willard School's PTA; wife of Oscar Brown, president of the Chicago chapter of the NAACP

Brown, Willa: teacher at Wendell Phillips High School in noncollege aviation; secretary of the National Airmen's Association

Browning, Alice: publisher and coeditor of *Negro Story Magazine* and a children's magazine; teacher, Forestville Elementary School

Bruce, Sadie: dancer and teacher of a children's dance troupe that performed at many community functions

Bryan, Mattie Elliott: director of Big Brothers

Buchanan, Eolis: president, Chicago Links, 1956–1959

Buckner, Jennnie: assistant residence director and building manager, PCH

Bullock, Carrie E.: nurse and Provident Hospital alumnus

Burroughs, Margaret Taylor Goss: founder, member of board of directors, and fund-raiser of the South Side Community Art Center (SSCAC); founder of DuSable Museum; art teacher and chair of Negro History Week at DuSable High School; writer of children's stories

Campbell, Lillian: prominent clubwoman

Carroll, Cora Eloise: first female mayor of Bronzeville, 1959

Carter, Fannie: administrator and counselor, YWCA; president, Chicago and Northern District Association (CNDA), 1943–1945; president, West Side Women's Club

Carter, Vivian: cofounder of Vee-Jay Records; Chicago's first black female disc jockey; also disc jockey with WJOB in Hammond, Indiana, and WORY in Gary, Indiana

Cayton, Irma: one of the first black WACs; social worker at PCH; wife of Horace Cayton

Clarke, Irma Frazier: Du Sable High School's first head librarian, who devoted the library to black history and literature; founder of Du Sable's Beta Club, a prestigious club for students who received good grades; member, Du Sable History Club

Clarke, Mrs. Thomas: chair, center committee, PCH

Coachman, Alice: president, Gaudeamus Charity Club; member, board of directors, CNDA

Cockrell, Oneida: principal of Rosenwald Apartments' nursery; consultant with University of Chicago Laboratory School

Coffin, Ollye: librarian, George Cleveland Hall Library; reviewer, Book Circle at SSCAC

Coleman, Genevieve: director, Old Folks' Home

Coles, Marie: community organizer; helped to organize neighborhood improvement clubs for the CUL

Compton, Eloise: book reviewer for the *Chicago Sunday Bee;* teacher

Cooper, Dr. Anna: chair, CNDA's Health and Hygiene Committee in 1932; volunteer doctor at a free health clinic during the Depression

Crank, Suejette: business and professional women's secretary, SPY

Crawford, Magdalene: employee, PCH

Crawford, Sadie: member, board of directors, CNDA

Cress, Ida Mae: newspaper columnist who wrote articles on parenting; teacher at Drake Elementary; chair of Woodlawn's 1958 World Fellowship night; fund-raiser for SSCAC; teacher at WPA nursery school, kindergarten, and elementary school

Cross, Beatrice: staff member, YWCA

Cummings, Rose: officer, CNDA

Danner, Margaret: poet; associate editor, *Poetry*

Davenport, Beatrice: chair, Maude E. Smith Social and Charity Club

Davis, Elizabeth Stubbs: fundraiser for Provident Hospital; wife of Allison Davis, University of Chicago Professor

Davis, Jessie Mae: officer, Douglas League of Women Voters; president, Rosa Gragg Educational and Civic Club, 1959

Delaney, Alva: president, CNDA, 1949–1951; president, Gaudeamus Woman's Club, 1942–1944

Demond, Willene: director, Young Adult Program, PCH

Dent, Jane: director, Old Folks' Home

De Ramus, Anna Louise: concert pianist

Dickerson, Mrs. Earl: committee chair, CUL; wife of Earl Dickerson

Diggs, Olive: editor of *Chicago Sunday Bee;* affiliated with PCH and YWCA; acting director, Illinois Commission on Human Relations

Dove, Lillian S.: medical doctor; cofounder of Business and Professional Women's Club; vice-president of a home (name unknown) for black working mothers, founded in 1930

Du Bois, Shirley Graham: director, Princess Theatre and Federal Theatre in Chicago; children's writer and playwright; composer of black opera; wife of W. E. B. Du Bois

Duggan, Frances: teacher, Doolittle Elementary

Dunham, Katherine: dancer and choreographer who studied Caribbean culture; researcher with the Illinois Writers' Project; director of several Chicago children's theatre and dance companies

Dunnegan, Marjorie: vice-chair, the publicity committee, the Negro American Labor Council of Chicago

Duster, Alfreda: secretary, Southside Community Committee (SCC); PTA president; daughter of Ida B. Wells

Elam, Melissa: founder of Elam Home for Girls

Ellis, Georgia Jones: lawyer, assistant corporation counsel

Euper, Elizabeth: founder of the first black YWCA in Chicago; professional corsetiere, designer, and store owner

Evans, Mary Green: pastor of Cosmopolitan Community Church, whose activities broadened to include a nursery, health clinics, youth programs, and membership drives for the NAACP and *Ebony Magazine;* in 1948, founded a community house with a nursery, kindergarten, kitchen, gym, health clinic, and home for the elderly

Faulkner, Georgia De Baptist: secretary, Chicago branch of the Association for the Study of Negro Life and History (ASNLH); prominent clubwoman

Flowers, Katherine: teacher of ballet, "primitive," and creative dance; had her own downtown studio

Ford, Thelma Sims: librarian; reviewed books at George Cleveland Hall Library

Foreman, Madeleine: staff member, Altgeld Gardens nursery

Foster, Mrs. A. L.: executive committee member, CUL; wife of A. L. Foster, president of the CUL

Fouche, Ruth Allen: musician, music educator; officer, CNDA

Fountain, Belle Graves: administrative board member, SPY; member, board of directors, CUL; helped purchase the headquarters for CNDA during her term as president; worked with the Old Folks' Home, Soldier Widow Rest, and Julia Johnson Home

Gaines, Irene McCoy: chair of hostesses of American Negro Exposition; social worker in women's division of the CUL's Employment Department, Cook County Hospital, and Cook County Bureau of Public Welfare; industrial secretary of the YWCA; committee member, Hoover's Housing Investigation; executive director of recreational project at the PCH, cosponsored with YWCA and YMCA; member of the Citizens Schools Committee, Citizens Advisory Committee to the Chicago Plan; president of the Chicago Council of Negro Organizations (CCNO); fifteenth president, National Association of Colored Women's Clubs (NACW) (three terms); president, Illinois Federation of the Republican Colored Women's Clubs; candidate in 1948 for delegate to the National Republican Nominating Convention; candidate in 1950 for the Republican nomination and election as member of Board of County Commissioners from Chicago; member of the Woman's Executive Committee of President Eisenhower's White House Conference on Highway Safety; board of director member, ASNLH; president, CNDA; candidate in 1940 for Illinois House of Representatives; 1950 candidate for Board of County Commissioners, Chicago; assistant secretary, *Defender* charities

Galbreath, Elizabeth: writer, *Defender*

Gardener, Mrs. Culbert: active YWCA member

Gayden, Fern: member of Parnassains and the SSCAC; co-editor, *Negro Story Magazine*

George, Maude Roberts: president, Douglas League of Women Voters; well-known soprano who performed in Chicago and nationally; chair, committee of management, SPY; chair, board of director member, Chicago Metropolitan YWCA;

chair, Music Department, NACW; member, Special Shelters Committee, CUL, 1931–1932; wife of Judge Albert George

Gitlin, Thyra Edwards: social worker; committee chair, Negro in Industry, Abraham Lincoln Center (ALC); journalist, Associated Negro Press; worked with the SPY to send black women to Bryn Mawr's summer school; received a fellowship to go to Denmark to attend the International People's College; affiliated with the Communist Party and labor unionists; leader, National Negro Congress, 1936; delegate, Social Workers' Committee to Aid Spanish Democracy; toured American cities with Salaria Kee, first black nurse sent to Spain, to help buy ambulances for Spanish Civil War

Glover, Geraldine: writer, lecturer, artist; junior supervisor, CNDA; president, Flying Squadron, youth auxiliary of the NAACP; active in Associated Business Women's Club, Chicago Art League; assistant children's librarian, George Cleveland Hall Library

Grammar, Juanita: organizer, Women's Community Club; PTA member

Gray, Mabel: president, American Rose Art and Charity Club

Green, Loraine Richardson: member, Chicago Public School board; chair, Public Affairs Committee, SPY; chair, Women's Division of the National Conference of Christians and Jews; chair, Human Relations Committee, Woman's City Club; Chicago Recreation Commission member, 1952; Advisory Committee, Chicago Board of Health, 1953; appointed by governor to the Advisory Board of the Illinois Training School for Girls, 1953; served on Chicago Commission on Human Relations, 1948 to 1967; chair, Division of Education and Recreation, Welfare Council of Metropolitan Chicago (WCMC); wife of Wendell Green, circuit court judge

Greene, Clara: chair, Finance Committee, Chicago branch, National Council of Negro Women (NCNW)

Griffin, Mrs. Mamie: president, Gaudeamus Woman's Club

Hansberry, Lorraine Vivian: writer especially known for her play, *Raisin in the Sun,* based on her family moving into a white neighborhood

Hardin Armstrong, Lilian: jazz musician who performed at Dreamland Café and Royal Gardens Theatre; member of King Oliver's Band; led two all-women bands; wife of Louis Armstrong

Harris, Mary: nursery director and fund-raiser, PCH

Harsh, Vivian: librarian, George Cleveland Hall Library; board member, Grace Presbyterian Church; committee member, SPY Girls Reserves; board member, PCH; involved in the Chicago chapter of the ASNLH; organized book reviews and lecture forums at library

Hedrick, Ursa: NACW secretary; president, Excelsior Social and Charity Club; president, Rosa Gragg Educational and Civic Club

Henderson, Ethel: staff member, Altgeld Gardens nursery

Hennigan, Mayme: director, annual membership, SCC; member, board of directors, United Charities

Hensley, Bertha: vice-president of a home (name unknown) for black working mothers, founded in 1930; involved in fund-raising for Provident Hospital

Hieber, Vivian Lockett: founder, Association of Colored Mannequins, first group of black models

Hill, Elizabeth Webb: medical doctor at Community Hospital, Evanston

Hill, Mae: president, South Parkway Improvement Club

Hillard, Rosa Mae: founder and director, Meatchem Youth Center, 1945

Hilliard, Ethel: second vice-president, SSCAC; art teacher; chair of annual tea fund-raiser for Chicago NAACP

Holmes, Margaret Flagg: teacher, Wendell Phillips High School; rated the best Latin teacher in Chicago by the North Central Association; history teacher, DuSable high School; involved with the CUL and the Chicago NAACP

Horton, Carrie: president, Cornell Charity Club; board member, Chicago Metropolitan YWCA; Special Shelters Committee, CUL, 1931–1932

Horton, Ella: president, Chicago Conference division of AME Layman's Organization

Howard, Helen: industrial secretary, SPY

Howe, Jane: cofounder, Howalton School, private black elementary school; art instructor, Englewood High School

Jackson, Charlotte: staff member, SPY; PCH board member

Jackson, Hattie: president, Phyllis Wheatley Association, 1941

Jackson, Mahalia: gospel singer with Thomas Dorsey; in 1956, sang for a benefit for the Montgomery bus boycott

Jackson, Pauline: fund-raiser for the Greater Provident Hospital drive; former president of the YWCA in Philadelphia

Jackson, Ruth: principal, Coleman Elementary School; PCH board member

Jackson, Thelma: president, Chicago Links, 1954–1956

Jackson, Mrs. J. H.: member, executive committee, SPY; wife of minister of Olivet Baptist Church

Jewell, Ruth Sykes: assistant principal, Douglas Elementary School

Johnson, Eloise: owner of hat boutique on East 47th Street for over sixty years; hat-maker for Eleanor Roosevelt, Pearl Bailey, and Lena Horne

Johnson, Irma: acting principal, Howalton School, 1949

Johnson, Isabel Joseph: gospel radio host for Sunday afternoon programs during the 1940s; active in the CUL and the Chicago NAACP

Jones, Dorothy: director, Altgeld Gardens Homes nursery

Jones, Faith Jefferson: supervisor, Washington Park District, Cook County Bureau of Public Welfare; acting director, PCH, 1949; Alpha Kappa Alpha member

Jones, Genevieve: assistant librarian, George Cleveland Hall Library

Jones, Jeanette: lifetime member, NCNW; president, CNDA

Jones, Mrs. Sidney: chair, Schools Committee, CUL

Joyner, Dr. Marjorie Stewart: founding member, NCNW; fund-raiser for Cosmopolitan Community Church; renowned beautician; head of *Defender* charities and co-organizer of the first Bud Billiken parade; chair, Women's Division, Democratic National Campaign Committee in 1944; founder, United Beauty School Owners and Teachers Association

Julian, Dr. Anna: medical doctor; member, executive committee, CUL; treasurer, national Links, 1958–1959

Kirk, Mildred: actress and director, Skyloft Players, PCH; teacher, Forestville Elementary school; also worked for Bureau of Child Study

Lane, Mrs. Frayser: committee chair, CUL

Lawrence, Pauline Jackson: staff member, SPY; member, YWCA Neighborhood Improvement Department; board member, PCH

Laws, Ida: establisher of community clubs to keep yards and homes in good condition

Lawson, Lula: executive member, Chicago YWCA; social worker, Michigan Boulevard Garden Housing; Women's Committee member, Wabash YMCA

Lewis, Bertha Moseley: playwright, director, actress in little theatres and children's theatre; chair, publicity committee, and active in vocational opportunity committee, CUL; chair, drama department, CNDA

Logan, Mrs. Odessa E.: president, Phyllis Wheatley Club

Lucus, Ethel Minnie: actress with Uptown Players and "Destination Freedom"; graduate of Chicago Conservatory of Music and Dramatic Art

Malone, Annie: founder and president of Poro College; advisory board member, CUL; member of the Chicago NAACP and SPY

Martin, Roberta Evelyn: gospel music singer and composer

Matlock, Frances: teacher, Chicago public school; archivist, Chicago Links

Maynor, Lygora: book reviewer; businesswoman; member of Chicago NAACP; involved with CUL membership drives

McBain, Gertrude: member, Fernwood Tenants Council

McBride, Mary: member of a dance troupe that performed in Europe

McCracken, Ethel: teacher; president of Illinois Association of Colored Women's Clubs, 1928 to 1930

McKenzie, Myrtle: chair of CNDA's Education Department

McKinley, Ada: prominent clubwoman since the turn of the century; organizer of the League of Women Voters of Chicago; founder, South Side Settlement House (SSSH), later the Ada McKinley Community House

McKissack, Pauline: president, Chicago branch, NCNW

McNeal, Estella Webster: staff member, SPY

Merrill, Iris Barbara: labor organizer and civil rights activist

Miller, Emily: program worker, PCH

Miller, Ida Mae: pastor, Metropolitan Community Church of Chicago; chaplain, NACW, 1928

Miller, Lucille: doctor who volunteered services for a free medical clinic during the Depression

Mitchell, Ella: president of CNDA, 1945–1947; paid off all indebtedness of CNDA's clubhouse during her term; president, Illinois Association of Colored Women's Club; president, Phyllis Wheatley Club

Mitchell, Mrs. Marion: first black staff member, Chicago Orphan Asylum; worked for the Chicago Welfare Administration and the Division of Aid to Dependent Children, Cook County Bureau of Public Welfare

Mitchell, Ruth: staff member, Altgeld Gardens nursery

Morgan, Rosa Whitlock: head of women's activities, PCH

Morrow, Ora Green: teacher, Hyde Park High School; member, SPY

Moseberry, Ella: staff member, SPY

Moten, Etta: nationally known singer; committee chair, CUL; wife of Claude Barnett

Murphy, Mrs. Callie: tenant leader, Ida B. Wells Homes

Nance, Olivia: owner of the Powell Funeral Home; former schoolteacher

Napolean, Ruth: head of women's activities and nursery, PCH

Nolan, Ethel Mae: schoolteacher; fund-raiser, SSCAC; secretary to Jesse Owen of the Illinois Youth Commission; board member, Du Saible Memorial Society

Obanion, Fannie B.: president, CNDA, 1941–1943; founder, Gaudeamus Woman's Club; founder, Enverite Progressive Club; during World War II sold $35,000 worth of war bonds and stamps; a millinery artist

Oldham, Ernistine: executive committee member, SPY; assistant director, Dunbar Vocational School

Oliver, Annie: president, Du Saible Memorial Society for thirty-three years; studied cosmetology and operated her own shop; member of the CNDA; treasurer, second vice-president, Chicago branch, NCNW

Overton, Sadie: supervisor of girls' activities in an NYA-sponsored organization in Chicago

Patton, Cora: chair, education committee, Chicago branch, NCNW; CUL officer; president, Gaudeamus Woman's Club

Payne, Ethel: international journalist, who once angered Eisenhower in 1954 by pressing him about ending segregation in interstate travel; called "First Lady of the Black Press"

Perry, Nixola F.: active member, Junior Women's Auxiliary, CUL

Philpott, Arcola: Lilydale's columnist, *Defender*

Pickney, Mrs. William: president, Giles Charity Club

Porter, Eva: matron of dormitories, PCH

Powell, Maude: president, Junior Women's Auxiliary, West Side Urban League

Powell, E. Ruth: renowned soprano; performed for Gaudeamus Woman's Club

Powell, Thelma: principal, Keith Elementary School; member, DuSable History Club

Prescott, Annabel Carey: dean, Wendell Phillips High School; assistant principal of DuSable High School; assistant principal, Medill High School (which consolidated and became McKinley High School in 1948); assistant principal at Cregier branch of Crane Technical High School (location of a pilot program in intergroup relations), 1948; member, education committee, Mayor's Commission on Human Relations; advisory member, Executive Committee of the Women's Council on Fair Education Practices; Chicago public schools' director for the Bureau of Human Relations from 1956 to 1959

Pressly, Elizabeth: staff member, Altgeld Gardens nursery

Price, Florence Beatrice Smith: composer who used rhythms from slave dances in her work

Redmond, Pauline: director, Youth and Social Welfare Department, CUL

Reed, Nannie: president, CNDA; active member of the CUL, Chicago NAACP, and SPY

Reed, Pauline Kligh: president and fund-raiser, SSCAC; Links, member

Rhea, LaJulia: classical music performer

Roberts, Mrs. Carl: board member, Woman's Auxiliary Board of Provident Hospital, chair of the Girls Reserve Committee; secretary of the Committee of Management, SPY

Robinson, Carrenne: publicity director, Regal Theatre

Robinson, Virginia: staff member, Altgeld Gardens nursery

Rollins, Charlemae: children's author and advisor for children's books; instrumental in having racist children's books removed from the Chicago public library; children's librarian, George Cleveland Hall Library; in 1942 she and Vivian Harsh worked with superintendent of the Chicago public schools on a research project to prepare materials for incorporating black history into the public school curricula

Sampson, Edith: probation officer and lawyer, Cook County Juvenile Court; board member, ALC; chair, executive committee, NCNW; in 1950 appointed by Truman as an alternate to the American delegation at the United Nations; member, U.S. Commission for UNESCO; in 1951 and 1952, guest lecturer for the State Department to speak about the social conditions of blacks; assistant corporation counsel, Chicago, 1955–1962; appointed judge, Chicago Municipal Court, 1962

Saunders, Doris: publishing executive, director, book division, Johnson Publishing Company; columnist, *Chicago Defender, Chicago Courier*

Sayre, Helen: recording secretary of a home for black working mothers, founded in 1930

Sayre-Lewis, Lydia: teacher, published articles about stereotypes of blacks in school textbooks

Scott, Florence: representative, CUL, for Metropolitan Housing and Planning; westside field worker, CUL

Searcy, Portia: first president of Chicago Links, 1950–1953

Seton, Marie: director, film department, ALC; producer of a movie in which Paul Robeson acted

Sherrod, Jessie: group social worker, PCH

Sherrod, Lilder: owner of dress shop; sewed clothing for jazz singers

Singleton, Frankie Raye: artist, lecturer, SSCAC

Skinner, Clementine: a WAAC, played in its band for two years; teacher and librarian at Wadsworth Elementary School

Smith, Alberta Moore: juvenile court officer

Smith, Ardella: daughter of Lucy Elder Smith, who was a minister of All Nations Pentecostal Church

Smith, Jeanette: superintendent of CNDA's club home in the early 1930s

Smith, Elder Lucy: preacher and healer of All Nations Pentecostal Church; pioneer in black gospel radio, which she used to help the poor

Smith Collier, "Little" Lucy: granddaughter of Elder Lucy Smith, who was a renowned gospel singer and organist on the radio

Smith, Mary: officer, SPY; vice-president, Metropolitan YWCA; group social worker, PCH; member, Special Shelters Committee, CUL, 1931–1932

Smith, Maude E.: founder, Maude E. Smith Children's Home; director, Junior Federation, CNDA; president, CNDA and the Illinois State Association of Colored Women's Clubs; president, Young Matrons Club

Smith, Naola Mae: corresponding secretary, CUL; chair, Civics Department, CUL; supervisor of the "Better Conduct Program," 1937

Smith, Ruth Moore: community secretary and director of residence, SPY; board member and fund-raiser, PCH

Snowden, Joanna: probation officer with Chicago's juvenile court

Spaulding, Helen: director, Skyloft Theatre at PCH; group worker and teacher, PCH

Spaulding, Marva Louis: big band singer who performed with Duke Ellington, Count Basie, and others; involved in Chicago March of Dimes Committee in the late 1940s; wife of boxer Joe Louis and Dr. Albert Lee Spaulding

Steele, Ruth: member, board of directors, CNDA; dramatist

Stratton, Charlotte: cofounder, Howalton School, a private black elementary school; member, board of directors, Howalton School; teacher, Douglas Elementary School

Stratton, Madeline: elementary teacher who started the Negro history curricula project in Chicago public schools, 1942–1945; member, DuSable History Club

Summers, Lillian Proctor: staff member, United Charities; board member, PCH; Chicago Council of the National Negro Congress; chair, stereotypes committee, CUL; field consultant, Illinois League for Planned Parenthood

Sutton, Dorothy: minister, Commonwealth Community Church and Cosmopolitan Community Church; vice-president, Chicago branch, NCNW

Switzer, Elaine: director, program department, PCH

Taylor, Corinne: supervisor, child welfare work; field worker, Institute of Juvenile Research; teacher, Howalton School

Taylor, Rebecca Stiles: editor, Women's Club Page, *Chicago Defender;* corresponding Secretary, NACW, 1930

Taylor, Mrs. Robert: committee chair, CUL

Thaddeus, Mrs. Winifred: president, National District Association of Colored Girls Clubs

Thomas, Izona: Y-Teen program director, PCH

Thompson, Era Bell: co-editor, *Negro Digest;* managing editor and international editor, *Ebony*

Thornton, Mattie: assistant pastor of First Church of Deliverance

Tivis, Vivian: social worker, Chicago Housing Authority (CHA)

Toles, Virginia: librarian, Wendell Phillips High School; member, DuSable History Club

Tompkins, Grace: music critic for *Chicago Defender*; editor of *Negro Musical;* associate editor of *Negro Story;* published poet

Tory, Suzanne: secretary to director, PCH

Waidell, Ethel: officer, United Colored Democratic Association of Chicago

Walker, Josephine: president and founder, American Friendship Club, formed in 1958, to promote "harmonious relations among all races and creed"; executive committee member, Chicago NAACP; board member, SCC; finance committee member, Woodlawn YWCA; board member, Chicago Area Friends of the Students for Nonviolent Coordinating Committee (SNCC)

Walker, Margaret: first black poet to win the Yale Poetry Prize; member, South Side Writers' group; member, Illinois Writers' Project

Waring, Mary: doctor; vice-president, NACW, 1930–1933; president, NACW, 1933–1937; chair, Social Hygiene Department, CNDA

Watson, Cora: officer of the Chicago branch of the NAACP

Weaver, Audrey: city editor, *Chicago Defender*, 1959

Weaver, Louise Overall: organist, New Covenant Baptist Church, where Mahalia Jackson sometimes sang

Weber, Mrs. James: president, woman's division, CUL

Wells, Eva: chair, near southside branch, Women's City Club; member, Chicago Recreation Commission; chair, Schools Department, CNDA; helped to introduce Negro history in the Chicago public schools

Wells, Grace: president, CNDA, 1953–1955; founder, Dorcas Art and Charity Club; organizer of women to volunteer in women's and juvenile courts and Provident Hospital

West, Cordelia: women's club leader; organizer, Chicago Federation Club

White, Alpha: secretary, Girls Reserve Committee, SPY

White, Delores: president, CNDA

Wilkinson, Florence: social worker; vice-president, Chicago Metropolitan YWCA

Williams, Essie Mae: president, Giles Avenue Neighborhood Improvement Club; president, East Side Woman's Club

Williams, Florence Chapman: an anti-tuberculosis activist; helped to establish health programs at Altgeld Gardens and Ida B. Wells Homes; director, Negro Health Education, Olivet Baptist Church; lecturer for tubercular institutes in the South

Williams, Gertrude Johnson: founder, Emanuel Baptist Church; president, Gertrude Johnson Williams Civic and Charity Club; mother of John Johnson, founder of Johnson Publishing Company

Williams, Mayme: president, CNDA, 1951–1953; president, Young Matron's Culture Club; established a camp fund for underprivileged children

Williams, Nannie Mae: president, CNDA, 1939–1941; treasurer of CNDA clubhouse

Williams, Violet: tenant activist, Cabrini Green

Willis, Bessie: president, CCNO

Wilson, Mrs.: chair, Finance Committee, PCH

Wilson, Halena: labor and civil rights activist

Woods, Bertha: pharmacist, owner of Woods-Robertson Pharmacy

Woods, Jeanette: chair, Social Welfare Committee, CNDA; set up classes for blacks at the Hull House

Woods, Sylvia Green: trade unionist and activist

Wright, Mrs. Sewall: president, Women's Joint Committee on Adequate Housing

Appendix B

Chicago Black Southside Community Organizations and Addresses, 1930–60

Churches

All Nations Pentecostal Church, 3716 S. Langley
Bethel A.M.E. Church, 45th St. and Michigan Ave.
Bethesda Baptist Church, 5301 S. Michigan Ave.
Church of the Good Shepherd, 5700 Prairie Ave.
Commonwealth Community Church, 140 W. 80th St.
Cosmopolitan Community Church, 53rd St. and Wabash Ave.
First Church of Deliverance, 4315 S. Wabash Ave.
Grace Presbyterian Church, 3600 Vincennes Ave.
Metropolitan Community Church, 4100 Parkway
Mt. Moriah Baptist Church, 50th St. and Indiana Ave.
Olivet Baptist Church, 401 E. 31st Street; 3101 S. Parkway
Pilgrim Baptist Church, 3932 S. Parkway; 3301 S. Indiana Ave.
Progressive Baptist Church, 3705 S. LaSalle
Quinn Chapel A.M.E. Church, 2401 S. Wabash Ave.
St. Elizabeth Catholic Church, 4049 Wabash Ave.
St. Mary's Baptist Church, 3235 Calumet Ave.
St. Stephen A.M.E. Church, 2000 Washington Blvd.
St. Thomas Episcopal Church, 3801 S. Wabash Ave.

Not all addresses are known. Addresses often changed as well.

Newspapers and Presses

Associated Negro Press, 3507 S. Parkway

Chicago Bee, 3655 S. State St.

Chicago Defender, 3435 S. Indiana

Negro Digest, 5619 S. State St.

Negro Story, 4019 Vincennes Ave.

Social Institutions

Abraham Lincoln Center (ALC), 700 E. Oakland

Chicago Council of Negro Organizations (CCNO), 3262 S. Vernon

Chicago Urban League (CUL), 2410 S. Michigan Ave.

CNDA's Federated Home for Dependent Children, 5650 Indiana Ave.

Elam Home of Girls, 4726 S. Parkway

Englewood YMCA, 6545 S. Union Ave.

George Cleveland Hall Library (GCHL), 4801 S. Michigan Ave.

Good Shepherd Community Center, 5700 Prairie Ave.

Home for the Aged and Infirm Colored People, 4430 Vincennes Ave.

Ida B. Wells Infant Welfare Station, 3704 S. Vincennes Ave.

Infant Welfare Station, 33 31st St.

Joint Negro Appeal, 5120 S. Parkway

Metropolitan Community Center, 4106 S. Michigan Ave.

Oakland Branch Library, 700 East Oakland Blvd.

Parkway Community House (PCH), 5120 South Parkway; 6301 S. Rhodes

Phyllis Wheatley Home, 5128 S. Michigan Ave.

Progressive Community Center, 56 E. 48th St.

Poro College, 4100 S. Parkway

Provident Hospital, 426 E. 51st Street

Southside Boys Club Foundation, 5740 S. Michigan Ave.

South Parkway YWCA (SPY), 4559 S. Parkway

South Side Community Art Center (SSCAC), 3831 S. Michigan Ave.

Southside Community (Juvenile Delinquent Prevention) Committee, 6156 S. Cottage Grove

South Side Housing Association, 3201 S. Wabash Ave.

South Side Settlement House (SSSH), 3201 S. Wabash Ave.

Wabash YMCA, 3763 S. Wabash Ave.

Washington Park YMCA, 5000 S. Indiana Ave.
Woodlawn YWCA, 1170 E. 63 St.

Public Housing

Altgeld Homes, 130th St and Ellis Ave.
Ida B. Wells Homes, 37th St. and Cottage Grove
Victor Olander Homes, 3939 Lake Park
Prairie Avenue Courts, 26th St. and South Parkway

Private Housing

Lake Meadows Development Site, 31–35th St., King Dr. to Lake Michigan
Michigan Blvd. Gardens Apts., Michigan Ave. and 47th St.

Entertainments

Café Montclare, 2903 S. State St.
Casbah Lounge, 6107 S. Parkway
Club Jimbob, 4700 Kenwood
Club Delisa, 5512–16 S. State St.
Delisa New Club, 5521 S. State St.
Dreamland Café, 3520 and 3616–18 S. State St.; 4700 S. State St.
Elite #1, 31–35 State St.
Elite #2, 31–35 State St.
Entertainers Club, 31–35 State St.
Grand Terrace, 3955 S. Parkway
Grand Theatre, 3110 S. State St.
Metropolitan Theater, 46th St. and South Parkway
Mid-Nite Club, 3140 S. Indiana Ave.
Park Theater, 3955 South Parkway
Pershing Hotel (and Ballroom), 743 W. 64th
Plantation Café, 338 E. 35th St.
Regal Theatre, 47th St. and Parkway
Rhumboogie Café, 343 Garfield Blvd.
Rialto, State St. and Van Buren St.
Royal Garden Café, 459 E. 31 St.
Savoy Ballroom, 47th St. and Parkway

Sunset Café, 31–35 State St.

The Peking, 31–35 State St.

Three Deuces, 222 N. State St.

White City Roller Rink, 63rd St. and Calumet

Men's Clubs

Appomattox Club, 3632 S. Parkway

Chicago Tuskegee Club, 4909 S. Parkway

Women's Clubs and Organizations

4 Leaf Clover Social Narrative Club

100 Dollar Social and Charity Club

AKA Sorority

American Friendship Club

American Rose Art Club[*]

Annie E. Oliver Civic and Charity Club

Associated Business Women's Club

Auga Caliente Club

Baby Relief Club

Bronze Americans

Carnation Study Club

Carrie S. Horton Civic and Study Club

Charmond Charity Club

Chicago Federation Club

Chicago Union Charity Club[*]

Chicago Young Woman's Club

Chrysanthemum Art and Charity Club

Clara Jessamine Civic Club[*]

Clio Culture and Civic Club

Clover Leaf Circle Club[*]

Clover Leaf Social and Charity Club[*]

Constant Climbers Art and Charity Club

Cornell Charity Club[*]

---

[*]Women's clubs in existence since the early twentieth century

Dardanell Civic Club

Die Lorellie Choral Club

Dorcas Art and Charity Club

Dorcas Narcissus Club

Douglas League of Women Voters

East Side Woman's Club[*]

Emma J. Andrews Woman's Club

En Avant Culture and Civic Club

En Verite Progressive Club

Ethel M. Cleaves Club

Excelsior Social and Charity Club

Fannie M. Carter Club

Gardenia Social and Civic Club

Gaudeamus Charity Club[*]

Georgia Martin Education Charity Club

Gertrude Johnson Williams Civic and Charity Club

Giles Charity and Study Club[*]

Grace Lee Stevens Civic and Charity Club

Hallie Q. Brown Civic Club

Harriet Tubman Civic Club

Henrietta Burr Social and Charity Club

Horton Art and Charity Club

Ida B. Wells Club[*]

Ideal Woman's Club[*]

Illa F. Summers Progressive and Civic Club

Imperial Art Club[*]

Irene McCoy Gaines Educational Club

Iroquois Community League[*] (Evanston)

Jeanette Smith Educational and Civic Club

Ladies Auxiliary of Brotherhood of Sleeping Car Porters

Lakota Welfare Club

League of States Club

Lelia E. Cannon Civic Club

Los Sonoras Social and Civic Club

Lou Art and Service Club

Loyal Charity Club

Madden Park Woman's Club

Mamye Williams Civic Club

Margaret Hayes Educational and Charity Club

Married Ladies Industrial and Charity Club

Mary B. Talbert Club

Mary E. Gaston Study Club

Matilda Dunbar Club (Evanston)

Maude E. Smith Club

Missouri Social and Charity Club

Nannie Reed Civic Club

New Green Pastures Club

New Pathfinders Club

North Side Woman's Club[*]

National Council of Negro Women, Chicago Branch

North Side Woman's Club

Octettes Club

One Fifty Girls Club

Oscar de Priest Charity Club

Ossie B. Wiley Charity Club

Phyllis Wheatley Club[*]

Progressive Mothers Club

Rosa Gragg Educational and Civic Club

Silent Workers Club

Silver Leaf Social and Charity Club[*]

Unique Ebonettes Charity and Social Club

Unique Workers Club

Violet Art and Charity Club

Volunteers Workers Charity Club[*]

West Side Woman's Club[*]

Woman's Progressive and Civic Club

Women's Civic League

Women's Welfare Club

Young Matrons' Culture Club (renamed Myra Hunter Reeves Culture Club)

Girls' Clubs

Clara Jessamine Gay Teenettes
Dardanella Teenettes
Distinguished Maidens
Elizabeth Lindsay Davis Juniors
Ida B. Wells Juniorettes
Ida's Girls
Iota Chi Mu
Phyllis Wheatley Junior Club
Sun Shine Club
Silent Cylindricas
Sophisticated Debs Club
Sophisticated Debutantes
Theta Phi Delta
Violet Art Buds

Schools

Carter Elementary School, 57th St. and Michigan Ave.
Coleman Elementary School, 4655 S. Dearborn St.
Doolittle Elementary School
Douglas School
Dunbar Vocational High School, 3000 S. Parkway
Doolittle Elementary School, 525 E. 35th St.
DuSable High School, 4934 S. Wabash St.; 24 E. 50th St.
Farren School, 51st St. and State St.
Keith Elementary School
Phillips High School, 244 S. Pershing Rd.
Raymond Elementary School
Webster Elementary School
Wendell Phillips High School, 39th St. and Indiana Ave.

Businesses and Business Associations

Ben Franklin Store, 436–44 E. 47th St.
Chicago Negro Chamber of Commerce, 449 East 47th St.

Douglas National Bank, 35th St. and State St.

Gladys, 4527 Indiana Ave.

Johnson Publishing, 820 Michigan Ave.

Jones Brothers (policy headquarters), 4724 Michigan Ave.

Metropolitan Life Insurance Company, 418 E. 47th St.

Morris Eat Shop, 410 E. 47th St.

National Association of Negro Business and Professional Women's Clubs, 4723 S. State St.

Negro Chamber of Commerce, 4043 S. Drexel Blvd.

Overton Hygienic Bldg., 3619–27 S. State St.

Poro College, 4415 S. Parkway

Provident Hospital, 500 E. 51st St.

Supreme Liberty Life Insurance, 3511 S. Parkway

Victory Life Insurance Company, 35th St. and State St.

Interracial Southside Social Institutions

Abraham Lincoln Center (ALC), 700 E. Oakwood Blvd.

Community Child Guidance Centers of Chicago, 700 E. Oakwood Blvd.

Sheil House, 4100 S. Michigan Ave.

Notes

Abbreviations

Chicago Historical Society, Chicago, Illinois

BWMWP   Black Women in the Middle West Project

CBP   Claude A. Barnett Papers

Harold Washington Public Library, Municipal Collections, Chicago, Illinois

CHAAR   Chicago Housing Authority. Annual Reports.

CHAMR   Chicago Housing Authority. Monthly Reports of the Executive Secretary to the Commissioners of the Chicago Housing Authority Chicago Housing Authority. Annual Reports

CSCP   Citizens Schools Committee Papers

CTUP   Chicago Teachers Union Papers

IMGP   Irene McCoy Gaines Papers

MM   Madeline Morgan Manuscript

PCHP   Parkway Community House Papers, 1937–1943

PPACP   Patrick B. Prescott and Annabelle Carey Prescott Papers

SLCP   Stella Levinkind Counselbaum Papers

TEP   Thyra J. Edwards Papers

WCMC   Welfare Council of Metropolitan Chicago

Northwestern University Archives, Evanston, Illinois

BA   Black Alumni

MHP   Melville Herskovits Papers

NBP   Neva Boyd Papers

Northwestern University Library, Evanston, Illinois

NACWCR   National Association of Colored Women's Clubs Records
Microfilm

Northwestern University, Special Collections, Evanston, Illinois

CCARRD   Chicago Council against Racial and Religious
Discrimination

Southern Illinois University, Special Collections, Carbondale, Illinois

KDP   Katherine Dunham Papers

University of Chicago, Regenstein Library, Chicago, Illinois

CCADN   Chicago Council against Discrimination Newsletters
CCTAR   Chicago Community Trust, Annual Reports, 1933–1959
CULAR   Chicago Urban League Annual Reports, 1929 to 1947
HAICPAR   Home for the Aged and Infirm Colored People Annual Reports,
1929–1944
WCMCRD   Welfare Council of Metropolitan Chicago, Research Department,
1955–1964

University of Chicago, Special Collections, Chicago, Illinois

ADP   Allison Davis Papers
IBWP   Ida B. Wells Papers
LWP   Louis Wirth Papers
MBWP   Mary Bolton Wirth Papers

University of Illinois at Chicago, Special Collections, Chicago, Illinois

ANDP   Annetta Dieckmann Papers
CFC   Community Fund of Chicago
CULP   Chicago Urban League Papers
MHPC   Metropolitan Housing and Planning Council
RHAP   Rose Haas Auschuler Papers
SAP   Saul Alinsky Papers
YWCA   Young Women's Christian Association

University of Iowa, Louise Noun Women's Archives, Ames, Iowa

KGWP   Katherine Gayle Williams Papers

*Vivian G. Harsh Research Collection of Afro-American History
and Literature, Woodson Regional Library, Chicago, Illinois*

ABP	Alice Browning Papers
ALP	Arthur Logan Papers
EMBP	Ebenezer Missionary Baptist Church Manuscripts
GCH	George Cleveland Hall Branch Library Archives
HSA	Howalton School Archives
IWP	Illinois Writers Project
LICC	Links, Inc., Chicago Chapter
LSCP	Lucy Smith-Collier Papers
MJP	Marjorie S. Joyner Papers
NIP	Negro in Illinois Papers
PCHPC	Parkway Community House Project Collection
RDP	Richard Durham Papers
SEEM	St. Edmund Episcopal Manuscripts
TCS	Theodore Charles Stone Papers
WMP	William McBride Papers

Newspapers

[*Defender*]	*Chicago Defender,* selected Years, 1930–60
[*Bee*]	*Chicago Sunday Bee,* 1943–48

Introduction

1. Bone, "Richard Wright and the Chicago Renaissance," 446–68; Walker, *Richard Wright: Daemonic Genius;* Fabre, *The Unfinished Quest of Richard Wright.*

2. Werner, "Chicago Renaissance," in *The Oxford Companion to African American Literature,* 132–33; Werner, *Playing the Changes;* Mullen, *Popular Fronts;* Mullen, "Popular Fronts: *Negro Story Magazine* and the African American Literary Response to World War II," 5–15; Bolden, *Urban Rage in Bronzeville.*

3. Hine, *Hine Sight,* 98.

4. Drake and Cayton, *Black Metropolis,* 379–80.

5. *Defender,* September 2, 1950, 10.

6. Statement by Irene McCoy Gaines to Trygve Lie, Secretary General, United Nations, May 19, 1947, box 2, file 6, IMGP.

7. Herskovits, *The Myth of the Negro Past;* Herskovits, "The Contribution of Afroamerican Studies to Africanist Research (1948)," 12–22. See Walker, ed., *African Roots/American Cultures,* which also discussed African retentions in the United States, the Caribbean, and Latin America.

8. Robeson, *Here I Stand,* 105.

Chapter 1: Models of Black Activism in Chicago

1. Annual Report—1944, box 23, GCH Archives 32/01 MSS; "Interest in Race History Increases," *Defender,* March 2, 1940. Black clubwomen, teachers, and librarians raised a significant proportion of the ASNLH's funds. Further, they became active in the collection and dissemination of black history through the ASNLH's publications and teacher kits. Des Jardins, *Women and the Historical Enterprise,* 155, 157–60. See also Goggin, *Carter G. Woodson: A Life in Black History;* Hine, "Carter G. Woodson, White Philanthropy and Negro Historiography." Book agents sold history books for the ASNLH in the Deep South and the rest of the United States. See Green, *Selling Black History for Carter G. Woodson.* In 1976 the ASNLH changed its name to the Association for the Study of African American Life and History.

2. Annual Report—1938, box 23, GCH Archives 32/01 MSS; *Bee,* January 28, 1945, 1–2; *Bee,* January 14, 1945, 1; 42; *Bee,* February 20, 1944, 12; *Bee,* February 10, 1946, 6; *Bee,* January 26, 1946, 11.

3. *Defender,* December 18, 1937, 17; Homel, *Down from Equality,* 144, 173.

4. Forum series, box 2, file 5, LWP; *Bee,* February 11, 1945, 11; *Bee,* January 7, 1945, 9.

5. Minutes of Management Committee, GSCC, May 29, 1941, box 1, file 1941, PCHP; *Bee,* May 5, 1946, 2; *Bee,* January 1, 1945, 12.

6. Minutes of Meeting of Program Advisory Committee of GSCC, February 16, 1942, box 1, 1942–1943 file, PCHP, 34; Yes—This is PCH-1942 file, PCHPC.

7. Woodson, *The Mis-Education of the Negro.*

8. Woodson, "Proceedings of the Annual Meeting of the Association for the Study of Negro Life and History Held in New York City, November 8–12, 1931," 4; Morgan, "Chicago School Curriculum Includes Negro Achievements," MM; Field, "Intercultural Education and Negro History during the Second World War," 79–81, 83; "Chicago Schools Include Negro History," 51, 60.

9. Morgan, "Chicago School Curriculum Includes Negro Achievements," MM.

10. Foreword: The Club Home, box 1, file 9, IMGP.

11. "Book Value," *Chicago Tribune,* April 30, 1991, sec. 5, 1–2; Flug, "Vivian Gordon Harsh," 542–43.

12. *Bee,* February 18, 1945, 9; *Bee,* January 17, 1945, 16–17; Shaw, "Charlemae Hill Rollins," 949–53.

13. *Defender,* January 8, 1938, 17; "National Du Saible Memorial Society," Interview with Annie Oliver, box 38, file 21, NIP, IWP.

14. "National Du Saible Memorial Society," Interview with Annie Oliver, box 38, file 21, NIP, IWP. Oliver also organized a club in 1939 in her own name, the Annie E. Oliver Social, Civic, and Charity Club. See Chicago and Northern District Association, *The Story of Seventy-Five Years of the Chicago and Northern District,* 49.

15. Editors of Freedomways, *Paul Robeson;* Du Bois, *The Autobiography of W. E. B. Du Bois;* Du Bois, "Pan-African and New Racial Philosophy," 237–40.

16. Editors of Freedomways, *Paul Robeson*, 51.

17. Paul Robeson, *Here I Stand*, 36.

18. Joy James, *Transcending the Talented Tenth*, 37. Robeson spoke in Chicago against Franco's Spain, sponsored by the "Win the Peace Committee of Chicago." *Bee*, May 26, 1946, 12. Ella Fitzgerald, too, refused to give a concert in Franco's Spain. *Bee*, June 2, 1946, 14.

19. Cayton, "The Morale of the Negro and National Defense," August 15, 1941, box 54, file 17, LWP; Cayton, "The Negro's Challenge," 10; Cayton, "Fighting for White Folks?" 267–70.

20. The *Defender* had a large readership not only in Chicago but also in the South. As such, the newspaper followed closely the violence in southern states as well as international news. As early as 1930, the *Defender* had published an article about African "civilization." See *Defender*, March 8, 1930, 5.

21. Robeson, *Here I Stand*, 74–76, 98, 105.

22. Letter to Frank Loomis from A. L. Foster, May 22, 1936, box 277, file 10, WCMC.

23. Herskovits, *The Myth of the Negro Past*, xxxvii–viii; Herskovits, "The Contribution of Afroamerican Studies to Africanist Research (1948)," 12–22. On the other hand, sociologist E. Franklin Frazier steadfastly argued that little of African culture was left in black American culture. He contended there was a "great poverty of traditions and patterns of behavior" among black Americans. However, Frazier emphasized that this "disorganization" of black Americans was not pathological but part of the "civilizational process." What he meant was that the stage of disorganization was cyclical, and it was experienced by other ethnic groups. Although his ideas may seem conservative today, Frazier was actually refuting the retrogressionist and hereditarian models of black inferiority. Frazier, "Traditions and Patterns of Negro Family Life in the United States," 194.

24. Bascom, *The Sociological Role of the Yoruba Cult-Group*; Bascom, "The Focus of Cuban Santeria," 64–68; Bascom and Gebauer, *Handbook of West African Art*; Bascom and Herskovits, *Continuity and Change in African Cultures*; Powdermaker, *After Freedom: A Cultural Study in the Deep South*; Smith, *The Economy of Hausa Communities of Zaria*; Turner, *Notes on the Sounds and Vocabulary of Gullah*; Davis and Dollard, *Children of Bondage*; Davis, Gardner, and Gardner, *Deep South*; Davis, "The Relation between Color Caste and Economic Stratification in Two Black Plantation Counties"; Davis, *Social Influences upon Learning*; Drake, *Churches and Voluntary Associations among Negroes in Chicago*; Dunham, *Journey to Accompong*.

25. Conference brochure, "The Crisis of Modern Imperialism in Africa and the Far East," box 7, file 38, MHP; *Defender*, March 8, 1930, 5; Brown, "Culture Contact and Race Conflict," 34–47. See also Cox, *Caste, Class, and Race*.

26. U.S. Work Projects Administration, Illinois, *Chicago Negro Community*.

27. The People's Forum Brochure, box 2, file 5, LWP.

28. Margaret T. Burroughs, "Saga of Chicago's South Side Community Art Cen-

ter (1938–1943), in SSCAC Fiftieth Anniversary Booklet (Chicago: SSCAC, 1991), 2, WMP; James Graff, "The SSCAC Offers a Rich Commentary on Civic Dedication in the Changing World of the Black Middle-Class," in SSCAC Fiftieth Anniversary Booklet, n.p.

29. Reynolds and Wright, *Against the Odds*, 20; 100; Vanterpool, "Open-Textured Aesthetic Boundaries," 149; and Locke, *The New Negro*.

30. Goss, "A Mother Looks at War," *Defender*, August 30, 1940, 13.

31. Craig, *Black Drama of the Federal Theatre Era*, 24, 113, 135–36; Aschenbrenner, "Katherine Dunham: Anthropologist, Artist, Humanist," 140; Fraden, *Blueprints for a Black Federal Theatre*, 125; Fraden, "The Cloudy History of Big White Fog: The Federal Theatre Project, 1938," 5–28; Shaw, "Charlemae Hill Rollins."

32. Craig, *Black Drama of the Federal Theatre Era*, 113, 135–36.

33. Plotkin, "Deeds of Mistrust: Race, Housing, and Restrictive Covenants in Chicago, 1900–1953," 140–41, 142, 146, 147–51; Waters, "Hansberry Decree Opens 500 New Homes to Race," *Defender*, November 23, 1940, 1; Cheney, *Lorraine Hansberry*; Nemiroff, *To Be Young, Gifted and Black*; and Wilkerson, "Hansberry, Lorraine," 338–39.

34. Schietinger, "Racial Succession and Values of Small Residential Properties," 833–34; Lahey, "Are Slum Landlords Criminals?" 75; Gries and Ford, "Property Depreciation and Negro Residence," box 37, file 6, NIP, IWP. Both black and white homeowners also formed neighborhood improvement associations to keep their neighborhoods clean and well kept. One black improvement association, the Five Hundred Block Club, even had a children's club, the Willing Workers' Club, who helped keep their yards and streets clean. The CUL encouraged the development of such black improvement associations by helping to organize neighborhood block clubs and improvement clubs to monitor zoning ordinances and violations. One such club, the Southside Improvement Club, tried to stop zoning that would permit barbershops and other businesses in their neighborhood. Not only were they worried about the devaluation of their property, they were also concerned that parks and playgrounds could not be built, since recreational facilities were illegal in areas zoned for businesses. These black associations, formed along social-class lines, tried to preserve their neighborhoods against encroaching businesses, as well as encourage civic responsibility. They were far different from most white neighborhood associations that usually reinforced segregation and were, in effect, restrictive covenant associations. Mikva, "The Neighborhood Improvement Association: A Counter-Force to the Expansion of Chicago's Negro Population," 19, 24; Flint, "Zoning and Residential Segregation: A Social and Physical History, 1910–40," 348; Chavers-Wright, *The Guarantee*, 326.

35. Segregation-Incorporated, box 3, RDP.

36. Reverend Archibald Carey, box 2, RDP.

37. Durham, "Millionaire Plots Tighter Noose on 'Black Ghetto,'" *Defender*, February 24, 1945, 9. Indeed, Chicago had its share of conservative whites who joined

restrictive covenant and improvement associations to keep blacks out. The first communities to do so were the southside communities of Kenwood, Oakland, Hyde Park, Woodlawn, and Englewood. Chicago Housing Authority (CHA) administrator Robert Taylor estimated that as much as 80 percent of Chicago was covenanted by 1939, although that estimate was unquestionably high. Nonetheless, by 1950, two years after restrictive covenants were declared illegal, there were still over 200 neighborhood improvement associations in Chicago. Plotkin, "Deeds of Mistrust," 96, 21; *Defender,* January 14, 1939, 4. Mikva cited in Plotkin, "Deeds of Mistrust," 62; Flint, "Zoning and Residential Segregation," 355; Sugrue, "Crabgrass-Roots Politics: Race, Rights, and the Reaction against Liberalism in the Urban North, 1940–1964," 551–52. See also the debate between Robert Weaver and Newton Farr, former president of the National Real Estate Association and the Chicago Real Estate Board. Farr, "Are Restrictive Covenants Justifiable?" 37; Weaver, "No," 39.

38. Postcard, July 6, 1944, box 2, file 3, IMGP.

39. Ibid. "Overcrowded" meant 1.51 or more persons per rooms. See WCMCRD Report 23 (October 1956): 4.

40. "Housing," box 37, file 1, NIP, IWP. By 1930, 90 percent of blacks lived in census tracts that were over 50 percent black, even though only 7 percent of Chicago's population was black. By 1940, 75 percent of blacks lived in census tracts with a black concentration of 90 percent or more. When the nonwhite population of Chicago increased by 80 percent from 1940 to 1950, further segregation ensued. By 1950, 79 percent of blacks lived in census tracts where 75 percent of the residents were black. Conversely, 84 percent of nonblacks lived in census tracts where less than 1 percent were black residents. In short, the color line remained drawn in Chicago. Wirth and Furez, *Local Community Fact Book, 1938,* chap. 7; Duncan and Duncan, *Chicago's Negro Population,* 1, 11; de Vise, *Chicago's Widening Color Gap,* 83.

41. Wirth and Furez, *Local Community Fact Book, 1938,* n.p.

42. Werner, *Playing the Changes,* 191.

43. Waters, "Everything Normal with These Folks Except They Have No Home," *Defender,* August 31, 1940, 5; Memorandum, December 16, 1948, box 74, file 20, MHPC. Kitchenettes consisted of a gas plate in a closet or simply sharing a common kitchen.

44. For further reading about the concept of caste and about Richard Wright, see Drake and Cayton, *Black Metropolis;* Cappetti, "Sociology of an Existence: Wright and the Chicago School," in *Richard Wright,* 255–71; Warner, *American Life;* Warner, Junker, and Adams, *Color and Human Nature,* 87–89, 98.

45. Sheppard, "Conflicting Business Associations," 11–12.

46. Weems, *Desegregating the Dollar,* 27–28; Sheppard, "Conflicting Business Associations," 26.

47. Morris, "The Chicago Negro and the Major Political Parties 1940–1948," 20; Travis, *An Autobiography of Black Chicago,* 37; Sheppard, "Conflicting Business Associations," 15.

48. Gould, cited in Sheppard, "Conflicting Business Associations," 16; Letter from

A. L. Foster to Frank Loomis, May 22, 1935, box 1, 1935 file, CULP; Frazier, "Chicago: A Cross-Section of Negro Life," 72. White businessmen owned most of the jazz clubs as well, although mostly black jazz musicians performed there. These clubs permitted interracial dancing but enforced segregated seating, reserving the best tables for white patrons. A number of restaurants and hotels, however, were black-owned and catered to black performers who were often refused service elsewhere. See Travis, *An Autobiography of Black Chicago;* Spillane, "The Making of an Underground Market: Drug Selling in Chicago, 1900–1940," 28, 39; *The Negro Travelers' Green Book for Hotels, Motels, Restaurants, Tourist Homes, Vacation Resorts.* For information on the clubs and nightlife on Chicago's southside, see Kenney, *Chicago Jazz.* On black female musicians in Chicago, see Placksin, *American Women in Jazz;* Floyd, *The Power of Black Music;* and Hanft, "Remarkable Iowa Women," box 1, KGWP.

49. Robertson, "A Study of Some Aspects of Racial Succession in the Woodlawn Community Area of Chicago," 32, 69. Black residents patronized white, as well as black, businesses. But black businesses took in less than one-tenth of all money spent by blacks in Bronzeville, in large part because black businesses offered limited and low-cost products. Morris, "The Chicago Negro," 8, 10; Sheppard, "Conflicting Business Associations," 23.

50. Sheppard, "Conflicting Business Associations," 13, 19, 20. The CUL helped to start the Negro Chamber of Commerce in the early 1930s; unfortunately, there is little information about the organization. Chicago Urban League, 1937 Annual Report, Part 1, p. 5, CULP.

51. Wolcott, *Remaking Respectability,* 237.

52. See chap. 5. In Scottsboro, Alabama, nine black men, including two boys, were accused of raping two white girls. Blacks were excluded from the jury; the accused were also not given adequate legal representation. See Carter, *Scottsboro: A Tragedy of the American South.*

53. Meier and Rudwick, *Along the Color Line,* 327.

54. Edley, "Strategies and Techniques of Politics," 2, 3; Third Ward News Clippings, 1957–1959, SAP, 401; Gosnell, *Negro Politicians,* chap. 7. Given the harsh restrictions of poll taxes and literacy tests, which severely prohibited southern blacks from exercising their right to vote, migrants were eager to participate in city, state, and national elections. Indeed, state legislator William King, speaking at Metropolitan Community Center on the "vigilance" of the ballot, stressed how important it was for northern blacks to vote because southern blacks could not. *Defender,* January 18, 1930.

55. See chap. 5 and Appendix A.

56. *Defender,* December 18, 1937, 17; Chicago and Northern District Association, *The Story of Seventy-Five Years of the Chicago and Northern District,* 10; *Defender,* December 18, 1937, 1; *Defender,* July 31, 1943, 17; *Bee,* February 27, 1944, 11.

57. Caldwell, *The Policy King,* iii, 255. Because it cost only a nickel to play the game, many blacks not only tried their luck but also could make their living by gambling; Caldwell, *The Policy King,* 236. Some blacks became wealthy by employing runners

and checkers. The Jones brothers reportedly earned almost $25,000 a day, in large part through the 250 persons they employed. In turn, they invested their profits in real estate in Bronzeville and opened one of the first black-owned department stores, the Ben Franklin Store. Similarly, "King" Cole became president of the Metropolitan Funeral Association, later the Chicago Metropolitan Mutual Assurance Company. He, too, turned his policy dollars toward legitimate businesses, including a recording studio that featured the "All Negro Radio Hour" and the "All Negro Children's Hour," as well as a publication, *Bronzeman Magazine*. See Weems, "Robert A. Cole and the Metropolitan Funeral Association," 3, 8. See also Haller, "Policy Gambling, Entertainment, and the Emergence of Black Politics: Chicago from 1900 to 1940," 719–39.

58. *Defender,* November 25, 1939, 13.

59. *Defender,* December 9, 1939, 13; Caldwell, *The Policy King,* 236–37.

60. Letter from Irene McCoy Gaines to Mayor Edward Kelly, September 22, 1937, box 1, file 12, IMGP; letter from Edward Kelly to Irene McCoy Gaines, October 4, 1937, box 1, file 12, IMGP.

61. "Federation of Women's Clubs Helps Defender in Vice War," *Defender,* March 8, 1930, 1; Letter from A. L. Foster to Irene McCoy Gaines, July 20, 1937, box 1, file 12, IMGP; Letter from Irene McCoy Gaines to Joe Jefferson, Better Conduct Program, the Chicago Urban League, box 1, file 12, IMGP. On clubwomen's involvement with prostitution, see also Smith, *Sin Corner and Joe Smith.*

62. *Defender,* March 1, 1930, 1; Reckless, *Vice in Chicago,* 192; "Fight Prostitutes Who Infest South Side," *Defender,* February 22, 1930, 3. See Spillane, "The Making of an Underground Market," 27–47.

63. Lincoln, *The Black Experience in Religion,* 200; Fisher, "Organized Religion and the Cults," 9; "Radio Special" and "The Pentecostal Ensign," box 1, LSCP. The First Church of Deliverance also started a radio program in 1934. See "First Church of Deliverance," box 2, LSCP.

64. "Faith Healer," 37–39; "And Churches," box 17, file 1, NIP, IWP. Smith's church exemplified Earl Lewis's idea that black people converted "segregation" into "congregation." Lewis cited in Kelley, *Race Rebels,* 45.

65. "Faith Healer," 37–39. See also "And Churches," box 17, file 1, NIP, IWP.

66. "In Testimony of the Faith of The Reverend Mary G. Evans, D. D. Banquet," November 4, 1949, box 2, MJP; "Lady Preacher," 31–33, box 45, file 3, NIP, IWP; Cosmopolitan Independent Community Church; 1947 Annual Report of the Cosmopolitan Independent Community Church, box 2, MJP; "Youthful Negro Woman Pastor's Church Expands," *Chicago Tribune,* March 14, 1943, box 2, file 3, IMGP.

67. "In Testimony of the Faith of The Reverend Mary G. Evans, D. D. Banquet," November 4, 1949, box 2, MJP.

68. Cosmopolitan Community Church, 1960 Annual Report, MJP; Cosmopolitan Community Church, "The Community House: The Grand Opening, Thanksgiving, November 25th, 1948," MJP. Evans also continued her outreach program to the sick

and elderly; in 1963 she established a home for the elderly, as the Old Folks' Home had closed during the 1940s. Cosmopolitan Community Church, 1955 Annual Report, box 1, MJP. The nursery's board of management was composed of prominent black women, including Marjorie Joyner, an avid fund-raiser for the church and cofounder of the National Council of Negro Women (NCNW). Similarly, the Ebenezer Missionary Baptist Church had outreach programs similar to the Cosmopolitan, such as a nursery, library, and various women's groups. See Sixtieth Anniversary Souvenir Book, box 1, EMBC.

69. "Youthful Negro Woman Pastor's Church Expands," *Chicago Tribune,* March 14, 1943, n.p., IMGP.

70. Strickland, *History of the Chicago Urban League.* As late as the 1950s, Ethel Payne wrote about job discrimination on State Street, yet many blacks continued to shop there. She suggested a "don't buy where you can't work" campaign. *Defender,* July 4, 1953, 9.

71. Johnson-Odim, "Gaines, Irene McCoy," in *Women Building Chicago: A Biographical Dictionary,* 296. In cooperation with Randolph, the CCNO advertised the Washington, D.C. march of 1941. Monthly Newsletter of the CCNO, April 1942, box 2, file 1, IMGP. A. Phillip Randolph's threat—to organize a mass protest in Washington, D.C. unless more blacks were given war-related industry jobs—had certainly paid off. He had forced Roosevelt's hand in issuing Executive Order 8802, which established a policy against hiring discrimination and also created the FEPC. Kersten, "March on Washington Committee," 322–24. As of 1958, there were thirteen states with FEPC statutes; Garfinkel, *When Negroes March,* 171. By 1949, such legislation was introduced in seventeen states, but failed to become law in Illinois; Guzman, Jones, and Hall, *1952 Negro Year Book,* 120.

72. See Appendix A.

73. Sitkoff, "Racial Militancy and Interracial Violence in the Second World War," 663; Bates, "A New Crowd Challenges the Agenda of the Old Guard in the NAACP, 1933–1941," 347–48; Meier and Rudwick, *Along the Color Line,* 343, 358; Reed, *The Chicago NAACP and the Rise of Black Professional Leadership;* CCADN (September 1955): 3; CCADN (October 1955): 2; CCADN (July 1955): 4. For further information about lynching during World War II, see Capeci, "The Lynching of Cloe Wright: Federal Protection of Constitutional Rights during World War II," 859–87.

74. CCADN (June 1945): n.p. Illinois's record on civil rights was "dismal." It was the only nonsouthern state that had not passed legislation to stop discrimination in private employment, that is, no FEPC. The American Jewish Congress of Chicago noted that there was no administrative agency to enforce civil rights laws. Since 1945, Chicago had an FEPC ordinance, but it was limited to private employment. See American Jewish Congress of Chicago, *The Lost Decade. An Analysis of Illinois Civil Rights Legislation, 1949–1959,* 1, 2.

75. Rieser, "An Analysis of the Reporting of Racial Incidents in Chicago, 1945 to 1950," 1, 11, 33, 34.

76. CCADN (April 1953): 2.

77. WJCAH, A Statement of the Joint Committee on Adequate Housing, January 1941, box 27, file 356, MHPC.

78. WJCAH, Minutes, May 4, 1944, box 28, file 358, MHPC, 68.

79. WJCAH, Minutes, March 13, 1941, March 27, 1941, May 8, 1941, box 27, file 356, MHPC.

80. WJCAH, Minutes, February 11, 1941, box 27, file 356, MHPC.

81. WJCAH, 1947 and 1948 Financial Reports, S. E. Ledger, 1942, box 27, file 333, MHPC.

82. Saul Alinsky, "In These 10 Cities," 1950, file 34, SAP; Saul Alinsky, Text of Testimony for the Civil Rights Housing Hearing, Commission on Civil Rights, May 5, 1959, file 34, SAP. The seminal book on Chicago's slum clearance and public housing is Hirsch, *Making the Second Ghetto*.

83. Chicago Housing Authority, *The Slum . . . Is Rehabilitation Possible?* 5.

84. *Defender*, March 30, 1957, 7. As early as 1941, the Neighborhood Redevelopment Corporation Act was passed to move toward clearance and redevelopment of blighted areas. (The term "blighted" referred to overcrowded areas with substandard housing, where there was no stable tax base.) See Chicago Planning Commission, *Housing Goals for Chicago,* 111. See also Fishbein, "The Expansion of Negro Residential Area in Chicago, 1950–60," 2; *Defender*, July 22, 1950, 14; *Defender*, November 27, 1954, 12. Another recommendation was occupancy standards, that is, placing limits on the number of persons per dwelling and maintaining strict rules on its upkeep. Black economist Robert Weaver hoped that this would prevent unsanitary and unhealthy living conditions, as well as undermine restrictive covenants. As he reasoned, if properties were well maintained, then whites would be less reluctant to sell real estate to blacks, at least to middle-class blacks. However, this recommendation was not embraced by city hall or landlords. Smith, "The Quest for Racial Democracy," 143; Mikva, "The Neighborhood Improvement Association," 19, 20. University of Chicago sociologist Louis Wirth agreed with Weaver, recommending that wealthier blacks be given "incentives" to buy homes in these neighborhoods to prevent further deterioration. See Plotkin, "Deeds of Mistrust," 127; Weaver, "Chicago: A City of Covenants," 75–78, 93.

85. Tom Jenkins, "South Side Public Housing and Expressway Redevelopment: An Implication for Businessmen," November 20, 1958, box 282, file 3, WCMC. The expressway later would be named the Dan Ryan Expressway.

86. Cook, *Sweet Land of Liberty?* 43–44.

87. Sitkoff, *A New Deal for Blacks;* Sitkoff, "Racial Militancy and Interracial Violence in the Second World War," 661–681; Cruse, *The Crisis of the Negro Intellectual*.

Chapter 2: Parkway Community House

1. Cayton, The Problem, Program, and Facilities of the Good Shepherd Community Center [hereafter GSCC], n.d., box 1, 1937–1943 file, PCHP.

2. Homel, *Down from Equality,* 165, 166.

3. Smith, *Community Renewal Society,* 71–72; "Yes—This is PCH," 1942 file, PCHPC; Good Shepherd Congregational Church, box 45, file 18, NIP, IWP. Du Bois's subject was "The Contribution of the Negro to American Civilization," in which he traced the communist idea of communal ownership back to African village life; *Defender,* March 22, 1930, 6.

4. GSCC, box 1, 1941 file, PCHP; Minutes of Board of Directors, box 1, 1937–1943 file, PCHP, 57, 85.

5. GSCC, box 1, 1941 file, PCHP; GSCC Programs, October 18, 1938, box 1, 1937–1943 file, PCHP, 1–2.

6. Preliminary—The Church of the Good Shepherd, January 29, 1937, box 1, 1937–1943 file, PCHP, 4; GSCC Program Committee, November 4, 1938, box 1, 1937–1943 file, PCHP, 2; Paul Healy, "Former Nomad Heads Largest Negro Center," box 67, file 6, LWP; Cayton, *Long Old Road,* 184, 236; Hobbs, *The Cayton Legacy,* 109. Cayton's abiding concern with labor is evident in two copublications: Cayton and Mitchell, *Black Workers and the New Unions;* and Drake and Cayton, *Black Metropolis,* 1993.

7. Moses, *The Negro Delinquent in Chicago,* 47; Moses, "Delinquency in the Negro Community," 304–7; Knupfer, *Reform and Resistance,* 28–29.

8. U.S. Work Projects Administration, Illinois, *Chicago Negro Community.* Warner, for example, would expand his typologies of black "personalities" to include thirty-two major ones, based on social class, gender, age, employment, nativity, and skin color. Warner, Junker, and Adams, *Color and Human Nature,* 4–7, 26.

9. Elizabeth Johns and Mary Elaine Ogden, under the direction of Horace R. Cayton, "Prospectus for the Study of the Migration and Adjustment of Negroes to Cities," March 31, 1939, box 54, file 17, LWP. For readings about the race-cycle theory, see Park, *The Collected Papers of Robert Ezra Park.*

10. Cayton, *Long Old Road,* 237; Mary Elaine Ogden and Horace Cayton, "Research on the Urban Negro," box 54, file 17, LWP; Hutton, "The Negro Worker and the Labor Unions in Chicago," 2; Chicago Housing Authority, *Information in Regard to the Proposed South Park Gardens,* 13.

11. In 1934, the Chicago Tuberculosis Institute finally established the Negro Health Education program. But one institute could not adequately care for all those in need. Chicago—Health, box 36, file 1, NIP, IWP; E. Jennings, "Report of Work Done on Negro Health Survey", box 36, file 13, NIP, IWP. Minutes of Board of Directors, box 1, 1937–1943 file, PCHP, 138, 186. The WPA had also started a sewing project that created jobs for 5,000 women, 90 percent of whom were black. The women sewed clothes for 200,000 persons in Chicago. *Defender,* June 8, 1940, 1.

12. Memorandum, Re: Chicago Orphan Asylum, April 6, 1940, box 1, 1937–1943 file, PCHP; Minutes, Management Committee, GSCC, February 5, 1941, box 1, 1941 file, PCHP; On Facilities—Parkway Community House, box 1, 1937–1941 file, PCHP; Horace Cayton, The Problem, Program, and Facilities of the GSCC, 1940, box 1, 1937–1941 file, PCHP. Given the age of the building and lack of repairs, accidents

did occur. An iron balustrade fell and cut a boy's head. Another time a window fell from the third story but fortunately no one was hurt. A section of a back wall had been pushed over by a group of young men, which could have hurt others. Letter from Cayton to the Executive Board Members, October 1, 1941 file, box 1, PCHP. A stone wall on the property had been vandalized so a Winnetka women's organization donated $100 for repair. Minutes of Management Committee, GSCC, May 29, box 1, 1941 file, PCHP. The 1940 budget indicated that actually only one-ninth of the funds came from rentals. The center tried various strategies for raising monies from the community, including a Marian Anderson concert. Apparently, this was not as successful as they had hoped; it brought in less than $900, although it was attended by at least 5,000 people. Minutes of Board of Directors, box 1, 1937–1943 file, PCHP, 177, 184.

13. Minutes of Board of Directors, box 1, 1937–1943 file, PCHP, 97; Herskovits, *The Myth of the Negro Past,* xv; see also correspondence among Cayton, Louis Wirth, and Myrdal in box 2, file 5, LWP; Myrdal, *An American Dilemma.* For an insightful analysis of who conducted the research and how they proceeded for the *American Dilemma,* Southern, *Gunnar Myrdal and Black-White Relations.*

14. Minutes of Meeting of Personnel Committee of GSCC, November 9, 1939, box 1, 1937–1943 file, PCHP.

15. Letter from Cayton to Vogler, October 13, 1939, box 1, 1937–1943 file, PCHP. Later in 1943, Cayton would recommend raising funds for a gymnasium that would be built after the war. He also hoped that a committee from the board would call on Marshall Field and ask for a "substantial" donation. Minutes of the Board of Directors Meeting, September 23, 1943, box 1, 1937–1943 file, PCHP.

16. Minutes of the Board of Directors, box 1, 1937–1943 file, PCHP, 127; Cayton, *Long Old Road,* 246. See also "Cayton Named Director of Good Shepherd Director," *Defender,* December 30, 1939, 7; "The Good Shepherd Congregational Church in Chicago," 2.

17. Minutes of the Board of Directors, 135, box 1, 1937–1943 file, PCHP; Memo Re. Trip to the East, September 8, 1940, box 1, 1937–1943 file, PCHP; Minutes, Executive Committee Meeting, GSCC, February 6, 1942, box 1, 1942–1943 file, PCHP; Memorandum, February 22, 1940, box 1, 1937–1943 file, PCHP.

18. Knupfer, *Toward a Tenderer Humanity and a Nobler Womanhood,* 56–58. Myles Horton, founder of the Highlander Folk School, had attended the University of Chicago's Sociology School in the early 1930s. Although there is no record of Cayton visiting the Highlander, he had taught at nearby Fisk University during the 1930s. See Horton, *The Highlander Folk School;* Glen, *Highlander: No Ordinary School 1932–1962.*

19. "Social Group Work," 80, 82.

20. Child Guidance Clinic and Allied Services at Abraham Lincoln Center, August 1942, box 242, file 1, WCMC. Sitting in a circle with Dreikurs, parents discussed parenting problems and offered advice to one another. Following discussion, Dreikurs

interviewed the children, while the parents observed, then listened to his interpretation of the children's behavior. Treatment included the placement of children in group activities, under the supervision of a group worker. The ALC's summer camp staff, too, kept family case records from the students about students and their families, health records, housing reports, correspondence from other social agencies, drawings and other material made by the children, and psychiatric reports. Group workers worked with some of the children as well. The camp director made over 300 summary reports on the adjustment of children referred by other social agencies to the camp from 1936 to 1941. Most were used later for interpretation by group workers. Records of the Center and Camp, 1933 through 1941, box 242, file 1, WCMC.

21. "Social Group Work," 82; Baker, "Social Work, Trade Unionism and the Negro," 20, 29; Wilson, *Group Work and Case Work,* 4; Kilpatrick, *Group Education for a Democracy,* 22; Boyd, *Social Group Work,* 6; Lindeman, "Group Work and Democracy—A Philosophical Note," 50.

22. Minutes of the Management Committee, January 29, 1940, box 1, 1937–1943 file, PCHP; Chicago Recreation Commission and Northwestern University, *Private Recreation;* Minutes of Meeting of the Personnel Committee, November 4, 1940, box 1, 1937–1943 file, PCHP; Neva L. Boyd, 1876–1964, Northwestern University Information Sheet, December 11, 1939, NBP; Adamczyk, "Neva L. Boyd (1876–1963)," 581–82; Good Shepherd Congregational Church, box 45, file 18, PCHP; Minutes of Board of Directors, box 1, 1937–1943 file, PCHP, 15. Neva Boyd held an eight-week training course in group work techniques at Parkway. Persons from YMCA, Abraham Lincoln Center, Friendship House, South Side Settlement House, and the Chicago Urban League were invited; *Defender,* February 18, 1945, 1. Cayton stressed that it was important to have "well-trained" black workers, although he would accept white workers, if they were temporary and well trained. Boyd agreed to work there but refused to accept a stipend because she had wanted full-time work. She recommended Elaine Switzer, who had been one of her students. Minutes, Executive Committee Meeting, GSCC, February 6, 1942, box 1, 1942–1943 file, PCHP.

23. See yearly budgets in box 1, 1937–1943 file, PCHP. The Chicago Community Trust supported the GSCC and PCH through 1959. See 1933–1959, CCTAR.

24. Minutes of Management Committee, GSCC, May 29, 1941, box 1, file 1941, PCHP. Ironically, the WPA project was organized by the WPA union, which was purportedly under communist control, although very few "real" communists participated in the study. Yet Kingsley did not complain about them; Cayton, *Long Hard Road,* 238. Communism did not have a strong hold in Chicago in the black community because of its white membership. When the National Negro Congress organized to protest inequitable conditions, communists, many of whom were white, infiltrated the organization. Randolph, as its first president, eventually quit the congress because it was not "truly a Negro congress." Of 1,200 delegates, over 300 were white. Gosnell, *Negro Politicians,* 352; Garfinkel, *When Negroes March,* 131. See also Record, *The Negro and the Communist Party.*

25. Minutes of Management Committee, GSCC, June 9, 1941, box 1, 1941 file, PCHP.

26. Minutes of Board of Directors, 216–17, box 1, 1937–1943 file, PCHP.

27. Ibid., 219. Under the leadership of Dorothy Rogers, the community activities department served over 95,000 people in 1944, 20 percent more than the preceding year. Annual Report of Activities, 1944–1945 file, PCHP; GSCC—News #41 file, PCHP; Minutes of the Board of the Directors, September 23, 1943, box 1, 1937–1943 file, PCHP, 265.

28. GSCC, Statement of Income and Expenses, Ending June 30, 1941, box 1, 1941 file, PCHP; Minutes, Executive Committee Meeting, GSCC, February 6, 1942, box 1, 1942–1943 file, PCHP; Minutes of Board of Directors, box 1, 1937–1943 file, PCHP, 215.

29. 1942 Budget Report, GSCC, box 1, 1942–1943 file, PCHP.

30. Minutes of Meeting of Program Advisory Committee of GSCC, February 16, 1942, box 1, 1942–1943 file, PCHP; Minutes, Executive Committee Meeting, GSCC, February 6, 1942, box 1, 1942–1943 file, PCHP; Parkway Minutes, box 1, 1937–1943 file, PCHP; Memorandum, October 6, 1943, Minutes of Board of Directors, box 1, 1937–1943 file, PCHP, 278–281. Prior to this funding, Parkway was one of forty nurseries in Chicago operated through the WPA. In 1943, funding ended and the Chicago public schools set up nurseries. In order to qualify for Lanham Fund monies, parents had to be employed in either war or essential civilian industries. But only one-fourth of the children's parents were employed in war and essential civilian industries. Duis and La France, *We've Got a Job to Do,* 11.

31. Memo Re Supplementary Agencies for Staffing Center for Cayton, box 1, 1937–1943 file, PCHP; 1948 Brochure, "They Need Parkway Community House," 1949–1957, file, PCHC; "Yes—This is PCH," 1942 file, PCHPC; News in the Making at PCH, 1944 file, n.p., PCHPC; Minutes of Management Committee, January 19, 1942, box 1, 1942 file, PCHP; Minutes of Program Staff Committee of the Teen Age Dance Project, South Parkway YWCA, April 5, 1946, box 2, file 5, IMGP; Teen Age Dance Project, box 2, file 10, IMGP; Letter from Mrs. John Hancock to Mrs. M. Davis, October 16, 1945, box 2, file 4, IMGP. Cayton requested further police protection because "hoodlums" had broken into Parkway during a dance. Sometimes these intruders were armed and so posed a danger to the staff and children. Through the 1950s, the staff would be proud of the "teen age canteen," a wholesome alternative for "unsupervised dance halls, ill-lighted taverns, and questionable dance halls." *Defender,* April 4, 1953, 9.

32. GSCC Program Committee, November 4, 1938, box 1, 1937–1943 file, PCHP.

33. Minutes of the General Committee on Noncommercial Recreation for Teen Age Youth Sponsored by the YWCA, the YMCA, and PCH, July 6, 1945, box 2, file 4, IMGP; Report of Irene M. Gaines, Committee Director of the Non-Commercial Recreation for Teen Age Youth, Sponsored by the YWCA, the YWCA, and PCH, June 4, 1945, box 2, file 4, IMGP; Minutes of Executive Committee of the Teen Age Dance Project Sponsored by the YWCA, YMCA, and PCH, June 4, 1946, box 2, file 5, IMGP.

34. "Yes—This is PCH," 1942 file, PCHPC.

35. Ibid.; Guzman, Jones, and Hall, *1952 Negro Year Book*, 120. Parkway's accommodations had a community service requirement, which differed from other working homes for young black women, such as the Phyllis Wheatley Home or the Elam Home.

36. Minutes of Board of Directors, box 1, 1937–1943 file, PCHP, 230, 239. The Chicago chapter of the National Council of Negro Women (NCNW) and the Chicago Council Against Racial and Religious Discrimination (CCARRD) had sent letters to the War Department in support of their policy. See *Defender*, July 7, 1945, 6. One room was designated as the "Irma Cayton Barracks," in honor of Cayton's wife who had enlisted. See *Bee*, February 21, 1943, 9. For information on black WACs, see Moore, *To Serve My Country, To Serve My Race*.

37. *Defender*, July 7, 1945, 6.

38. The People's Forum Brochure, box 2, file 5, LWP.

39. Ibid.; September 1945 CCNO Newsletter, box 2, file 4, IMGP; Du Bois, "Pan-African and New Racial Philosophy," 247.

40. Forum series, box 2, file 5, LWP; *Bee*, February 11, 1945, p. 11; *Bee*, January 7, 1945, 9.

41. Cayton, "The Morale of the Negro and National Defense," August, 15, 1941, box 54, file 17, LWP; Cayton, "The Negro's Challenge," 10; Cayton, "Fighting for White Folks?" 267–70. See also Logan, "The Negro Wants First-Class Citizenship," 1–30. Following the war, many of these ideas would still be raised. See Logan, *The Negro and the Post-War World Primer*.

42. According to one Department of Labor report, there was an increase of 350,000 more black women in the labor force nationally in 1947 than existed several years earlier. Black women's work in factories increased by almost 12 percent. Guzman, Foster, and Hughes, *Negro Year Book*, 138; Weaver, "Negro Labor Since 1929," 34; Fehn, "African-American Women and the Struggle for Equality in the Meatpacking Industry, 1940–1960," 53; Anderson, "Last Hired, First Fired: Black Women Workers during World War II," 83; Guzman, Jones, and Hall, *1952 Negro Year Book. A Review of Events Affecting Negro Life*, 116–20; Kahn, "Chicago Hits the Job Jackpot," 6. For further information on women's World War II employment, see Hartmann, *The Home Front and Beyond: American Women in the 1940s*. For more information on black women and wartime employment, see Rosenberg, "Womanpower and the War," 35–36; Jeffries, "Step Up, Lady—Want a War Job?" 39–40; Yeyarwood, "Women Volunteers Unite To Serve," 60–62, 88; Harris, "A Challenge to Negro Women," 72, 95; "Women at War," 4–5; Honey, *Bitter Fruit: African American Women in World War II;* Foner and Lewis, *The Black Worker from the Founding of the CIO to the AFL-CIO Merger, 1936–1955*, 239–50. Dorothy Porter stressed that black women had always served in wars, including the Revolutionary and Civil wars; "Negro Women in Our Wars," 195–96, 215.

43. Guzman, Jones, and Hall, *1952 Negro Year Book*, 120. See also Kahn, "Chicago Hits the Job Jackpot," 4–6.

44. *Bee,* April 29, 1945, 15; *Bee,* January 2, 1944, 7; "After the War WHAT?" *Bee,* January 2, 1944, 7. For biographical information on Marjorie Joyner, see Smith, *Notable Black American Women,* 367–69; and "Profiles of a Legend: A Historical Tribute to Marjorie Stewart Joyner," *Chicago Tribune,* February 4, 1987, sec. 5, 1–2; *Bee,* March 17, 1946, 9; data, *1950 U.S. Census.*

45. *Bee,* May 20, 1945, 10; "Skyloft,"—1942 file, PCHPC.

46. "Skyloft," 1942 file, PCHPC.

47. Ibid.

48. *Bee,* May 5, 1946, 2; *Bee,* January 1, 1945, 12; box 8, file 14, IBWP. The woodshop center designed and made the stage settings, as well as assisted the art department with artwork and posters for Skyloft Players.

49. *Bee,* May 20, 1945, 10.

50. Diary entry, box 1, IMGP; Management Committee Minutes, February 17, 1942, box 1, 1942–1943 file, PCHP; S. E. Ledger, box 2, 1944–1957 file, PCHP; *Bee,* May 19, 1946, 14. For example, Esther Wood's *If Left is Right* was directed by fellow troupe member, Lester Chung. Some of the plays were performed for the benefit of the nursery or for other facilities; S. E. Ledger, box 2, 1944–1957 file, PCHP.

51. Craig, *Black Drama of the Federal Theatre Era;* Mathews, *The Federal Theatre, 1935–1939;* Flanagan, *Arena.*

52. *Bee,* January 1, 1945, 12. Parkway's children's theatre also performed a Chinese play; *Bee,* April 14, 1946, 15.

53. *Bee,* June 30, 1946, 10; *Bee,* May 5, 1946, 15; March 3, 1946, 15; *Bee,* April 28, 1946, 10; Minutes of Management Committee, May 4, 1942, box 1, 1942–1943 file, PCHP. In 1945, there were fifty-two nursery school centers in Chicago, and eight on the southside that would soon close. One-third of the nursery enrollment was on the southside. *Defender,* September 15, 1945, 3.

54. These companies and philanthropies were strong supporters during the war years. See 1942 Budget Report, box 1, 1942–1943 file, PCHP; Statement Showing Financial Position, August 31, 1943, box 1, 1937–1943 file, PCHP.

55. Letter from Cal Axford to Marion Craine, October 8, 1954, box 44, file 11, PCHP.

56. Letter from Mrs. James Sloss to Linn Brandenberg, July 27, 1955, box 44, file 11, PCHP.

57. Cayton, *Long Old Road,* 309. Cayton recalled how once a minister of a suburban congregation asked him what his congregation could do for him personally. Cayton said he would love a little place in the suburbs where he could write on the weekends. The minister looked startled and replied: "And you realize that I couldn't ask my congregation to break the zoning laws. But they do want to do something for you. How about a little car to run around the city in?" Cayton, *Long Hard Road,* 389.

58. Ibid., 257; see also *Defender,* November 3, 1945, 14.

59. Cayton, *Long Old Road,* 322, 326.

60. Ibid., 380.

61. The ALC actually offered more programs than the PCH or the SSSH. For example, there was a Friday Morning Forum, a Sunday Evening Discussion Club, and parent-teacher groups. The Men's and Boy's Department sponsored sports, woodwork activities, boy scouts, lectures, tournaments, and parties. The Women's and Girls' Department organized a rhythm band, games, stories, a doll club, singing, swimming, a child care club, journalism, folk dancing, trips, a "better housewives'" club, and mothers' clubs. Although it was forced to relocate because of slum clearance, the ALC continued to thrive because of its large endowment. Additional Information to Members of Appeals Committee, April 16, 1959, box 242, file 1, WCMC.

62. Ada McKinley Community Home, Minutes of the Meeting of the Group Reviewing Committee, December 20, 1955, box 34, file 2, CFC; Report of Application for Membership, August 24, 1950, box 698, file 8, CFC; Ada McKinley Community Home, 1955 Annual Report, box 34, file 2, CFC.

63. Parkway relocated to 6301 South Rhodes. Charles Webb, affiliated with the Urban League of Marion, Indiana, became director after Cayton.

64. Minutes of the Group Work Reviewing Subcommittee, May 24, 1955, box 44, file 11, CFC; Ada McKinley Community House, Minutes of the Meeting of the Group Work Reviewing Committee, November 20, 1958, box 75, file 3, CFC.

Chapter 3: Community Sponsorship of Literature and the Arts

1. Hughes, "The Negro Artist and the Racial Mountain," 92.

2. Walker, *For My People*; see Wright, *Native Son*.

3. Hughes, *The Return of Simple*, xv, xvi; Nichols, *Arna Bontemps-Langston Hughes Letters*, 70. Simple is a actually a version of Gramsci's street intellectual. See also De Santis, *Langston Hughes and the Chicago Defender*.

4. Woolley, *American Voices of the Chicago Renaissance*, 122. Frazier claimed that Chicago was "more representative" than New York "of Black society and culture" because of the crossroads of southern life. Frazier cited in Meyerowitz, "The Negro in Art Week: Defining the 'New Negro' through Art Exhibition," 78.

5. Werner, *Playing the Changes*, 244–45.

6. Conroy, "A Reminiscence," 33; Wixson, *Worker-Writer in America*, 445, 446, 457; Ward, "Walker, Margaret," 753; Bontemps and Conroy, *Any Place But Here*; Wright, "Early Days in Chicago," 52–68; Alexander, "Richard Wright," 47–67; Fabre, *The Unfinished Quest of Richard Wright*; Bontemps, "Famous WPA Authors," 45–46.

7. Bone, "Richard Wright and the Chicago Renaissance," 446–68. I take issue with Bone's contention that the Chicago Black Renaissance was influenced by the sociological ideas of Robert Park. Instead, I contend that the Chicago School had its own cadre of black sociologists who reshaped and enlarged the School's theories to include concepts of caste and racism. See Knupfer, *Reform and Resistance*, chap. 1. For another perspective, see Cappetti, "Sociology of an Existence: Wright and the Chicago School," 255–71.

8. Nichols, *Arna Bontemps-Langston Hughes Letters*, 148, 165.

9. Walker, *For My People;* Wright, *Native Son;* Drake and Cayton, *Black Metropolis.*

10. Penkower, *The Federal Writers' Project*, 80, 121, 142. In the Illinois guidebook, Chicago was overly emphasized, as were institutions such as the University of Chicago. In fact, the president of the university, Robert Hutchins, was interested in publishing the guide.

11. "Expect Next Literary Renaissance to Come from Chicago Group," General File, BA; Engelhardt, "Fenton, Johnson," 402; Bolden, *Urban Rage in Bronzeville*, 5; Brooks, *A Street in Bronzeville*. As early as 1935, there was concern that the ALC was involved with communism. However, as one staff member countered, the ALC had always been liberal and inclusive, and so supported organizations for workers and the unemployed, just as other settlements did. He knew of no activities "bent upon the destruction of the capitalistic system." There were some interracial problems, although the nature of those problems were not disclosed. Letter from Lea D. Taylor to Frank Loomis, May 18, 1935, box 242, file 1, WCMC.

12. Woolley, *American Voices of the Chicago Renaissance*, 409; Roberts, "Thompson, Era Bell"; The Martha Washington Guild, Provident Hospital by Dorothy Jones, February 23, 1938, box 36, file 2, NIP, IWP; Edwards, "The Mulzac School of Seamanship," 73–75; Long, "Burroughs, Margaret Taylor Goss," 111. One of Bonner's stories, "Nothing New," described life on Chicago's southside. See Dillon, "Bonner, Marita," 91. See also Harriott, "The Life of a Pulitzer Poet," 14–16, on Brooks and the Pulitzer Prize. Edwards (later Gitlin), who had worked at the ALC, wrote several vignettes in the style of reportage and case record reports, which depicted poor housing and working conditions in Chicago. Government officials later questioned her about her possible affiliation with the Communist Party, as well as possible communist meetings at the ALC. See box 1, files 1 and 2, TEP. On Hansberry, see Nemiroff, *To Be Young, Gifted and Black;* Cheney, *Lorraine Hansberry*. Lastly, one should not forget the role that Wendell Phillips High School played during the 1920s in cultivating the creative talents of so many artists and activists of the Chicago Black Renaissance. I am thankful to Michael Flug for showing me the school's yearbooks, located in boxes 1 and 2, ALP.

13. Radio Log, Destination Freedom, box 1, RDP; Savage, *Broadcasting Freedom*. Actors for "Destination Freedom" included Studs Terkel, Harris Gaines, Oscar Brown Jr., and Ollye Coffin. Destination Freedom, Memorabilia, RDP.

14. Segregation-Incorporated, box 3, RDP.

15. Reverend Archibald Carey, box 2, RDP.

16. Housing, Chicago, box 2, RDP.

17. W. E. B. Du Bois, "Krigwa Players Little Negro Theatre," 134; Edmonds, "The Negro Little Theatre Movement," 85; Lawson, "The Negro in America Drama," 173.

18. Edmonds, "The Negro Little Theatre Movement," 83; Chapelle, "Drama—Dance—Cinema," box 47, file 6, NIP, IWP.

19. Goss, "Negro Theatre Movement Thrives on Southside," *Bee,* May 26, 1946, 15. Supported largely through the WPA, the Chicago Park District encouraged the growth of nearly fifty little theaters, with their own theater organizations and staff. Chicago Recreation Commission and Northwestern University, *Private Recreation,* 146.

20. "Opinion of W. E. B. Du Bois: In Black," 263–64.

21. "The Negro Theatre," 16–17.

22. Grant, "The Negro in Dramatic Art," 28; Curtis, *The First Black Actors on the Great White Way,* 120, 127, 134; Edmonds, "The Negro Little Theatre Movement," 94.

23. Colored Culture in Chicago, box 47, files 6 and 7, NIP, IWP. It was not unusual for black theater groups to adapt works by Eugene O'Neill, George Bernard Shaw, and Oscar Wilde; see Mathews, *The Federal Theatre,* 143.

24. Wixson, *Worker-Writer in America,* 452; Aschenbrenner, "Katherine Dunham: Anthropologist, Artist, Humanist," 140.

25. Colored Culture in Chicago, box 47, file 7, NIP, IWP. See Alain Locke's *The New Negro.*

26. Program brochure, "Tropics: Impressions and Realities," box 7, file 12, MHP.

27. Achenbrenner, "Katherine Dunham," 141; Letter from Dunham to Herskovits, June 18, 1933, box 7, file 12, MHP; Announcement, box 1, file 3, KDP; Biographical Sheet, KDP. Chavers-Wright had enrolled in a dancing school started by Dunham. She had wanted to become a professional dancer with Dunham's dance troupe but her parents would not let her show her legs. But she did start her own dance school, "Madrue's School of Dancing." One of her students was Lorraine Hansberry. See Chavers-Wright, *The Guarantee,* 374, 380, 382.

28. Letter from Dunham to Herskovits, March 9, 1932, box 7, file 12, MHP; Letter from Herskovits to Dunham, March 23, 1932, box 7, file 12, MHP. See Dunham, *Journey to Accompong.*

29. Letter from Dunham to Herskovits, June 18, 1933, box 7, file 12, MHP; Aschenbrenner, "Katherine Dunham," 145; box 7, file 12, MHP; Letter from Herskovits to Dr. Price-Mars, May 30, 1935, box 32, file 41, MHP; Letter from Dunham to Herskovits, September 23, 1936, box 32, file 41, MHP; Letter from William Grant Still to Dunham, June 20, 1936, box 1, file 4, KDP.

30. Letter from Robert Redfield to Herskovits, January 4, 1936, box 7, file 12, MHP; Letter from Herskovits to Dunham, January 4, 1937, box 32, file 41, MHP; Guzman, Foster, and Hughes, *Negro Year Book,* 444.

31. Letter from Dunham to Herskovits, January 6, 1937, box 7, file 12, MHP. Regarding Northwestern University, the dean upheld housing segregation of black students through the 1940s. In 1947, nearly half of the forty-one black undergraduates lived in their own homes, the YWCA, or the YMCA. See *Defender,* March 8, 1947, 12.

32. Colored Culture in Chicago, box 47, file 7, NIP, IWP; Chicago and Northern District Association of Colored Women's Clubs, 1937–1938 Annual Report, 47–48, box

11, file 11, IMGP. At least fifty women, many from the women's clubs, assisted in these children's productions. Actors Guild, box 7, file 9, NIP, IWP. The Princess Theatre, too, had its own children's theatre. Lucille La Verne Officer, an actress trained at the University of Chicago, assisted Graham with this endeavor. Officer had previously organized a children's troupe, the Peter-Pan Players, who performed regularly in the grammar schools, churches, and at PTA meetings. Chapelle, "Drama—Dance—Cinema," box 47, file 7, NIP, IWP. Several sororities also assisted in children's theater productions. The Phi Delta Kappa Mu chapter wrote and produced a children's play composed of short skits about slavery, emancipation, and World War II. The Phi Delta Kappa sorority sponsored *Popo and Fifina*, a play about Haitian children written by Arna Bontemps and Langston Hughes. Brunetta Mouzon, an actress for many of Hughes's plays, collaborated with the authors on this presentation. The Lambda Chapter of the Delta Sigma Theta Sorority sponsored "Jabberwack," an annual variety show at DuSable High School, from which local talent was later recruited. Entries included musical comedies, boogie-woogie piano, recitations, and solo performances. The judges were usually local, and they included Horace Cayton, Olive Diggs, and Willa Brown. See *Bee,* February 4, 1945, 5; *Bee,* May 2, 1943, 9; *Bee,* February 21, 1943, 13.

33. Nichols, *Arna Bontemps-Langston Hughes Letters,* 133.

34. Du Bois, *His Day Is Marching On,* 38; Guzman, Foster, and Hughes, *Negro Year Book,* 427; Hamalian and Hatch, *The Roots of African American Drama,* 364. For plays of Graham, see Hamalian and Hatch, *The Roots of African American Drama;* and Perkins, *Black Female Playwrights.*

35. Letter from Graham to Herskovits, November 6, 1936, box 8, file 9, MHP; Letter from Herskovits to George Kondolff, November 6, 1936, box 8, file 9, MHP.

36. Letter from Graham to Herskovits, April 12, 1937; Letter from Graham to Herskovits, December 24, 1936; Letter from Herskovits to Graham, February 24, 1937; Letter from Graham to Herskovits, December 24, 1936, box 8, file 9, MHP.

37. Letter from Graham to Herskovits, December 24, 1936, box 8, file 9, MHP; Letter from Herskovits to Graham, January 4, 1937, box 8, file 9, MHP; Letter from Herskovits to Graham, February 24, 1937, box 8, file 9, MHP.

38. Avery, ed., *A Paul Green Reader* (Chapel Hill: University of North Carolina Press, 1998), 80.

39. Letter from Graham to Herskovits, January 18, 1937, box 8, file 9, MHP.

40. Letter from Graham to Herskovits, January 16, 1937; Letter from Graham to Herskovits, January 16, 1937, box 8, file 9, MHP; Letter from Graham to Herskovits, January 18, 1937, box 8, file 9, MHP.

41. Kenny, *Paul Green,* 69–72.

42. Craig, *Black Drama of the Federal Theatre Era,* 113, 135–36.

43. Horne, *Race Woman,* 77.

44. Fraden, *Blueprints for a Black Federal Theatre,* 125; Fraden, "The Cloudy History of Big White Fog: The Federal Theatre Project, 1938," 5–28.

45. See Fraden, *Blueprints for a Black Federal Theatre;* Craig, *Black Drama of the Federal Theatre Era,* 61.

46. Horne, *Race Woman,* 74.

47. Letter from Herskovits to Graham, n.d., box 8, file 9, MHP; Workers of the Writers' Program of the WPA in the State of Illinois, *Cavalcade of the American Negro,* 53; Letter from Graham to Herskovits, n.d., box 8, file 9, MHP; Chorpenning, "Dramatics and Personality Growth," 143; Hamalian and Hatch, *The Roots of African American Drama,* 365.

48. Horne, *Race Woman,* 76.

49. Letter from Dunham to Arthur Mitchell, July 8, 1938, KDP.

50. Workers of the Writers' Program of the WPA in the State of Illinois, *Cavalcade of the American Negro,* 53.

51. Horne, *Race Woman,* 81. At Yale's drama school, Graham thrived. She wrote a number of plays, including *Dust to Earth,* a three-act tragedy about black coal miners. Yale's theater troupe performed at least three of her plays: *It's Morning, Elija's Raven,* and *Track Thirteen,* the last a radio play published in *Yale Radio Plays* (1940). She also wrote music for and danced in the Yale drama school production of *The Garden of Time* by a black writer, Owen Dodson. In 1940, she moved back to her hometown of Indianapolis, where she directed a YMCA troupe for a time. Within several years, though, she left for New York City, where she worked as an NAACP field secretary. In this position, she drew on her Chicago theater experiences: "As supervisor of the Negro Unit of the Chicago Federal Theatre, I had guided that group of discouraged recipients of 'relief' from despair and disintegration by drawing out their inner resources, restoring their confidence and welding them together into the first 'human orchestra' heard in Chicago." Hamalian and Hatch, *The Roots of African American Drama,* 365–66; Du Bois, *His Day Is Marching On,* 52.

52. Letter from Alfred Edgar Smith to Dunham, April 28, 1938, box 1, file 6, KDP; Letter from Hallie Flanagan, Director of Federal Theatre Project, to Edwin Embree, July 20, 1938, box 1, file 7, KDP; Letter from Dunham to Bethune, July 3, 1938, box 85, file 3, KDP.

53. Spear, *Black Chicago,* 72–73.

54. "Book Value," *Chicago Tribune,* April 30, 1991, sec. 5, 1–2; Flug, "Vivian Gordon Harsh," 542–43. Prior to Harsh's library work, the only black to have been affiliated with the Chicago public library system was Fannie Barrier Williams, a board member from 1924 to 1926; *Bee,* March 12, 1944, 2.

55. Annual Report—1935, box 23, GCH Archives 32/01 MSS; Annual Report—1932, box 23, GCH Archives 32/01 MSS; Annual Report—1939, box 23, GCH Archives 32/01 MSS.

56. *Bee,* February 6, 1944, 12.

57. *Bee,* February 18, 1945, 9.

58. *Bee,* March 11, 1945, 15.

59. *Bee,* June 10, 1945, 15.

60. *Bee,* February 6, 1944, 11.

61. Bolden, *Urban Rage in Bronzeville,* 3. I am grateful, again, to Michael Flug for showing me the Notes on Social Institutions, Bronzeville, from the Vivian Harsh Collection Conference.

62. Nichols, *Arna Bontemps-Langston Hughes Letters,* 253.

63. *Bee,* January 7, 1945, 16–17; Shaw, "Charlemae Hill Rollins," 949–53. The late Chicago Mayor Harold Washington's tribute to Rollins and Harsh indicated the librarians' powerful influence during his youth; see Travis, *"Harold," The People's Mayor,* 21.

64. "About Books on the Negro," *Bee,* January 7, 1945, 16–17.

65. Shaw, "Charlemae Hill Rollins," 949–53. A number of Chicago black writers wrote for children. Most notable were Arna Bontemps, Langston Hughes, Charlemae Rollins, Shirley Graham Du Bois, and Margaret Goss Burroughs. Hughes's children's plays were performed in Washington Park during the summer; children sometimes performed Bontemps's *We Have Tomorrow* during Negro History Week. There was also Ellen Tarry, children's writer and codirector at Chicago's Friendship House, where she organized a children's story hour. She, too, noted the distinctions between Bronzeville and Harlem, especially "the south side of Chicago, with its strong racial pride bordering on nationalism." Tarry, *The Third Door,* 202.

66. Annual Report—1933, box 23, GCH Archives 32/01 MSS.

67. The Oakland branch also displayed artwork by black artist Laura Wheeler Waring and white artist Betsy Graves Reyneau. (The latter had done portraits of prominent blacks, including Alain Locke.) *Bee,* February 20, 1944, 1; *Bee,* February 17, 1946, 4; Annual Report—1940, box 23, GCH Archives 32/01 MSS.

68. Annual Report—1942, box 23, GCH Library Archives 32/01 MSS.

69. *Bee,* February 6, 1944, 11; *Bee,* March 28, 1943, 9; *Bee,* February 20, 1944, 4.

70. Annual Report—1944, box 23, GCH Archives 32/01 MSS; "Interest in Race History Increases," *Defender,* March 2, 1940, 4. Historian Julie Des Jardins has discussed how black women were historians in their own right, upholding this responsibility through library work, as well as through their teaching and club meetings. See Des Jardins, *Women and the Historical Enterprise,* 7.

71. Workers of the Writers' Program of the WPA in the State of Illinois, *Cavalcade of the American Negro; Bee,* February 10, 1946, 11.

72. Annual Report—1951, box 23, GCH Archives 32/01 MSS; Annual Report—1954, box 23, GCH Archives 32/01 MSS; Annual Report—1955, box 23, GCH Archives 32/01 MSS.

73. Although its national circulation reached 50,000 subscribers, the *Bee* closed its office as of 1947.

74. Wesley, "The Negro Has Always Wanted the Four Freedoms," in *What The Negro Wants,* 110. Perhaps the best-known set of photographs about black life during the 1930s are those from the Farm Security Administration that accompany Wright's *Twelve Million Black Voices.*

75. See *Bee* editions from 1943 to 1947.

76. Annual Report—1938, box 23, GCH Archives 32/01 MSS; *Bee*, January 28, 1945, 1–2; *Bee*, January 14, 1945, 1.

77. *Negro Story Magazine*, 1, 3; Mullen, "Popular Fronts: *Negro Story Magazine* and the African American Literary Response to World War II," 5–15.

78. "Letter to Our Readers," *Negro Story*, 1.

79. Ibid.

80. Ibid.

81. "Letter to Our Readers," *Negro Story*, n.p. Copies of the children's magazine are in the ABP.

82. Burroughs, "Saga of Chicago's South Side Community Art Center (1938–1943)," 2, WMP; Graff, "The SSCAC Offers a Rich Commentary on Civic Dedication," n.p., WMP.

83. Mavigliano and Lawson, *The Federal Art Project in Illinois, 1935–1943*, Plate 27; *Bee*, March 21, 1943, 4; Burroughs, "Saga of Chicago's South Side Community Art Center (1938–1943)," 2, 5; Graff, "The SSCAC Offers a Rich Commentary on Civic Dedication," n.p., WMP.

84. Graff, "The SSCAC Offers A Rich Commentary on Civic Dedication," n.p., WMP.

85. Burroughs, "Saga of Chicago's South Side Community Art Center (1938–1943)," 2, WMP. For further information on black art and art centers during the 1930s and 1940s, see O'Connor, *Art for the Millions;* and Porter, *Modern Negro Art.*

86. Burroughs, "Saga of Chicago's South Side Community Art Center (1938–1943)," 2, WMP.

87. Ibid., 10.

88. McKinzie, *The New Deal for Artists*, 141–42; SSCAC Report, January 30, 1946, box 403, file 6, WCMC.

89. McKinzie, *The New Deal for Artists*, 141–42.

90. Nipson, "The South Side Community Art Center: A 'Soul' Survivor in the History of American Art," in SSCAC Fiftieth Anniversary Booklet, 4, WMP; Burroughs, "Saga of Chicago's South Side Community Art Center (1938–1943), 3–5, 13, WMP; Mattock, "The Spectacular Artists and Models Balls of 50 Years Ago," in SSCAC Fiftieth Anniversary Booklet, n.p., WMP; *Bee*, April 4, 1943, 5; *Bee*, April 29, 1945, 1; *Defender*, November 4, 1939, 16.

91. *Bee*, April 2, 1944, 11; *Bee*, May 21, 1944, 3.

92. *Bee*, March 25, 1945, 20; *Bee*, April 2, 1944, 11.

93. *Bee*, May 21, 1944, 3; *Bee*, May 13, 1945, 9; *Bee*, June 9, 1946, 9; Burroughs, "Saga of Chicago's South Side Community Art Center (1938–1943)," 12, WMB; Reed, "Letter," December 30, 1940, in SSCAC Fiftieth Anniversary Booklet, WMB; "Excerpts from Artists," in SSCAC Fiftieth Anniversary Booklet, n.p., WMB. At the SSCAC, Marion Perkins taught sculpture; Charles White and Gordon Parks worked in the darkroom.

94. *Bee*, April 29, 1945, 11; Burroughs, "Saga of Chicago's South Side Community

Art Center (1938–1943)," 12, WMB. Poetry classes at SSCAC were first taught by Inez Cunningham, a reader for *Poetry Magazine*. See Brooks, *Front Line Report From Part One*, 174.

95. *Bee*, May 28, 1944, 9; *Bee*, April 22, 1944, 9; Burroughs, "Saga of Chicago's South Side Community Art Center (1938–1943)," 1, WMP.

96. *Bee*, May 28, 1944, 9; *Bee*, March 25, 1945, 20.

97. Goss, "A Mother Looks at War," *Defender*, August 30, 1940, 13.

98. Reynolds and Wright, *Against the Odds*, 20.

99. Locke, "Excerpts from Artists," in SSCAC Fiftieth Anniversary Booklet, n.p., WMP.

100. Vanterpool, "Open-Textured Aesthetic Boundaries," 149.

101. "An Exhibition of African Art and Craft," booklet, box 30, file 28, MHP; *Bee*, February 13, 1944, 9. The tea committee for the exhibit included Ethel Hilliard, Jessica Anderson, Kathryn Dickerson, Dorothy Taylor, Mrs. Gonzales Motts, and Estelle Reid. "An Exhibition of African Art and Craft," booklet, box 30, file 28, MHP. The *Chicago Defender* had published news about African art, such as work by the African painter Kalifa Sidibe, who had exhibited in Paris, as early as 1930. See *Defender*, March 1, 1930, 13.

102. *Bee*, February 17, 1946, 1; *Bee*, January 27, 1946, 9; *Bee*, May 12, 1946, 9; *Bee*, February 24, 1946, 10; "Exhibit of Twenty-Seven Outstanding Americans," box 319, file 2, CBP.

103. Letter to Mrs. Fred Singleton from Lucy Carner, June 4, 1946, box 403, file 6, WCMC; *Bee*, June 2, 1946, 2, 9.

104. "Home Decorating Exhibit and Contest," box 403, file 6, WCMC; Letter from Carner to Mr. Jacob, August 10, 1945, box 403, file 6, WCMC. Director Gorleigh also wrote an article for the *Bee*, in which he reviewed a home decoration book; see Gorleigh, "Home Decorations Books Informative, Practical," *Bee*, April 21, 1946, 16.

105. McKinzie, *The New Deal for Artists*, 145; Nipson, "The South Side Community Art Center," 4, WMP; Burroughs, "Saga of Chicago's South Side Community Art Center (1938–1943)," 14, WMP. See Mavigliano and Lawson, *The Federal Art Project in Illinois*, 68. Another possible complication, according to Bernard Goss, was the Red Scare. Although most black artists he knew were procommunist, they were not members of the party; Mavigliano and Lawson, *The Federal Art Project in Illinois*, 69.

106. McKinzie, *The New Deal for Artists*, 129.

107. Penkower, "Federal Writers' Project," 270.

108. Ferrell, "Wright Discusses Function of the Writer in Interview," *Bee*, April 29, 1945, 15.

109. *Defender*, April 16, 1949, 22.

Chapter 4: Schools as Sites of Activism

1. James B. McCahey, "A 1944 Message about Chicago's Schools," box 21, file 2, LWP.

2. Ibid.; Berman and Baber, *Report of the Commission on Intercommunity Relationships of the Hyde Park-Kenwood Council of Churches and Synagogues,* 17.

3. Citizens Schools Committee, Data on Negro Schools in Chicago as of September 1943, box 5, file 2, CSCP.

4. "Council Wages War on Unfair Shift System," *Defender,* December 3, 1939, 1; Homel, *Down from Equality,* 82.

5. *Defender,* December 16, 1939, 1; Graham, Halpern, Herson, and Jerison, "An Investigation of the Chicago School Redistricting Program," 4, 19.

6. Citizens Schools Committee, "From Crowded Homes to Crowded Schools," 1, 4; Baron, "History of Chicago School Segregation to 1953," 17–18.

7. Mayor's Committee on Race Relations, 1945, "Districting and the Use of School Facilities" box 5, file 4, CSCP; Homel, *Down from Equality,* 144, 173.

8. *Defender,* December 18, 1937, 17.

9. "Vote for Irene McCoy Gaines," brochure, box 2, file 1, IMGP.

10. Letter from Dorothy Hayes to Gaines, April 1, 1949, box 1, file 9, IMGP; Letter from Ishmael Madison to John Cunningham, April 2, 1949, box 1, file 9, IMGP.

11. Pinderhughes, *Race and Ethnicity in Chicago Politics,* 217.

12. Homel, *Down from Equality,* 171.

13. McCahey, "A 1944 Message about Chicago's Schools," box 21, file 2, LWP.

14. Herrick, *The Chicago Schools,* 233–34, 236–37; Levit, "The Chicago Citizens Schools Committee," 18, 67.

15. Strassman, "The Activities of Parent-Teacher Associations in Elementary Schools in Chicago," 40; Homel, *Down from Equality,* 145. Black schools with PTAs included Coleman, Forestville, Burke Doolittle, Douglas, Fuller, Keith, Oakland, Phillips, and Raymond Elementary Schools. Du Sable High School also had a PTA. Alfreda Duster, Ida B. Wells's daughter, was the PTA president for Douglas School. McGrath, "Negro Leaders Protest McCahey School Views," box 1, file 3, IMCP; see also box 7, file 10, IBWP.

16. Homel, *Down from Equality,* 144–47.

17. Ibid., 166–69; Homel, "The Lilydale School Campaign of 1936," 232, 236, 237–38. By 1947 Lilydale's newly built school had double shifts. Gaines wrote to Hunt on behalf of the Lilydale and West Chesterfield Improvement Associations. Letter from Gaines to Hunt, November 15, 1947, box 2, file 6, IMGP.

18. Field, "Intercultural Education and Negro History during the Second World War," 75–85; January 13, 1942 Meeting, box 5, file 1, CSCP; Homel, *Down from Equality,* 120–21. During the 1950s, Dunbar School offered courses in nursing, commercial cooking, commercial art, dressmaking, beauty culture, tailoring, drafting, cabinetmaking, and sheet-metal work. But credits from the school could not be transferred to other high schools because Dunbar was considered a vocational center, not a high school. When students completed their beauty culture course, many could not get licenses because they could not pass the state examination. Gaines, a member of the Dunbar Trade School Citizens' Committee, along with Robert Taylor and Oscar

Brown, asked for more appropriations for the school. Dunnegan, "Vocational Education at Dunbar," 29–35; Homel, *Down from Equality,* 121; Minutes of the Dunbar Trade School Citizens' Committee, October 19, 1949, box 1, file 9, IMGP.

19. January 13, 1942 Meeting, box 5, file 1, CSCP.

20. McCahey, "A 1944 Message about Chicago's Schools," box 21, file 2, LWP.

21. School in Ward 3, June 12, 1946, box 5, file 5, CSCP.

22. City of Chicago, *Chicago Conference on Home Front Unity,* 23.

23. Homel, *Down from Equality,* 41; 1937 CULAR, 6.

24. Memorandum Re: School, Gaines to Oscar Brown, May 29, 1945, box 7, file 4, IMGP.

25. Committee on Education, Training and Research in Race Relations Records, box 13, file 8, LWP; Baron, "History of Chicago School Segregation to 1953," 19.

26. Herrick, "Negro Employees of the Chicago Board of Education," 9–10, 32, 86; Citizens Schools Committee, Significant Activities, 1933–1965," box 3, file 34, ANDP.

27. *Defender,* January 13, 1934, 4.

28. Memorandum Re: School, Gaines to Oscar Brown, May 29, 1945, box 7, file 4, IMGP; Berman and Baber, *Report of the Commission on Intercommunity Relationships.*

29. Winget, "Teacher Inter-School Mobility Aspirations Elementary Teachers, Chicago Public School System, 1947–48," 2–3, 51, 73–78, 166–68, 173.

30. Becker, "Role and Career Problems of the Chicago Public School Teachers," 54.

31. Davis, *Social Influences upon Learning;* see also Davis, "The Relation between Color Caste and Economic Stratification in Two Black Plantation Counties"; Hess cited in Becker, "Role and Career Problems of the Chicago Public School Teachers," 102.

32. "'Study Negro History' Says Stratton to Group," *Defender,* December 28, 1940, 19. By 1951, there were six DuSable History Clubs with 120 members. Annual Report—1951, box 23, GCL 32/01 MSS.

33. "Three Years of the Negro History Bulletin," 44.

34. Between 1934 and 1944, nearly two hundred articles were published about intercultural education in forty-two journals. Field, "Intercultural Education and Negro History during the Second World War," 76. Examples of intercultural publications include Davis-DuBois, *Adventures in Intercultural Education;* Davis-DuBois and Okorodudu, *All This and Something More;* Davis-DuBois, *Get Together Americans;* Powdermaker, *Probing Our Prejudices.*

35. Morgan, "Chicago School Curriculum Includes Negro Achievements," MM; Field, "Intercultural Education and Negro History during the Second World War," 79.

36. Morgan, "Chicago School Curriculum Includes Negro Achievements," MM. See also Bethune, "The Adoption of the History of the Negro to the Capacity of the Child," 9–13.

37. Morgan, "Chicago School Curriculum Includes Negro Achievements," MM.

38. Thorpe, *Negro Historians in the United States,* 106. For another example of black literature for students, see Cromwell, Turner, and Dykes, *Readings from Negro Authors, for Schools and Colleges.*

39. Morgan, "Chicago School Curriculum Includes Negro Achievements," MM; Field, "Intercultural Education and Negro History during the Second World War," 79–81, 83; "Chicago Schools Include Negro History," 51, 60. Although the Chicago schools adopted these social studies curricula for three years, that does not necessarily mean that all Chicago public school teachers were enthusiastic about teaching them. Unfortunately, no records exist of how Chicago public school teachers used the curricula. Morgan's later works built upon these curricula. See Stratton, *Negroes Who Helped Build America,* and Morgan, "A Bank Project," 83–84. Morgan was not the only teacher to revise textbooks. See Sayre-Lewis, "Caricature and Portrait in Children's Books," 41.

40. *Bee,* January 22, 1944, 2; *Bee,* February 10, 1946, 11; *Bee,* March 12, 1944, 12; *Bee,* March 3, 1946, 9.

41. Bullard, "Roberta Bell, A Monograph," BWMWP; *Bee,* January 6, 1946, 10. Chicago black authors featured in the *Chicago Schools Journal* included Arna Bontemps, Margaret Taylor Burroughs, and Charlemae Rollins. See Jacobs and Lulu, "Chicagoland Authors and Illustrators of Children's Literature," 1–45; Burroughs, "Holidays in Mexico," 159–63; Burroughs, "Survey Indicates Student Attitudes toward Art," 224–26.

42. *Bee,* February 20, 1944, 12; *Bee,* February 10, 1946, 6; *Bee,* January 27, 1946, 11.

43. Biographical Sketches on Tributes to Founder, box 1, HSA; Gladly Learn and Gladly Teach, box 1, Historical Sketches on Howalton School file, HSA; WPA Nursery News, box 1, file 10, RHAP.

44. Biographical Sketches on Tributes to Founder, box 1, HSA; Gladly Learn and Gladly Teach, box 1, Historical Sketches on Howalton School file, HSA.

45. Biographical Sketches on Tributes to Founder, box 1, HSA; Gladly Learn and Gladly Teach, box 1, Historical Sketches on Howalton School file, HSA.

46. Gladly Learn and Gladly Teach, box 1, Historical Sketches on Howalton School file, HSA; Meeting Notes from 1948, box 5, Memorabilia file, HSA; Dewey, *The School and Society.* A religious school similar to Howalton was St. Edmund Episcopal School. Founded in 1948, Maudelle Bousfield chaired the school committee. Like Howalton, St. Edmund started small, first with a kindergarten and five grades. Then a grade was added each year until there were eight grades. Like Howalton, classes were intentionally small, so teachers could give individual attention to students. See boxes 2 and 4, SEEM.

47. Brochure, 1950–1951, box 1, Brochures file, Promotional Literature, HSA.

48. Meeting Notes from 1948, box 5, Memorabilia file, HSA; Dewey, *How We Think,* 102–6.

49. Meeting Notes from 1948, box 5, Memorabilia file, HSA; Dewey, *How We Think,* 102–6; Gladly Learn and Gladly Teach, box 1, Historical Sketches on Howalton School file, HSA.

50. Gladly Learn and Gladly Teach, box 1, Historical Sketches on Howalton School file, HSA.

51. Ibid.; Letter from PCH to Allen-Anderson, July 1, 1952, box 3, Correspondence, Allen-Anderson file 1946–1975, HSA; Letter from PCH to Allen-Anderson, August 8, 1952, box 3, Correspondence, Allen-Anderson file 1946–1975, HSA.

52. Meeting Notes from 1948, box 5, Memorabilia file, HSA.

53. Gladly Learn and Gladly Teach, box 1, Historical Sketches on Howalton School file, HSA; "Howalton News," box 1, Financial Statements, Howalton School (1951–1975), HSA; "Howalton Students Play Santa Claus for Little Chums at Provident," box 2, News Clippings file, HSA.

54. One student gave her own harp recital. She continued to study harp later in Switzerland. Some parents also served on the board of directors, along with the co-founders, the teachers, *Chicago Defender* editor John Sengestacke, and University of Chicago professor Allison Davis. See box 1, Financial Statements, Howalton School, 1951–1975 file, HSA.

55. Ibid; Gladly Learn and Gladly Teach, box 1, Historical Sketches on Howalton School file, HSA.

56. Gladly Learn and Gladly Teach, box 1, Historical Sketches on Howalton School file, HSA. At the University of Chicago's Laboratory School, black students were not accepted until several women drew up a petition to support their enrollment. Nearly 80 percent of the parents whose children attended the school signed the petition. As of 1943, the school admitted a few black children to the kindergarten and elementary school. De Pencier, *The History of the Laboratory Schools,* 154–55.

57. Box 9, file 12, ADP.

58. Davis had studied anthropology at Harvard under Lloyd Warner, and it was through Warner that he was offered a faculty position at the University of Chicago. See Browne, "Across Class and Culture: Allison Davis and His Works," in *African-American Pioneers in Anthropology,* 171–72. But Davis was not the first to study school achievement of poor black children. Maudelle Bousfield's study of black children at Keith Elementary School noted that most, if not all, lived in a fairly poor neighborhood. In her study she found no correlation among students' IQs, school achievement, and their home conditions. Bousfield, "The Intelligence and School Achievement of Negro Children," 390–91.

59. Chicago Teachers Union, Report of the Workshop in Intergroup Education for Chicago Public Schools, June 28–June 30, 1948, box 26, file 4, CTUP.

60. Hunt, "Chicago's Intercultural Relations Program," 113.

61. Graham, Halpern, Herson, and Jerison, "An Investigation of the Chicago School Redistricting Program," 4, 19; Minutes of the December 5, 1949 Meeting of the Citizens' Advisory Committee on the Chicago Public Schools, box 21, file 2, LWP; Report of the Inter-Cultural Relations Program in the Chicago Public Schools, 1949, box 1, file 9, IMGP.

62. Minutes of Meeting of the Technical Committee on Chicago Public Schools, of the Committee on Education, Training, and Research in Race Relations, February 3,

1950, box 21, file 2, LWP; Helen E. Amerman, "The Intergroup Relations Significance of Certain Items in Chicago School Bulletins 1947–1951," May 7, 1951, box 13, file 1, LWP; Helen E. Amerman, "Survey of Human Relations Problems and Projects in the Chicago Public Schools," box 13, file 6, LWP; Bishop, "Education for Democracy," 136.

63. Hafemann, "Vitalizing Intercultural Relations," 54–61; Herrick, *The Chicago Schools,* 296.

64. Margaret Burroughs recalled how she was "called down" before a committee of the Chicago school administrators and asked about her political views. One question was her view of Robeson because he was considered a "communist sympathizer." Editors of Freedomways, *Paul Robeson,* 269–71; Fleming and Burroughs, "Dr. Margaret T. Burroughs," 38–39.

65. Various letters from Louis Wirth to Harold Hunt, late 1940s and early 1950s, box 21, file 1, LWP.

66. Lord, "Herrick, Mary Josephine," 383–84; Notice, August, 20, 1944, box 5, file 3, CSCP.

67. "Columbia Cites Chicago Teacher," *Chicago Tribune,* n.d., file 3, PPACP; Rice, "Prescott, Annabel Carey," in *Women Building Chicago, 1790–1990,* 713–15.

68. Herrick, *The Chicago Schools,* 312.

69. Other community groups, especially the Catholic Interracial Council, held teachers' workshops. CCADN (November 1953), 4; Human Relations Department, Chicago Council Against Racial and Religious Discrimination, The Trumbull Park Homes Committee, August 1953–September 1954, file 649, CULP; Chicago Council against Discrimination, Minutes of Trumbull Park Committee of the Council against Discrimination, September 2, 1954, file 649, CULP.

70. Rice, "Prescott, Annabel Carey," 713–15. She was a member of the Chicago Commission on Human Relations and a board member of the South Side Settlement House.

71. "Climate in the Classroom Panel," box 1, file 4, PPACP.

72. "Teachers Study Pupils of Minority Groups" (1958), box 1, file 4, PPACP. Northwestern University sponsored a six-week session for teachers, supervisors, and principals on human relations. Speakers were from the Chicago Commission on Human Relations, the Anti-Defamation League, the National Conference of Christians and Jews, and the Japanese-American Association. Field trips were planned to show teachers problems in housing. "42 Attend Six-Week Workshop," box 1, file 4, PPACP.

73. "Teachers Study Pupils of Minority Groups" (1958), box 1, file 4, PPACP. Like Ina Brown, Prescott emphasized human rights, not just "minority" rights. As such, schools could be sites of democracy; for example, principals would treat teachers and students in a democratic manner. Brown, "The Role of Education in Preparing Children and Youth to Live in a Multi-Racial Society," 386–87.

74. Annabel Carey Prescott, "Comments on Human Relations," box 1, file 4, PPACP.

75. Frank Hayes, "How 'Stepchild' School Makes Brisk Comeback," box 1, file 4, PPACP; "Human Relations in Our Schools," April 22, 1958, box 1, file 4, PPACP.

76. "2 Groups Oppose Daley's Appointee," *Chicago American,* April 3, 1959, box 6, file 3, IMGP; *Defender,* April 9, 1962, 1. Yet Green had completed a master's thesis on race consciousness. See Green, "The Rise of Race-Consciousness in the American Negro."

77. Strickland, "The Schools Controversy and the Beginning of the Civil Rights Movement in Chicago," 717; Danns, *Something Better for Our Children.*

78. Homel, *Down from Equality,* 177.

79. Pinderhughes, *Race and Ethnicity in Chicago Politics.*

Chapter 5: Black Women's Clubs

1. See, for example, Blair, *The Clubwoman as Feminist;* Gere, *Intimate Practices;* Freedman, "Separatism Revisited," 170–88; Anderson, *After Suffrage.*

2. Hendricks, *Gender, Race, and Politics in the Midwest,* 29; Davis, *Lifting as They Climb,* 134, 137, 138; Knupfer, *Toward a Tenderer Humanity and a Nobler Womanhood.* The CNDA started in 1906 with fifteen clubs. Its district included Chicago Heights, Robbins, Elgin, Aurora, Batavia, Hinsdale, LaGrange, Maywood, Oak Park, Evanston, and Joliet.

3. *Defender,* May 4, 1935, 34; *Defender,* April 26, 1930, 19; Thirty-First Annual Session of the Illinois State Federation of Colored Women's Clubs, July 22–July 25, 1930, box 1, file 9, IMGP. As of 1986, the Gaudeamus Women's Club and the Clara Jessamine Civic and Charity Club were still active. See Brochures, box 1, TCS.

4. Pardee, "A Study of the Functions of Associations in a Small Negro Community in Chicago," 46.

5. *Bee,* June 2, 1946, 10; *Bee,* June 9, 1946, 6; President's Message, 1939, box 1, file 12, IMGP. Poignantly, McKinley died the day the cornerstone for a new community house was laid in 1955.

6. Funeral brochure for Mamie Ellis Kelly, 1960, box 6, file 4, IMGP.

7. Box 1, file 12, IMGP; Burk, *The Eisenhower Administration and Black Civil Rights,* 7.

8. National Du Saible Memorial Society, box 38, file 21, NIP, IWP; "Violette Neatley Anderson (1882–1937)," 12–15; Knupfer, *Toward a Tenderer Humanity and a Nobler Womanhood,* 145, 146; 1929 to 1944 HAICPAR. For this and other accomplishments, the NACW would honor Oliver. See Letter from Gaines to President and Members of the National Du Saible Memorial Society, April 20 1954, box 4, file 1, IMGP.

9. *Defender,* July 13, 1937, 17; Davis, *Lifting as They Climb,* 182.

10. Knupfer, *Toward a Tenderer Humanity and a Nobler Womanhood,* 120–21; Colored Culture in Chicago, box 47, files 6 and 7, NIP, IWP.

11. List of NCNW, Chicago Chapter Life Members, box 363G, file 1944–49, SLCP; Chicago Metropolitan Council of Negro Women, International Good Will Tea and Objets d'Art Exhibit, June 6, 1948, box 363G, file 1944–49, SLCP.

12. List of NCNW, Chicago Chapter Life Members, box 363G, file 1944–49, SLCP.

13. *Defender,* February 5, 1935, 15.

14. *Bee,* March 24, 1946, 11. Gaines did not say that Congressman William Dawson had done "nothing about the Tennessee riot." She had only stated that Dawson was not in Washington, D.C., when she wanted to visit with him about the matter and only added that he "must have been attending to local campaign duties." Letter from Gaines to Diggs, n.d., box 2, file 4, IMGP. In all fairness, the Chicago NCNW, too, had its own posh events, for example, a "dripping in mink" extravaganza in 1954. Although the purpose of the fund-raiser was to aid school desegregation nationally, the show featured mink that was "plush ranch, silver blue, royal pastel, cerulean, luteticia, Canadian wild, butter beige, white and the new heather." "NCNW in Show of Mink Wraps," *Defender,* October 2, 1954, 14.

15. See, for example, *Defender,* February 4, 1950, 9.

16. Anderson, "National Council of Negro Women," 446–49.

17. Incorporation Papers, Chicago Chapter, 1957, box 14, 99/06, Manuscripts, LICC; 1956 Financial Reports, Budget Report, November, 5, 1958, box 15, LICC; "Celebrating 50 Years of Friendship and Service: The Chicago Chapter of the Links, Inc.: 1950–2000," box 17, LICC.

18. "Brief Summary of the Report of the Chicago and Northern District Federation of Colored Women's Club for the Biennial Ending July 1926," box 259, file 8, WCMC; *Defender,* January 18, 1930, 17–19; box 1, file 12, IMGP; *Defender,* October 30, 1937, 17; *Defender,* May 28, 1938, 17; 1929 to 1944 HAICPAR.

19. "Open Children's Clinic at Provident Hospital," *Defender,* March 22, 1930, 1; *Defender,* February 1, 1930, 1; *Defender,* January 11, 1930, 5; Chicago and Northern District Association, *The Story of Seventy-Five Years of the Chicago and Northern District,* 41.

20. Hughes, "Autumn Visit to Chicago Where There's Always Something New," *Defender,* November 14, 1954, 9; "Windy City Elite Defies Overcast Sky, Dons Smartest for WABPH Tea," *Defender,* July 18, 1953, 6.

21. See Knupfer, *Toward a Tenderer Humanity and a Nobler Womanhood; Defender,* May 8, 1954, 16.

22. Knupfer, *Toward a Tenderer Humanity and a Nobler Womanhood;* Davis, *Lifting as They Climb,* 136.

23. NACWCR, Part 1, Reel 7, n.d.

24. Ibid.

25. *Defender,* June 19, 1937, 17.

26. Announcements, box 1, file 12, IMGP.

27. Interview with "Mr. X" Concerning Depression-Era Evictions on the South Side, box 37, file 18, NIP, IWP, n.p. This event occurred in June 1931.

28. Letter to Miss Webster from Ruth Powell, Memo, October 24, 1931, box 259, file 8, WCMC.

29. *Defender,* May 4, 1935, 26; Knupfer, *Toward a Tenderer Humanity and a Nobler Womanhood,* 78, 146.

30. Knupfer, *Toward a Tenderer Humanity and a Nobler Womanhood,* 156.

31. Mary Waring had a history of NACW involvement at the city, state, and national levels. She had been chair of the executive board, as well as secretary and treasurer for the Illinois State Federation of Colored Women's Clubs. Given her medical background, we should not be surprised that she chaired the NACW's Health and Hygiene Committee. See Hendricks, *Gender, Race, and Politics in the Midwest,* 86; Davis, *Lifting as They Climb,* 40.

32. Chicago and Northern District Association of Colored Women Family Relief Committee, Relief Committee Report, 1932, box 1, file 11, IMGP.

33. See Knupfer, *Toward a Tenderer Humanity and a Nobler Womanhood;* Thompson, *Ida B. Wells-Barnett: An Exploratory Study of an American Black Woman;* Schechter, *Ida B. Wells-Barnett and American Reform;* Hine and Thompson, *A Shining Thread of Hope.*

34. Chicago and Northern District Association of Colored Women Family Relief Committee, Relief Committee Report, 1932, box 1, file 11, IMGP.

35. Foreword: The Club Home, box 1, file 9, IMGP.

36. *Defender,* January 25, 1930, 7; box 1, file 11, IMGP; "Sunshine Home Completes Fourth Year of Existence," *Defender,* January 25, 1936, 20.

37. *Defender,* January 5, 1957, 12; "Maude E. Smith Nursery School Report," December, 4, 1950, box 3, file 1, IMGP; "Maude E. Smith Nursery School," January, 24, 1951, box 3, file 2, IMGP; 1929 to 1944 HAICPAR.

38. "A Scrap Book for Women in Public Life," *Defender,* March 15, 1930, 24.

39. Wesley, *The History of the National Association of Colored Women's Clubs,* 104.

40. Brasher, "Citizens of Morgan Park to Have Gala Community Event," *Defender,* April 5, 1930, 6.

41. Newspaper excerpt, April 18, 1937, box 11, file 11, IMGP; Note, December 10, 1937, box 11, file 11, IMGP; *Bee,* January 7, 1945, 9.

42. Knupfer, *Toward a Tenderer Humanity and a Nobler Womanhood,* 116–21.

43. Gaines, "Women in Politics," *Fisk News,* November 1936, box 1, file 11, IMGP.

44. "Mrs. Irene McCoy Gaines Prominently Connected with Every Movement in This City for the Welfare and Advancement of the Colored Race, Delivers Address," source unknown, March 1930, box 1, file 9, IMGP. See also Gaines, "Colored Authors and Their Contributions to the World's Literature," 261–70.

45. Article about Snowden, February 19, 1939, newspaper unknown, box 1, file 12, IMGP.

46. *Defender,* August 14, 1943, 17.

47. *Defender,* February 2, 1937, 19; *Bee,* April 4, 1943, 9; *Bee,* March 13, 1943, 13; *Bee,* January 9, 1944, 9.

48. *Bee,* January 20, 1946, 10; *Bee,* January 27, 1946, 9. Gaines and Ella Mitchell were judges of the youth contests.

49. CNDA, Report of the Department of Fine Arts and Literature, December 5, 1927, box 1, file 8, IMGP.

50. Workers of the Writers' Program of the WPA in the State of Illinois, *Cavalcade of the American Negro,* 10, 94, 91, 92; "American Negro Exposition," 175. President Roosevelt pressed a button in his home, which lit the Chicago Coliseum. *Defender,* July 13, 1940, 12.

51. Program of Exhibit, box 319, folder 2, CBP; Hostesses of American Negro Exposition, Plans of Organization, box 2, folder 1, IMGP. See also Prospectus, box 2, folder 1, IMGP, which outlined plans for the various exhibits at the American Negro Exposition; also see "American Negro Exposition," 175, 178. Burroughs and Reed were also active in this event.

52. "Northwestern Professor to Lecture at Art Show January 15," no source, box 1, file 12, IMGP. The list of all the women involved included Gaines, Nannie Mae Williams, Margaret Joyner, Maude Roberts George, Anna Crisp, Lillian Dove, Mary Waring, Mrs. Robert R. Jackson, Mary Evans, Mrs. Earl Dickerson, and Mrs. William Dawson. "Hostesses of American Negro Exposition, Plans of Organization," box 2, file 1, IMGP.

53. "Women Open War on Mrs. Ruth McCormick," source unknown, October 19, 1929, box 1, file 8, IMGP; Letter from Gaines to Mrs. Jacob Burr, May 4, 1931, box 1, file 9, IMGP.

54. "Mrs. Irene M. Gaines Organizer Heads Republican Women," *Defender,* April 26, 1930, 19; "Sixth Annual Convention of Colored Women's Republican Clubs of Illinois, Inc., Held Forth for Two Days in Chicago This Week," box 1, file 9, IMGP. Report of Irene M. Gaines, Chairman, State Work Among Colored Women, Week Ending March 22nd, 1930, box 1, file 9, IMGP. In appreciation of Gaines's work, McCormick in turn contributed $200 to the CNDA's working mothers' home. See box 1, file 9, IMGP.

55. Letter from Gaines to Honorable Roscoe Simmons, May 1, 1932, box 1, file 11, IMGP; Letter from Gaines to Honorable Roscoe Simmons, July 31, 1932, box 1, file 11, IMGP.

56. Johnson-Odim, "Gaines, Irene McCoy," 294–96.

57. Smith, "Address Delivered before National Labor Conference," *Defender,* February 10, 1930, 18.

58. Ibid.

59. *Defender,* July 22, 1933, 15; "Women Push Campaign for Phone Jobs," *Defender,* November 11, 1939, 11.

60. Chicago and Northern District Association, *The Story of Seventy-Five Years of the Chicago and Northern District,* 10.

61. Letter to *Chicago Tribune* from Gaines and CNDA, December 8, 1938, box 1, file 1, IMGP; Letter from Manager of Research and Promotion of *Chicago Tribune* to Helen Brascher, Honorary President of CNDA, December 16, 1938, box 1, file 12, IMGP; see Winter Travel and Resorts Section, *Chicago Tribune,* December 5, 1938, 8.

62. Garfield L. Smith, "Civic Leaders Fill Morris Cafe to See, Hear Famous Woman,"

newspaper unknown, box 7, file 7, IMGP; Letter from Charles Browning, Assistant State Director in Charge of Negro Affairs, National Youth Administration of Illinois to Gaines, July 7, 1937, box 1, file 12, IMGP; *Defender,* December 6, 1937, 17.

63. Letter from Everett Dirksen to Gaines, February 1, 1943, box 2, file 3, IMGP; Letter to William Dawson from Gaines, January 27, 1943; box 2, file 3, IMGP; Dawson to Gaines, February 9, 1943, box 2, file 3, IMGP.

64. Letter from Robert R. Taylor to Gaines, November, 27, 1939, box 1, file 12, IMGP; *Defender,* March 26, 1938, 17.

65. *Defender,* December 18, 1937, 17. In 1946, two black men were lynched in Georgia, setting off nationwide protests. That summer, the NACW picketed the White House and also stepped up their advocacy of an anti-lynching bill. Murray, *The Negro Handbook 1949,* 99.

66. *Defender,* January 1, 1938, 17.

67. *Defender,* December 18, 1937, 1; *Defender,* July 31, 1943, 17; *Bee,* February 27, 1944, 11.

68. Souvenir Program of the Illinois Association of Colored Women and Illinois Association of Colored Girls, May 9, 1943, box 2, file 3, IMGP. So much of the NACW's activism had been built upon motherhood. In 1947, when an NACW member was chosen as "American Mother of the Year," the NACW declared that they had been vindicated of the 1895 accusation of womanhood and motherhood. "They Lift as They Climb: The NACW," box 5, file 1, IMGP.

69. *Defender,* March 1, 1947, 14.

70. Statement by Gaines to Trygve Lie, Secretary General, United Nations, May 19, 1947, box 2, file 6, IMGP. But Trygve Lie emphasized that the UN could not solve any countries' domestic problems. Murray, *The Negro Handbook 1949,* 239.

71. "Interracial Commissions," *Pittsburgh Courier,* September 12, 1944.

72. Letter from Mayor Edward Kelly to Gaines, January 18, 1944, box 2, file 3, IMGP; Letter from Mayor Kelly to Gaines, May 7, 1945, box 2, file 4, IMGP.

73. Letter to Mayor Kennelly from the Chicago Crime Commission, February 10, 1948, box 2, file 7, IMGP.

74. Article, newspaper unknown, February 11, 1950, box 3, file 1, IMGP.

75. Rita Fitzpatrick, "3 G.O.P. Women Seeking County Board Positions," *Chicago Tribune,* April 6, 1950, box 3, file 1, IMGP.

76. Report on the Community Forum's Meeting on Trumbull Park, May 23, 1954, box 4, file 1, IMGP; CCADN (December 1953), 4; "Thousands Urge Action on Civil Rights Bills," source unknown, box 6, file 3, IMGP; "Women's Day" at Monumental Baptist Church, box 6, file 3, IMGP. For further context about Trumbull Park, see Hirsch, "Massive Resistance in the Urban North: Trumbull Park, Chicago, 1953–1966," 522–50; and the novel by Frank London Brown, *Trumbull Park.*

77. Davis, *Lifting as They Climb,* 78–82.

78. Moreno, "President's Committee on Government Employment Policy," 590; Krislov, *The Negro in Federal Employment,* 35. Gaines's stance seemed contradictory

because Eisenhower had been opposed to a national FEPC. Further, Eisenhower eschewed a direct legislative approach to most civil rights issues because he did not want to alienate his white southern constituency. Nonetheless, he was praised for his President's Committee on Government Contracts in 1953, which oversaw equal employment opportunity with companies that had government contracts. In truth, this committee had simply replaced Truman's Committee on Government Contract Compliance and was only an advisory board.

79. Statement by Mrs. Irene McCoy Gaines, President of the NACW, Before the Subcommittee of the Senate Committee on Labor and Public Welfare, March 2, 1954, box 4, file 1, IMGP.

80. Letter from Gaines to Eisenhower, September 29, 1954, box 4, file 2, IMGP.

81. Letter from Maxwell Abbell, Chair of President's Committee on Government Employment Policy to Gaines, April 16, 1956, box 5, file 1, IMGP; no title or source (1955), box 5, file 1, IMGP.

82. Letter from Gaines to President Eisenhower, May 4, 1955, box 5, file 1, IMGP.

83. Letter from Gaines to Carey, November, 14, 1957, box 5, file 5, IMGP; Letter from Carey. to Gaines, November 15, 1955, box 5, file 5, IMGP.

84. Letter from Arthur B. Caldwell, Chief, Civil Right Section, and Warren Olney III, Assistant Attorney General, Criminal Division, U.S. Department of Justice to Gaines, October 11, 1955, box 5, file 1, IMGP.

85. News Release from Gaines, box 5, file 2, IMGP; Letter from Gaines to Rosa Parks, n.d., box 5, file 2, IMGP.

86. News Release from Gaines, box 5, file 2, IMGP.

87. Letter from Mabel Neely, April 21, 1956, box 5, file 2, IMGP.

88. "Emergency Faces Negro Hospital in Mississippi," NACW Press Release, June 28, 1956, box 5, file 2, IMGP; Letter from Gertrude Reese Hicks, Campaign Manager of Genevieve Weaver for NACW President, n.d., box 7, file 7, IMGP.

89. Speech of Gaines at the Prayer Demonstration at Lincoln Memorial Plaza, Washington, D.C., May 17, 1957, box 5, file 4, IMGP. Following her talk, Mahalia Jackson sang.

90. See Laville, *Cold War Women;* "Another Milestone on the Road of Progress by the NACW—Representation in the United Nations," box 5, file 1, IMGP; Letter from Eric Johnston of the White House to Gaines, February 4, 1958, box 6, file 1, IMGP.

91. Letter from Gaines to Carey, November 14, 1957, box 5, file 5, IMGP; Letter from Carey to Gaines, November 15, 1957, box 5, file 5, IMGP.

92. *Defender,* November 2, 1946, 17; *Defender,* November 11, 1945, 19; "Mrs. Jane Morrow Spaulding," box 6, file 3, IMGP.

93. "National Grapevine, Windy City Notes," *Defender,* January 7, 1956; Jane Spaulding, "The Community Project Contest to Improve Homes and Neighborhoods," box 5, file 2, IMGP; Irene Powers, "Post Prizes to Improve Home Areas," *Chicago Tribune,* January 8, 1956, Part 7, 2. Jane Spaulding's son, Dr. Albert Lee Spaulding, was a doctor at Provident Hospital; he had also married Marva Louis. See brochure, box 1, TCS.

94. Letter from John Weatherwax of the John Henry and Mary Louisa Dunn Bryant Foundation to Gaines, May 2, 1956, box 5, file 2, IMGP; 1957 NACW Annual Report, box 5, file 3, IMGP; "Supplementary Report of President Gaines Made at the Miami Convention of the NACW Clubs, August 1, 1956," box 5, file 3, IMGP; Letter from Gaines to Spaulding, August 12, 1956, box 5, file 3, IMGP; Letter from Ruby Kendrick to Gaines, September 16, 1956, box 5, file 3, IMGP. Gaines appointed Ora Stokes Perry as the new project director. A lawyer from Virginia, Perry had been Bethune's assistant for the National Youth Administration. See Treadway, "Stokes, Ora Brown (1882–1957)," 1118–19.

95. Ethel Payne, "Jane Spaulding on Her Way Out," *Defender,* January 23, 1954, 1; Burk, *The Eisenhower Administration and Black Civil Rights,* 29.

96. Letter from Gaines to Harold Stassen, June 1, 1955, box 5, file 1, IMGP.

97. Burk, *The Eisenhower Administration and Black Civil Rights,* 80; Letter from Gaines to Mary Dawson, Director of Music of the NACW, July 24, 1954, box 4, file 1, IMGP.

98. Resolutions at the NACW Twenty-Ninth Biennial Convention, July 31 to August 6, 1954, box 4, file 1, IMGP.

99. Letter from Gaines to Dirksen, November 21, 1955, box 5, file 5, IMGP; Burk, *The Eisenhower Administration and Black Civil Rights,* 112.

100. Editorial, *Afro American,* November 20, 1954, box 4, file 2, IMGP.

101. Minutes of the NACW, Inc. and the NACG, 1956, box 5, file 3, IMGP; 1957 NACW Annual Report, box 5, file 3, IMGP; Letter from Gaines to Ella Stewart, July 3, 1956, box 5, file 2, IMGP; Letter from Susan Blockson to Officers and Members of the Past President's Council, May 15, 1957, box 5, file 5, IMGP; Letter from Harris Gaines to George Hayes, September 24, 1956, box 5, file 3, IMGP.

102. 1957 NACW Annual Report, box 5, file 3, IMGP; "80 Block Clubs Join NACW Neighborhood Improvement Contest," June 23, 1956, box 5, file 2, IMGP. Over eighty black leaders had convened at Kenwood-Ellis Community Center to discuss the Sears projects.

103. "Politics and Shenanigans," *Defender,* April 14, 1956, box 5, file 2, IMGP. Not surprisingly, Gaines wrote *Defender* publisher John Sengestacke to complain about the article. She reminded him that she had been a "good friend" of the *Defender,* for example, she had been the only woman on its Fiftieth Anniversary Celebration Committee. Sengestacke promised to correct the problem. Letter from Gaines to Sengestacke, November 20, 1956, box 5, file 3, IMGP; Letter from Sengestacke to Gaines, November 29, 1956, box 5, file 3, IMGP.

104. Jones, "Terrell, Mary Eliza Church," 1158–59; Letter from Gaines to Valores Washington, National Republican Committee, June 12, 1956, box 5, file 2, IMGP. Gaines had previously acknowledged Terrell's activism against the Washington, D.C. restaurants, hotels, and theaters and had invited her to be guest speaker at a Chicago event. Letter from Gaines to Terrell, March 17, 1953, box 3, file 5, IMGP. See also Burk, *The Eisenhower Administration and Black Civil Rights,* 45–46, 49, 52.

105. Letter from Gaines to Valores Washington, National Republican Committee, June 12, 1956, box 5, file 2, IMGP; Burk, *The Eisenhower Administration and Black Civil Rights*, 137, 141–42.

106. See, for example, Letter from Gaines to Ella P. Stewart, July 8, 1956, box 5, file 2, IMGP; Letter from Gaines to James C. Worthy, Director, Sears Roebuck Foundation, August 12, 1956, box 5, file 3, IMGP; Memorandum, September 10, 1956, box 5, file 3, IMGP; Letter from Gaines to Inez Tinsley, December 26, 1957, box 5, file 5, IMGP.

Chapter 6: Women's Activism in Public Housing

1. Chicago Housing Authority, *Facts about Public Housing in Chicago,* 6, 8. The CHA would also become increasingly involved in the debate over slum clearance, since most low-rent housing was built in slum areas or on vacant sites.

2. Bowly, *The Poorhouse,* 27; Chicago Housing Authority, *Five War Homes a Day,* 8. See also Abrams, "Does Interracial Housing Work?" 34.

3. Chicago Housing Authority, *Facts about Public Housing in Chicago,* 24; Chicago Housing Authority, *Five War Homes a Day,* 11; 1939 CHAAR, 6, 26, 28. One family requesting housing at the Wells Homes had its case publicized by a Chicago newspaper story. Their three-month-old was bitten by rats in a slum southside district. Tragically, this family's situation was not unique. CHAMR (November 15, 1944), 1.

4. Of the first 1,900 applicants to the Wells Homes in 1941, 1,600 of them had an average annual income of $750. Chicago Housing Authority, *Facts about Public Housing in Chicago,* 24. Some white restrictive covenant associations opposed public housing in or near their neighborhoods. When CUL president Foster submitted an application for the Ida B. Wells Homes in 1937, property owners in Hyde Park, Kenwood, and Oakland protested. They called public housing "un-American" and "socialistic" because public-housing residents didn't have to pay taxes. At one association meeting in 1950, a member complained about tax monies given to unmarried mothers, saying, "If we got rid of this A.D.C. business, there wouldn't be no housing shortage and over 60,000 people would go back to Dixie where they belong." The associations used various strategies to protest the building of public housing. Representatives from the associations attended city council meetings whenever there was discussion of public-housing projects. Mikva, "The Neighborhood Improvement Association: A Counter-Force to the Expansion of Chicago's Negro Population," 29, 31–32, 93.

5. 1945 CHAAR, n.p.; 1950 CHAAR, 18.

6. 1950 CHAAR, 6; Chicago Housing Authority, *Five War Homes a Day,* 3, 5. After seventeen years, Wood would be fired as executive secretary because of her efforts to desegregate Trumbull Park and other projects. See Robert Gruenberg, "Trumbull Park: Act II," September 18, 1954, box 4, file 2, IMGP.

7. Exhibit A of Fernwood Housing Project, box 317, file 10, WCMC; Chicago Housing Authority, *Facts about Public Housing in Chicago,* 6, 23; 1945 CHAAR, n.p.

8. 1947 CHAAR, 10.

9. Chicago Housing Authority, *Manager and Builder of Low-Rent Communities,* 25.

10. Chicago Housing Authority, *Flowers Grow Where Slums Once Stood,* n.p.

11. Bowly, *The Poorhouse,* 3.

12. 1940–1941 CHAAR, 30; 1943–1944 CHAAR, n.p.

13. Chicago Housing Authority, *Manager and Builder of Low-Rent Communities,* 25.

14. The nursery was mostly subsidized through private philanthropy and WPA funds, just as the later public-housing projects would be. Drake and Cayton, *Black Metropolis,* 661; *Five Year Report of the Michigan Boulevard Garden Apartments Building Corporation, February 1935,* box 37, file 27, NIP, IWP; "Michigan Boulevard Gardens Fulfill Dreams of Founder," *Defender,* March 22, 1930, 1; *Five-Year Report of the Michigan Boulevard Garden Apartments Building Corporation.,* box 7, file 8, RHAP, Supplement.

15. See CHAMR (1949), 8, 11.

16. History of CHA, box 3, file 5, MBWP; Flint, "Zoning and Residential Segregation: A Social and Physical History, 1910–40," 413; Memo, box 1, file 12, MBWP. The great migration exacerbated the availability of public housing as well. In some years during the 1950s, an estimated 1,700 blacks migrated to Chicago weekly. Most came to Chicago because of work opportunities, given the projection of 300,000 jobs there in the next ten years. Memorandum of Record, March 21, 1956, box 1, file 1, MBWP.

17. Memorandum, July 9, 1956, box 1, file 1, MBWP. The CHA, in fact, had hired Mary Wirth as a social work consultant in the tenant selection division; her main responsibility was to approve or reject applications by the established criteria. There were also black women who were CHA staff, such as Vivian Tives. When she was appointed manager of Wentworth Gardens Project, it was the first time a black woman was put in such a position of authority. She had previously worked at Altgeld Gardens and the Wells Homes as a tenant selector. *Defender,* April 24, 1954, 12.

18. Notes on Mr. Downs's Comments on Public Housing in Chicago, July 18, 1956, box 1, file 1, MBWP. As of 1956, the CHA established new income requirements, starting at a $4,500 annual income for a two-person family, with incremental rises for additional family members. Memorandum to the Commissioners, November 27, 1957, box 3, file 5, MBWP.

19. Mary Wirth, Standards of Social Eligibility, March 1, 1957, box 282, file 3, WCMC; The Housing Managers' Proposals for Community and Tenant Relations, CHA, June 11, 1958, box 2, file 13, MBWP.

20. Mary Wirth, Standards of Social Eligibility, March 1, 1957, box 282, file 3, WCMC. Eighty percent of the white families were classified as "normal," that is, nuclear, compared to 70 percent of black families. Memorandum, May 22, 1952, box 1, file 13, MBWP.

21. Notes on Mr. Downs's Comments on Public Housing in Chicago, July 18, 1956, box 1, file 1, MBWP.

22. Letter to the Chicago Housing Authority from the Welfare Council of Metropolitan Chicago Advisory Committee, December 1956, box 2, file 13, MBWP.

23. Hirsch, *Making the Second Ghetto.* Wirth rightly claimed that community building could not occur in high-rises. She argued that high-rises "froze" the social structure and individual living standards.

24. 1939 CHAAR, 29–30; 1940–1941 CHAAR, 25.

25. Bowly, *The Poorhouse,* 27. The Oakland Business Men's Association and southside realtors opposed the building of the Wells Homes. See Gibbs, "The Life Cycle of Oakland Community," 219.

26. "Protest Delay on Ida Wells Housing," box 1, file 12, IMGP.

27. Letter from A. L. Foster to Irene McCoy Gaines, December 12, 1938, box 1, file 12, IMGP; "Let's Make History" flyer, box 9, file 4, IBWP; "Ida B. Wells Fiftieth Anniversary" article, box 8, file 12, IBWP; "Dedication Program," *Defender,* November 2, 1940.

28. Bowly, *The Poorhouse,* 31; 1940–1941 CHAAR, 8, 11.

29. Chicago Housing Authority, *Facts about Public Housing in Chicago;* 1947 CHAAR, 10, 31.

30. 1940–1941 CHAAR, 24.

31. Ibid., 13, 24; WJCAH, Minutes, January 16, 1941, box 27, file 365, MHPC. As of 1947, most families with an income of under $1,500 were female-headed. Chicago Housing Authority, *What Is a Low-Income Family?* 17.

32. See, for example, 1940–1941 CHAAR, 30; 1943–1944 CHAAR, n.p.; 1947 CHAAR, 35.

33. Programs Operated by Health and Welfare Agencies in Housing Developments Operated by the CHA, box 282, file 3, WCMC; CHAMR (April, 1950), n.p. In the projects, the infant mortality rate was 35 per 1,000 live births, compared to 59 per 1,000 in Chicago's slums. The death rate of Wells Homes' tenants at 9.3 per 10,000 was half that of nearby neighborhoods. 1948 CHAAR, 25.

34. CHAMR (October 9, 1944), 10; 1945 CHAAR, n.p.; 1940–1941 CHAAR, 28.

35. 1939 CHAAR, 25.

36. CHAMR (October 9, 1944), 3.

37. See Knupfer, *Toward a Tenderer Humanity and a Nobler Womanhood;* White, *Too Heavy a Load.*

38. CHAMR (January 24, 1946), 11; 1945 CHAAR, n.p.

39. Playhouse Nursery, 1956–1957, box 380, file 12, WCMC.

40. Collins, *Black Feminist Thought;* Chicago Housing Authority, *Handbook for Residents of Altgeld Gardens,* 9. The Wells Homes' model was used to encourage Altgeld residents to do the same.

41. CHAMR (February 26, 1946), 8; CHAMR (March 27, 1946), 22; CHAMR (July, 1946), 14; *Wellstown Crier* 1 (February 1949), box 8, file 14, IBWP.

42. See chaps. 2 and 3 of this book.

43. South Parkway YWCA, Decentralized Program at the Olander Homes, April,

1957, box 427, file 1, WCMC; Programs Operated by Health and Welfare Agencies in Housing Developments Operated by the CHA (1954), box 282, file 3, WCMC.

44. CHAMR (February 26, 1946), 17.

45. Community Contacts, October, 1947 to February, 1948, box 426, file 5, WCMC.

46. WJCAH, February 11, 1941 Minutes, box 27, file 356, MHPC; WJCAH, March 13, 1941, March 27, 1941, May 8, 1941 Minutes, box 27, file 356, MHPC.

47. CHAMR (October 9, 1944), 12; CHAMR (May 27, 1946), 11. High school students from the wealthy suburb, Winnetka, also toured the Lathrop Homes.

48. CHAMR (May 27, 1946), 11.

49. Letter from Mrs. Jasper King to Parkway YWCA Committee, January 26, 1953, box 5, file 10, YWCA; Lease for Community Activity and Non-Commercial Space in Housing Development, box 5, file 10, YWCA; Letter from Hattie Droll to Elizabeth Wood, April, 27, 1953, box 5, file 10, YWCA.

50. South Parkway Announcement, Getting to Know You Series, box 12, file 10, YWCA.

51. South Parkway, Center Committee Meeting, October 26, 1954, box 12, file 10; Saul Alinsky, "In These 10 Cities," 1950, file 34, SAP; Saul Alinsky, "Text of Testimony for the Civil Rights Housing Hearing of the Commission on Civil Rights," May 5, 1950, file 34, SAP.

52. Summary of Services Available in CHA Community Space, n.d., box 282, file 3, WCMC.

53. Monthly Report of Teen-Age Clubs, September and October 1953, box 9, file 1, YWCA; The Y-Teener Newsletter, March 19, 1955, box 12, file 10, YWCA.

54. Brochure of Teenage Director, Parkway YWCA, box 5, file 10, YWCA; The South Parkway Story, n.d., box 9, file 1, YWCA.

55. Letter from Regina Saxton to Janet Sharp, June 25, 1958, box 21, file 1, YWCA.

56. Letter from Regina Saxton to Bernard Shiffman, July 24, 1957, box 426, file 3, WCMC; Parkway Center Committee Minutes, September 11, 1957, box 21, file 1, YWCA.

57. Hard to Reach Youth Project and Ourselves, January 6, 1959, box 24, file 13, YWCA. Other Wells Homes' gangs were less involved in these planned social activities. The Rams, also called the Bad Boys, were known more for their vandalism. Memorandum, September 9, 1953, box 9, file 1, YWCA.

58. South Parkway YWCA, Decentralized Program at the Olander Homes, April 1957, box 427, file 1, WCMC, 2.

59. Shack, "Social Change in an Isolated Negro Community," 11, 13, 15; Chicago Housing Authority, Facts about Public Housing in Chicago, 12; 1950 CHAAR, 18; Pellow, Garbage Wars, 68.

60. CHAMR (March 27, 1946), 19.

61. CHAMR (November 10, 1946), 21; CHAMR (August 1949), 13; Untitled Booklet, n.d., box 3, file 2, MBWP.

62. Memorandum, May 22, 1952, box 1, file 13, MBWP; Shack, "Social Change in an Isolated Negro Community," 13, 16.

63. Chicago Housing Authority, *Handbook for Residents of Altgeld Gardens,* 2.

64. Ibid.; CHAMR (November 15, 1944), 4; "Altgeld Gardens to Have Huge Shopping Center," *Bee,* March 5, 1944, 1.

65. 1945 CHAAR, n.p.; Memorandum to Alexander Ropchan from Milton L. Shurr, June 19, 1947, box 244, file 17, WCMC. Altgeld's elementary school also extended its services to include an evening program of adult education, which would lead to an elementary school diploma. The Chicago board of education also sponsored a series of school social nights, with games and dances for children. CHAMR (January 24, 1946), 13. At several school assemblies, Paul Robeson spoke; *Bee,* May 13, 1945, 1.

66. Shack, "Social Change in an Isolated Negro Community," 19, 21, 23, 24, 33; "Exhibit B," Fernwood Housing Project, 1947–1948, box 317, file 10, WCMC. There was a Fernwood-Bellevue Civic Association opposed to blacks moving into the neighborhood. A community goodwill council was formed for the protection of blacks, which endorsed the CHA's plan for Fernwood Project. On June 9, 1947, the *Calumet Index* newspaper published an editorial about the restrictive covenant bill, "Protect Your Homes." The editor warned about protecting white neighborhoods. One letter to the editor stated, "If we have to have a show-down with them to protect our homes and families, I'm in favor of it. God knows, I wouldn't want one alongside of me." Record of Events Prior to Move-In Day at Fernwood Park Homes, box 317, file 10, WCMC. With plans for integrated housing in Fernwood Park for veterans, riots ensued. See also Reiff, "Rethinking Pullman: Urban Space and Working-Class Activism," 6.

67. 1947 CHAAR, 35.

68. Memorandum from Milton L. Shurr to Alexander Ropchan, June 19, 1947, box 244, file 17, WCMC; Minutes of Meeting of Committee on Altgeld Gardens, December 3, 1953, box 244, file 17, WCMC; CHAMR (November 15, 1944), 4, 7; CHAMR (July 26, 1946), 11; CHAMR (July 1949), 9.

69. Minutes of Meeting of Committee on Altgeld Gardens, September 25, 1953, box 244, file 17, WCMC.

70. Letter from Louise H. Coggs to Elizabeth Wood, April 23, 1953, box 244, file 17, WCMC.

71. Letter from Community Fund of Chicago to Robert MacRae, April 9, 1954, box 244, file 18, WCMC; Report from Cal Axford to Marion Craine, January 5, 1955, box 244, file 18, WCMC; Minutes of the Executive Committee Division II, February 3, 1955, box 244, file 17, WCMC; Meeting of Committee of the Health Division of the Welfare Council of Metropolitan Chicago, September 22, 1953, box 244, file 17, WCMC.

72. Report on Application for Membership of Altgeld Nursery School Parent Council, Inc. to Altgeld Nursery School Parent Council, August 26, 1946, box 600, file 7, CFC, 3, 4.

73. Ibid., 3.

74. Ibid., 4–5.

75. Ibid., 4.

76. Ibid.

77. Board of Directors Meeting, box 1, file 7, WCMC; Treasurer Report, Altgeld Nursery School Council, July, 1960, box 1, file 7, WCMC.

78. Special Meeting of the Day Nurseries Reviewing Committee, September 21, 1956, box 53, file 4, CFC; Description of School, March 1956, box 53, file 4, CFC; Questions Which the Committee Wants Agency to Answer Prior to Its Conference, December 16, 1959, box 120, file 4, CFC; Cohen, *Making a New Deal,* 335–36, 442–43.

79. Altgeld Nursery School, Special Meeting of the Day Nurseries Reviewing Committee, September 21, 1956, box 53, file 4, WCMC; Altgeld Nursery School Council, Report on Visit to Agency Regarding Functional Budgeting, September 30, 1957, box 76, file 7, WCMC; Untitled, 1951 and 1952, box 245, file 2, WCMC.

80. Altgeld Nursery School Council's Service Report, September 24, 1958, box 120, file 4, WCMC; Altgeld Nursery School Council, Description (unnamed), October 1959, box 1, file 7, WCMC.

81. Description of School, March 1956, box 53, file 4, CFC.

82. 1960 Board of Directors' Meeting, Altgeld Nursery School Council, box 1, file 7, CFC.

83. Shack, "Social Change in an Isolated Negro Community," 59, 61–62. Mary Wirth agreed that lack of middle-class tenants was a problem in public housing. Untitled Booklet, n.d., box 3, file 2, MBWP.

84. Shack, "Social Change in an Isolated Negro Community," 31–32.

85. Ibid.; various correspondence in MBWP; Letter from John Ballard to Mrs. E. Kuh, April 7, 1959, box 282, file 3, WCMC.

86. Shack, "Social Change in an Isolated Negro Community," 50; Bontemps and Conroy, *Any Place but Here,* chap. 14. Communism was not only a concern at Altgeld Gardens but also at all of Chicago's housing projects, where tenants were required to sign loyalty oaths in the late 1950s. Some tenants at the Addams Homes were confused, and those who couldn't read didn't respond. "Reminiscences of my Assignment as an 'Aide'—1953–1954," box 2, file 14, MBWP.

87. Essien-Udom, *Black Nationalism,* 90–91.

88. Letter from Robert MacRae to Lillian Taylor, Program Supervisor, Women's Service Division, United Charities of Chicago, April 2, 1959, box 282, file 3, WCMC.

Chapter 7: The Chicago YWCAs

1. Interracial Practices of Girl Reserve Department, box 40, file 10, YWCA. The Westside Y was located at 101 South Ashland Avenue.

2. Ibid. Camp Sagawau accommodated 176 girls of various ethnic backgrounds.

3. Boynton, "Fighting Racism at the YWCA," 28.

4. Inter-Racial Progress in the Chicago YWCA, 1930–36, box 40, file 10, YWCA.

5. Boynton, "Fighting Racism at the YWCA," 31.

6. Ibid.

7. Ibid., 31, 33.

8. January 1945 Report, box 40, file 10, YWCA.

9. Boynton, "Fighting Racism at the YWCA," 33. Like all applicants, residents had to meet a salary range requirement, as well as an age limit. Minutes of Meeting of Residence Directors, January 17, 1945, box 40, file 10, YWCA.

10. Questionnaire about Interracial Practices in YWCA, Form B, May, 1943, box 40, file 10, YWCA.

11. Minutes of Meeting of Residence Directors, December 14, 1944, box 40, file 11, YWCA; Residences, n.d., box 40, file 10, YWCA.

12. Inter-Racial Sub-Committee Girl Reserve Department, November 30, 1944, box 40, file 10, YWCA.

13. Minutes of Meeting of Residence Directors, December 14, 1944, box 40, file 11, YWCA.

14. Inter-Racial Sub-Committee Girl Reserve Department, November 30, 1944, box 40, file 10, YWCA; January, 1945 Report, box 40, file 10, YWCA.

15. Questionnaire about Interracial Practices in YWCA, Form B, May 1943, box 40, file 10, YWCA.

16. Inter-Racial Sub-Committee Girl Reserve Department, November 30, 1944, box 40, file 10, YWCA; *Defender,* August 14, 1943, 5.

17. Letter from Barbara Abel to Mrs. Sundry, June 20, 1937, box 40, file 10, YWCA.

18. Interracial Practices Committee, January 19, 1945, box 40, file 10, YWCA.

19. Ibid.

20. *Bee,* February 3, 1946, 5.

21. Questionnaire about Interracial Practices in YWCA, Form A, May, 1943, box 40, file 10, YWCA.

22. Ruth M. Smith, Statement of Inter-Racial Policies of the YWCA of Chicago, n.d., box 40, file 10, YWCA.

23. *Defender,* October 9, 1937, 14; *Bee,* February 7, 1943, 10; "YWCA Membership Drive Opens," *Defender,* March 8, 1930, 17.

24. *Defender,* September 30, 1933, 7; *Defender,* May 27, 1937, 23; Bates, "A New Crowd Challenges the Agenda of the Old Guard in the NAACP, 1933–1941," 347.

25. The History of the Young Women's Christian Association, box 38, file 5, NIP, IWP; Chicago Recreation Commission and Northwestern University, *Private Recreation* vol. 3 of *The Chicago Recreation Survey, 1937* (Chicago: n.p., 1937). Long-term residents were charged weekly rates of $5 to $9. Those who needed housing for only a few nights paid as little as 50 cents per night. There were clearly a number of the latter, as the SPY accommodated 147 young women in 1936 alone. Chicago Recreation Commission and Northwestern University, *The Chicago Recreation Survey.*

26. Inter-Racial Discussion Group, December 1936, box 40, file 10, YWCA.

27. *Defender,* March 22, 1930, 20; Notice, 1938, YWCA, box 8, file 2, YMCA.

28. Extracts from Annual Industrial Reports, box 40, file 10, YWCA.

29. "YWCA to Open Room Registry Service for Girls," *Bee,* February 7, 1943, 10.

30. Report of the Metropolitan Industrial Department for the Year Ending August 31, 1936, box 40, file 10, YWCA; Boynton, "Fighting Racism at the YWCA," 26; *Defender,* November 6, 1937, 11.

31. Questionnaire about Interracial Practices in YWCA, Form A, box 40, file 10, YWCA.

32. Report, YWCA Health Education Project, 1944–1949, box 426, file 5, WCMC.

33. Report to the Community Fund on the South Parkway Counseling Service, September 1945, box 427, file 1, WCMC.

34. Ibid. See also Hughes, *On Work, Race, and the Sociological Imagination,* 97–99.

35. Report to the Community Fund on the South Parkway Counseling Service, September 1945, box 427, file 1, WCMC.

36. Letter from Helen Bull to Lucy Carner, December 16, 1943, box 427, file 1, WCMC.

37. Report to the Community Fund on the South Parkway Counseling Service, September, 1945, box 427, file 1, WCMC.

38. Ibid.

39. Report on Three Year Project Counseling Services at South Parkway YWCA, box 427, file 1, WCMC.

40. 1952–53 Narrative Report, South Parkway, Center, box 5, file 10, YWCA Supp.

41. South Parkway Center Committee Minutes, May 20, 1958, box 21, file 1, YWCA.

42. Ibid. The Woodlawn Y, organized in June of 1953, was located at 1170 East 63rd Street.

43. Minutes, South Side Building Committee Minutes, September 24, 1962, box 427, file 2, WCMC.

44. Minutes, South Side Steering Committee, September 1, 1959, box 427, file 2, WCMC; Minutes, South Parkway YWCA Center, March, 17, 1959, box 24, file 13, YWCA. Olive Diggs was chair of the South Side Steering Committee for the YWCA; Memo, January 19, 1959, box 427, file 2, WCMC.

45. South Side Study Report, May 1959, box 427, file 2, WCMC; Exhibit III: Things We Need To Know, October, 1959, box 427, file 2, WCMC; Letter from Minnie Levinson and Mary Lewis to Julia Ann Spenney, May 26, 1958, box 21, file 1, YWCA.

46. Ada S. McKinley Community House, October 1954, box 34, file 2, CFC; Community Service to Older People: A Project of Ada S. McKinley Community House in Prairie Avenue Courts, April 1956, box 53, file 2, CFC; Summary Report, January 3, 1958, box 76, file 4, CFC. Elizabeth Wood had suggested that perhaps there could be teen programs in the Trumbull Homes for "character building" that would use

the Wells Homes' youth programs as a model. Letter to Hattie Droll from Thomas Colgan, October 8, 1953, box 11, file 5, YWCA.

47. Letter from Mildred Jones and Regina Saxton to Daisy Bates, December 5, 1957, box 21, file 1, YWCA; Letter from Daisy Bates to Mildred Jones and Regina Saxton, December 12, 1957, box 21, file 1, YWCA; Letter from Mildred Jones and Mrs. Samuel Jones to Chicago Metropolitan YWCA, March 10, 1958, box 21, file 1, YWCA. In soliciting funds for the Wells Homes' community center, the SPY staff found that there were bitter feelings about the Wells Homes because some persons had had to move in order for it to be built. Center Committee Meeting Minutes, June 22, 1954, box 9, file 1, YWCA.

48. Bowly, *The Poorhouse,* 87.

49. South Parkway YWCA, Decentralized Program at the Olander Homes, April 1957, box 427, file 1, WCMC, 1.

50. Ibid., 2.

51. Ibid.

52. Ibid.

53. Ibid., 3–5.

54. Ibid.

55. Ibid., 6

56. Ibid.

57. Appendix 4, Profile of Members and Services—January, 1959, box 427, file 2, WCMC.

Conclusion

1. Naples, "Activist Mothering," 446. See also Naples, "Just What Needed to Be Done," 478–94.

2. "They Lift as They Climb: The NACW," box 5, file 1, IMGP.

3. Untitled Booklet, n.d., box 3, file 2, MBWP.

4. Naples, "Activist Mothering," 441–63; Naples, "Just What Needed to Be Done," 478–94; Venkatesh, *American Project.*

5. Essien-Udom, *Black Nationalism.*

6. See Black, *Bridges of Memory.*

Bibliography

Abrams, Charles. "Does Interracial Housing Work?" *Negro Digest* 6 (November 1947): 27–36.

Adamczyk, Janina. "Neva L. Boyd (1876–1963)." *American Sociological Review* (August 1964): 581–82.

Alexander, Margaret Walker. "Richard Wright." In *Richard Wright: Impression and Perspectives,* ed. David Ray and Robert M. Farnsworth, 47–67. Ann Arbor: University of Michigan Press, 1973.

American Jewish Congress of Chicago. *The Lost Decade: An Analysis of Illinois Civil Rights Legislation, 1949–1959.* Chicago: American Jewish Congress, 1959.

"American Negro Exposition." *The Crisis* 47 (June 1940): 175, 178.

Anderson, Karen. "National Council of Negro Women." In *Organizing Black America: An Encyclopedia of African American Associations,* ed. Nina Mjagkij, 446–49. New York: Garland Publishing, 2001.

Anderson, Karen Tucker. "Last Hired, First Fired: Black Women Workers during World War II." *Journal of American History* 69 (June 1982): 82–97.

Anderson, Kristi. *After Suffrage: Women in Partisan and Electoral Politics before the New Deal.* Chicago: University of Chicago Press, 1996.

Andrews, William L., Frances Smith Foster, and Trudier Harris, eds. *The Oxford Companion to African American Literature.* New York: Oxford University Press, 1997.

Aschenbrenner, Joyce. "Katherine Dunham: Anthropologist, Artist, Humanist." In *African-American Pioneers in Anthropology,* ed. Ira. E. Harrison and Faye V. Harrison, 137–53. Urbana: University of Illinois Press, 1999.

Avery, Laurence G., ed. *A Paul Green Reader.* Chapel Hill: University of North Carolina Press, 1998.

Baker, James H., Jr. "Social Work, Trade Unionism and the Negro." *Opportunity* 16 (January 1936): 19–22, 29.

Baron, Harold. "History of Chicago School Segregation to 1953." *Integrated Education Review* 1 (January 1963): 17–19, 30.

Bascom, William R. "The Focus of Cuban Santeria." *Southwest Journal of Anthropology* 6 (1950): 64–68.

———. *The Sociological Role of the Yoruba Cult-Group.* Menasha, Wis.: American Anthropological Association, 1944.

Bascom, William R., and Paul Gebauer. *Handbook of West African Art.* Milwaukee: Bruce Publishing, 1954.

Bascom, William R., and Melville J. Herskovits, eds. *Continuity and Change in African Cultures.* Chicago: University of Chicago Press, 1959.

Bates, Beth Tompkins. "A New Crowd Challenges the Agenda of the Old Guard in the NAACP, 1933–1941." *American Historical Review* (April 1997): 340–77.

Becker, Howard S. "Role and Career Problems of the Chicago Public School Teachers." Ph.D. diss., University of Chicago, 1951.

Berman, Rabbi Morton, and Zonia Baber. *Report of the Commission on Intercommunity Relationships of the Hyde Park-Kenwood Council of Churches and Synagogues on "The Negro Problems of the Community to the West."* Chicago: n.p., 1940.

Bethune, Mary McLeod. "The Adoption of the History of the Negro to the Capacity of the Child." *Journal of Negro History* 14 (January 1939): 9–13.

Bishop, L. K. "Education for Democracy." *Chicago Schools Journal* 31 (1949): 136–38.

Black, Timuel D., Jr. *Bridges of Memory: Chicago's First Wave of Black Migration.* Evanston, Ill.: Northwestern University Press, 2003.

Blair, Karen J. *The Clubwoman as Feminist: True Womanhood Redefined, 1868–1914.* New York: Homes and Meier Publishers, 1980.

Bolden, B. J. *Urban Rage in Bronzeville: Social Commentary in the Poetry of Gwendolyn Brooks, 1945–1960.* Chicago: Third World Press, 1999.

Bone, Robert. "Richard Wright and the Chicago Renaissance." *Callaloo* 9 (Summer 1986): 446–68.

Bontemps, Arna. "Famous WPA Authors." *Negro Digest* 8 (June 1950): 43–47.

Bontemps, Arna, and Jack Conroy. *Any Place but Here.* 1945. Reprint. New York: Hill, 1966.

Bousfield, Maudelle B. "The Intelligence and School Achievement of Negro Children." *Journal of Negro Education* 1 (October 1932): 388–95.

Bowly, Devereux, Jr. *The Poorhouse: Subsidized Housing in Chicago, 1895–1976.* Carbondale: Southern Illinois University Press, 1978.

Boyd, Neva. *Social Group Work: A Definition with a Methodological Note.* Chicago: University College, Northwestern University, 1937.

Boynton, Virginia R. "Fighting Racism at the YWCA." *Chicago History* (Summer 2000): 22–39.

Brooks, Gwendolyn. *Front Line Report from Part One.* Detroit: Broadside Press, 1972.

———. *A Street in Bronzeville.* New York: Harper and Brothers Publishers, 1945.

Brown, Frank London. *Trumbull Park.* Chicago: Henry Regnery, 1959.

Brown, Ina Corrinne. "The Role of Education in Preparing Children and Youth to Live in a Multi-Racial Society." *Journal of Negro Education* 19 (Summer 1950): 384–87.

Brown, W. O. "Culture Contact and Race Conflict." In *Race and Culture Contacts,* ed. Edward B. Reuter, 34–47. New York: McGraw-Hill, 1934.

Browne, Dallas L. "Across Class and Culture: Allison Davis and His Works." In *African-American Pioneers in Anthropology,* ed. Ira. E. Harrison and Faye V. Harrison, 168–90. Urbana: University of Illinois Press, 1999.

Burk, Robert Fredrick. *The Eisenhower Administration and Black Civil Rights.* Knoxville: University of Tennessee, 1984.

Burroughs, Margaret Taylor. "Holidays in Mexico: Mexican Festivals Provide Interesting Settings for Teaching Units." *Chicago Schools Journal* 37 (January–February 1956): 159–63.

———. "Survey Indicates Student Attitudes toward Art: Teenagers Prefer Handicraft Activities to Drawing." *Chicago Schools Journal* 50 (February 1950): 224–26.

Caldwell, Lewis A. H. *The Policy King.* Chicago: New Vistas Publishing House, 1945.

Capeci, Dominic J., Jr. "The Lynching of Cloe Wright: Federal Protection of Constitutional Rights during World War II." *Journal of American History* 72 (March 1986): 859–87.

Cappetti, Carla. "Sociology of an Existence: Wright and the Chicago School." In *Richard Wright: Critical Perspectives Past and Present,* ed. Henry Louis Gates Jr. and K. A. Appiah, 255–71. New York: Amistad, 1993.

Carter, Dan T. *Scottsboro: A Tragedy of the American South.* Baton Rouge: Louisiana State University Press, 1969.

Cayton, Horace R. "Fighting for White Folks?" *The Nation* 155 (September 26, 1942): 267–70.

———. *Long Old Road.* New York: Trident Press, 1965.

———. "The Negro's Challenge." *The Nation* 157 (July 3, 1943): 267–70.

Cayton, Horace R., and George S. Mitchell. *Black Workers and the New Unions.* Chapel Hill: University of North Carolina Press, 1939.

Chavers-Wright, Madrue. *The Guarantee: P. W. Chavers, Banker, Entrepreneur, Philanthropist in Chicago's Black Belt of the Twenties.* 2d ed. New York: Wright-Armstead Associates, 1987.

Cheney, Anne. *Lorraine Hansberry.* Boston: Twayne Publishers, 1984.

Chicago and Northern District Association. *The Story of Seventy-Five Years of the Chicago and Northern District.* Chicago: Chicago Northern District Association, 1981.

Chicago Housing Authority. *Facts about Public Housing in Chicago.* Chicago: Chicago Housing Authority, 1947.

———. *Five War Homes a Day.* Chicago: Chicago Housing Authority, 1942.

———. *Flowers Grow Where Slums Once Stood.* Chicago: Chicago Housing Authority, 1942.

———. *Handbook for Residents of Altgeld Gardens.* Chicago: Chicago Housing Authority, 1944.

———. *Information in Regard to the Proposed South Park Gardens.* Chicago: Chicago Housing Authority, 1938.

———. *The Slum: Is Rehabilitation Possible?* Chicago: Chicago Housing Authority, 1946.

———. *What Is a Low-Income Family? An Analysis of Incomes of Urban Families of Various Types.* Chicago: Chicago Housing Authority, 1947.

Chicago Planning Commission. *Housing Goals for Chicago.* Chicago: Chicago Planning Commission, 1946.

Chicago Recreation Commission and Northwestern University. *Private Recreation.* Vol. 3, *The Chicago Recreation Survey, 1937.* Chicago: n.p., 1938.

"Chicago Schools Include Negro History." *The Crisis* 50 (February 1943): 51, 60.

Chorpenning, Charlotte B. "Dramatics and Personality Growth." In *New Trends in Group Work,* ed. Joshua Lieberman, 140–51. New York: Association Press.

Citizens Schools Committee. "From Crowded Homes to Crowded Schools." *Chicago's Schools* (February–March 1941): 1, 4.

City of Chicago. *Chicago Conference on Home Front Unity, 1945: Mayor's Committee on Race Relations* Chicago: n.p., 1945.

———. *City Planning in Race Relations: Proceedings of the Mayor's Conference on Race Relations, February, 1944.* Chicago: n.p., 1944.

Cohen, Lizabeth. *Making a New Deal: Industrial Workers in Chicago, 1919–1939.* Cambridge, United Kingdom: Cambridge University Press, 1990.

Collins, Patricia Hill. *Black Feminist Thought.* New York: Routledge, 1990.

Conroy, Jack. "A Reminiscence." In *Richard Wright: Impression and Perspectives,* ed. David Ray and Robert M. Farnsworth, 31–34. Ann Arbor: University of Michigan Press, 1973.

Cook, Robert. *Sweet Land of Liberty? The African-American Struggle for Civil Rights in the Twentieth Century.* London and New York: Longman, 1998.

Cox, Oliver C. *Caste, Class, and Race: A Study in Social Dynamics.* 1948. Reprint. New York: Modern Reader Paperbacks, 1970.

Craig, E. Quita. *Black Drama of the Federal Theatre Era: Beyond the Formal Horizons.* Amherst: University of Massachusetts Press, 1980.

Cromwell, Otelia, Lorenzo Dow Turner, and Eva B. Dykes. *Readings from Negro Authors, for Schools and Colleges.* New York: Harcourt, Brace, 1931.

Cruse, Harold. *The Crisis of the Negro Intellectual: A Historical Analysis of the Failure of Black Leadership.* New York: Quill, 1967.

Curtis, Susan. *The First Black Actors on the Great White Way.* Columbia: University of Missouri Press, 1998.

Danns, Dionne. *Something Better for Our Children: Black Organizing in Chicago Public Schools, 1963–1971.* Routledge: New York and London. 2003.

Davis, Allison. "The Relation between Color Caste and Economic Stratification in Two Black Plantation Counties." Ph.D. diss., University of Chicago, 1942.

———. *Social Influences upon Learning.* Cambridge, Mass.: Harvard University Press, 1948.

Davis, Allison, and John Dollard. *Children of Bondage: The Personality Development of Negro Youth in the Urban South.* Washington, D.C.: American Council on Education, 1940.

Davis, Allison, Burleigh B. Gardner, and Mary R. Gardner. *Deep South: A Social Anthropological Study of Caste and Class.* 1941. Reprint. Los Angeles: Center for Afro-American Studies, University of California, 1988.

Davis, Elizabeth Lindsay. *Lifting as They Climb.* 1933. Reprint. New York: G. K. Hall, 1996.

Davis-DuBois, Rachel. *Adventures in Intercultural Education: A Manual for Secondary School Teachers.* New York: Progressive Education Association and Commission on Intercultural Education, 1938.

———. *Get Together Americans: Friendly Approaches to Racial and Cultural Conflicts through the Neighborhood-Home Festival.* New York: Harper and Brothers, 1943.

Davis-DuBois, Rachel, and Corann Okorodudu. *All This and Something More: Pioneering in Intercultural Education.* Bryn Mawr, Penn.: Dorrance, 1984.

De Pencier, Ida B. *The History of the Laboratory Schools: The University of Chicago, 1896–1965.* Chicago: Quadrangle Books, 1967.

De Santis, Christopher C., ed. *Langston Hughes and the Chicago Defender: Essays on Race, Politics, and Culture, 1942–62.* Urbana: University of Illinois Press, 1995.

Des Jardins, Julie. *Women and the Historical Enterprise: Gender, Race, and the Politics of Memory, 1880–1945.* Chapel Hill: University of North Carolina Press, 2003.

de Vise, Pierre. *Chicago's Widening Color Gap.* Chicago: Interuniversity Social Research Committee, 1967.

Dewey, John. *How We Think.* Boston: Houghton Mifflin, 1998.

———. *The School and Society; The Child and the Curriculum.* 1902. Reprint. Chicago: University of Chicago Press, 1990.

Dillon, Kim Jenice. "Bonner, Marita." In *The Oxford Companion to African American Literature,* ed. William L. Andrews, Frances Smith Foster, and Trudier Harris, 90–91. New York: Oxford University Press, 1997.

Drake, St. Clair. *Churches and Voluntary Associations among Negroes in Chicago.* Chicago: Works Public Administration, 1940.

Drake, St. Clair, and Horace Cayton. *Black Metropolis: A Study of Negro Life in a Northern City.* Rev. ed. Chicago: University of Chicago Press, 1993.

Du Bois, Shirley Graham. *His Day Is Marching On: A Memoir of W. E. B. Du Bois.* Philadelphia: J. B. Lippincott, 1971.

Du Bois, W. E. B. *The Autobiography of W. E. B. Du Bois: A Soliloquy on Viewing My Life from the Last Decade of Its First Century.* New York: International Publishers, 1968.

———. "Krigwa Players Little Negro Theatre." *The Crisis* 32 (July 1926): 134.

———. "Pan-African and New Racial Philosophy." *The Crisis* 40 (November 1933): 237–40.

Duis, Perry, and Scott La France. *We've Got a Job to Do: Chicagoans and World War II.* Chicago: Chicago Historical Society, 1992.

Duncan, Otis, and Beverly Duncan. *Chicago's Negro Population: Characteristics and Trends.* Chicago: University of Chicago, 1956.

Dunnegan, Marjorie Lord. "Vocational Education at Dunbar." *Integrated Education Review* 1 (June 1963): 29–35.

Dunham, Katherine. *Journey to Accompong.* Westport, Conn.: Negro Universities Press, 1946.

Editors of Freedomways. *Paul Robeson: The Great Forerunner.* New York: Dodd, Mead, 1978.

Edley, Lucille. "Strategies and Techniques of Politics: A Study of Ten Selected Precinct Captains from Chicago's Third Ward." Master's thesis, University of Chicago, 1955.

Edmonds, R. "The Negro Little Theatre Movement." *Negro History Bulletin* 12 (January 1949): 82–86, 92–94.

Edwards, Thyra. "The Mulzac School of Seamanship." *Negro Digest* 3 (February 1945): 73–75.

Engelhardt, Elizabeth Sanders Delwiche. "Fenton, Johnson." In *The Oxford Companion to African American Literature,* ed. William L. Andrews, Frances Smith Foster, and Trudier Harris, 402–3. New York: Oxford University Press, 1997.

Essien-Udom, E. U. *Black Nationalism. A Search for an Identity in America.* Chicago: University of Chicago Press, 1962.

Fabre, Michael. *The Unfinished Quest of Richard Wright.* New York: William Morrow, 1973.

Farr, Newton D. "Are Restrictive Covenants Justifiable?" *Negro Digest* 9 (February 1946): 37–38.

Fehn, Bruce. "African-American Women and the Struggle for Equality in the Meatpacking Industry, 1940–1960." *Journal of Women's History* 10 (Spring 1998): 45–69.

Field, Sherry L. "Intercultural Education and Negro History during the Second World War." *Journal of the Midwest History of Education Society* 22 (1995): 75–85.

Fishbein, Annette. "The Expansion of Negro Residential Area in Chicago, 1950–60." Master's thesis, University of Chicago, 1962.

Fisher, Miles Mark. "Organized Religion and the Cults." *Crisis* (January 1937): 9–12.

Flanagan, Hallie. *Arena.* New York: Duell, Sloan and Pearce, 1940.

Fleming, John E., and Margaret T. Burroughs. "Dr. Margaret T. Burroughs: Artist, Teacher, Administrator, Writer, Political Activist, and Museum Founder." *Public Historian* 21 (Winter 1999): 31–55.

Flint, Barbara J. "Zoning and Residential Segregation: A Social and Physical History, 1910–40." Ph.D. diss., University of Chicago, 1977.

Floyd, Samuel A., Jr. *The Power of Black Music: Interpreting Its History from Africa to the United States.* New York: Oxford University Press, 1995.

Flug, Michael. "Vivian Gordon Harsh." In *Black Women in America: An Historical Encyclopedia.* Vol. 1, ed. Darlene Clark Hine, Elsa Barkley Brown, and Rosalyn Terborg-Penn, 542–43. Brooklyn: Carlson, 1993.

Foner, Philip S., and Ronald L. Lewis, eds. *The Black Worker from the Founding of the CIO to the AFL-CIO Merger, 1936–1955.* Vol. 7, *A Documentary History from Colonial Times to the Present.* Philadelphia: Temple University Press, 1983.

Fraden, Rena. *Blueprints for a Black Federal Theatre, 1935–1939.* Cambridge, United Kingdom: Cambridge University Press, 1994.

———. "The Cloudy History of Big White Fog: The Federal Theatre Project, 1938." *American Studies* 29 (Summer 1989): 5–28.

Frazier, E. Franklin. "Chicago: A Cross-Section of Negro Life." *Opportunity* 7 (March 1929): 70–73.

———. "Traditions and Patterns of Negro Family Life in the United States." In *Race and Culture Contacts,* ed. Edward B. Reuter, 191–207. New York: McGraw-Hill, 1934.

Freedman, Estelle B. "Separatism Revisited: Women's Institutions, Social Reform, and the Career of Miriam Van Waters." In *U.S. History as Women's History: New Feminist Essays,* ed. Linda Kerber, Alice Kessler-Harris, and Kathryn Kish Sklar, 170–88. Chapel Hill: University of North Carolina Press, 1995.

Gaines, Irene M. "Colored Authors and Their Contributions to the World's Literature." In *The Messenger Reader: Stories, Poetry, and Essays from The Messenger Magazine,* ed. Sondra Kathryn Wilson, 261–70. New York: Modern Reader, 2000.

Garfinkel, Herbert. *When Negroes March: The March on Washington Movement in the Organizational Politics for FEPC.* Glencoe, Ill.: Free Press, 1959.

Gates, Henry Louis, Jr., and K. A. Appiah, eds. *Richard Wright: Critical Perspectives Past and Present.* New York: Amistad, 1993.

Gere, Anne Ruggles. *Intimate Practices. Literacy and Cultural Work in U.S. Women's Clubs, 1880–1920.* Urbana: University of Illinois Press, 1997.

Glen, John. *Highlander: No Ordinary School 1932–1962.* Lexington: University of Kentucky Press, 1988.

Goggin, Jacqueline. *Carter G. Woodson: A Life in Black History.* Baton Rouge: Louisiana State University Press, 1993.

Gosnell, Harold F. *Negro Politicians. The Rise of Negro Politics in Chicago.* Chicago: University of Chicago Press, 1935.

Graham, Polly, Ruth Weaver Halpern, Muriel Herson, and Irene Landkof Jerison. "An Investigation of the Chicago School Redistricting Program." Master's thesis, University of Chicago, 1952.

Grant, George C. "The Negro in Dramatic Art." *Journal of Negro History* 17 (June 1932): 19–29.

Green, Loraine Richardson. "The Rise of Race-Consciousness in the American Negro." Master's thesis, University of Chicago, 1919.

Green, Lorenzo J. *Selling Black History for Carter G. Woodson: A Diary, 1930–1933.* Ed. Arvarh E. Strickland. Columbia: University of Missouri Press, 1996.

Guzman, Jessie Parkhurst, Vera Chandler Foster, and W. Hardin Hughes, eds. *Negro Year Book: A Review of Events Affecting Negro Life, 1941–1946.* Tuskegee, Ala.: Department of Records and Research, Tuskegee Institute, 1947.

Guzman, Jessie Parkhurst, Lewis W. Jones, and Woodrow Hall, eds. *1952 Negro Year Book: A Review of Events Affecting Negro Life.* New York: Wm. H. Wise, 1952.

Hafemann, Henrietta. "Vitalizing Intercultural Relations." *Chicago Schools Journal* 28 (January 1947): 54–61.

Haller, Mark H. "Policy Gambling, Entertainment, and the Emergence of Black Politics: Chicago From 1900 to 1940." *Journal of Social History* 24 (Summer 1991): 719–39.

Hamalian, Leo, and James V. Hatch, eds. *The Roots of African American Drama: An Anthology of Early Plays, 1858–1938.* Detroit: Wayne State University Press, 1991.

Harriott, Frank. "The Life of a Pulitzer Poet." *Negro Digest* 8 (1950): 14–16.

Harris, Leonard, ed. *The Critical Pragmatism of Alain Locke.* Lanham, Mass.: Rowman and Littlefield Publishers, 1999.

Harrison, Ira. E., and Faye V. Harrison, eds. *African-American Pioneers in Anthropology.* Urbana: University of Illinois Press, 1999.

Hartmann, Susan M. *American Women in the 1940s: The Home Front and Beyond.* Boston: Twayne Publishers, 1982.

Hatch, James V., and Leo Hamalian, eds. *Lost Plays of the Harlem Renaissance 1920–1940.* Detroit: Wayne State University, 1996.

Hendricks, Wanda A. *Gender, Race, and Politics in the Midwest: Black Club Women in Illinois.* Bloomington: Indiana University Press, 1998.

Herrick, Mary J. *The Chicago Schools: A Social and Political History.* Beverly Hills, Calif.: Sage Publications, 1971.

———. "Negro Employees of the Chicago Board of Education." Master's thesis, University of Chicago, 1931.

Herskovits, Frances S., ed. *The New World Negro*. Bloomington: Indiana University Press, 1966.

Herskovits, Melville J. *The Myth of the Negro Past*. 1941. Reprint. Boston: Beacon, 1990.

———. "The Contribution of Afroamerican Studies to Africanist Research (1948)." In *The New World Negro*, ed. Frances S. Herskovits, 12–22. Bloomington: Indiana University Press, 1966.

Hine, Darlene Clark. "Carter G. Woodson, White Philanthropy and Negro Historiography." *History Teacher* 19 (November 1985): 405–25.

———. *Hine Sight : Black Women and the Re-Construction of American History*. Brooklyn: Carlson, 1994.

Hine, Darlene Clark, Elsa Barkley Brown, and Rosalyn Terborg-Penn, eds. *Black Women in America: An Historical Encyclopedia*. Vols. 1 and 2. Brooklyn: Carlson, 1993.

Hine, Darlene Clark, and Kathleen Thompson. *A Shining Thread of Hope*. New York: Broadway Books, 1998.

Hirsch, Arnold R. *Making the Second Ghetto: Race and Housing in Chicago, 1940–1960*. Cambridge, United Kingdom: Cambridge University Press, 1983.

———. "Massive Resistance in the Urban North: Trumbull Park, Chicago, 1953–1966." *Journal of American History* 8 (1982): 522–50.

Hobbs, Richard S. *The Cayton Legacy: An African American Family*. Pullman: Washington State University Press, 2002.

Homel, Michael W. *Down from Equality: Black Chicagoans and the Public Schools, 1920–41*. Urbana: University of Illinois Press, 1984.

———. "The Lilydale School Campaign of 1936: Direct Action in the Verbal Protest Era." *Journal of Negro History* 59 (July 1974): 228–41.

Honey, Maureen, ed. *Bitter Fruit: African American Women in World War II*. Columbia: University of Missouri Press, 1999.

Horne, Gerald. *Race Woman: The Lives of Shirley Graham Du Bois*. New York: New York University Press, 2000.

Horton, Aimee Isgrig. *The Highlander Folk School: A History of Its Major Programs*. Brooklyn: Carlson Publishing, 1989.

Hughes, Everett C. *On Work, Race, and the Sociological Imagination*. Edited and with an Introduction by Lewis A. Coser. Chicago: University of Chicago Press, 1994.

Hughes, Langston. "The Negro Artist and the Racial Mountain." In *The Portable Harlem Renaissance Reader*, ed. David Levering Lewis, 91–95. New York: Penguin Books, 1984.

———. *The Return of Simple*. New York: Hill and Wang, 1994.

Hunt, Herold C. "Chicago's Intercultural Relations Program." *Chicago Schools Journal* (1949): 113–16.

Hutton, Oscar D. "The Negro Worker and the Labor Unions in Chicago." Master's thesis, University of Chicago, 1939.

Jacobs, Louise M., and Mabel Thorn Lulu. "Chicagoland Authors and Illustrators of Children's Literature." *Chicago Schools Journal* 32 (May-June 1951): 1–45.

James, Joy. *Transcending the Talented Tenth: Black Leaders and American Intellectuals.* New York: Routledge, 1997.

Jeffries, LeRoy W. "Step Up, Lady—Want a War Job?" *Opportunity* 21 (April 1943): 39–40.

Johnson-Odim, Cheryl. "Gaines, Irene McCoy." In *Women Building Chicago 1790–1990,* ed. Rima Lunin Schultz and Adele Hast, 294–96. Bloomington: Indiana University Press, 2001.

Jones, Beverly. "Terrell, Mary Eliza Church." In *Black Women in America.* Vol. 2, ed. Darlene Clark Hine, Elsa Barkley Brown, and Rosalyn Terborg-Penn, 1158–59. Brooklyn: Carlson, 1993.

Kahn, Dorothy. "Chicago Hits the Job Jackpot." *Negro Digest* 6 (July 1948): 4–6.

Kelley, Robin D. G. *Race Rebels. Culture, Politics, and the Black Working Class.* New York: Free Press, 1996.

Kenney, William Howland. *Chicago Jazz: A Cultural History 1904–1930.* New York: Oxford University Press, 1993.

Kenny, Vincent S. *Paul Green.* New York: Twayne Publishers, 1971.

Kerber, Linda, Alice Kessler-Harris, and Kathryn Kish Sklar, eds. *U.S. History as Women's History: New Feminist Essays.* Chapel Hill: University of North Carolina Press, 1995.

Kersten, Andrew E. "March on Washington Committee." In *Organizing Black America: An Encyclopedia of African American Associations,* ed. Nina Mjagkij, 322–24. New York: Garland Publishing, 2001.

Kilpatrick, William Heard. *Group Education for a Democracy.* New York: Association Press, 1940.

Knupfer, Anne Meis. *Reform and Resistance: Gender, Delinquency, and America's First Juvenile Court.* London and New York: Routledge, 2001.

———. *Toward a Tenderer Humanity and a Nobler Womanhood: African American Women's Clubs in Turn-of-the-Century Chicago.* New York: New York University Press, 1996.

Krislov, Samuel. *The Negro in Federal Employment.* Minneapolis: University of Minnesota Press, 1987.

Lahey, Edwin. "Are Slum Landlords Criminals?" *Negro Digest* 6 (April 1947): 75–76.

Laville, Helen. *Cold War Women: The International Activities of American Women's Organizations.* Manchester and New York: Manchester University Press, 2002.

Lawson, Hilda Josephine. "The Negro in America Drama." Ph.D. diss., University of Illinois, 1939.

Levit, Martin. "The Chicago Citizens Schools Committee: A Study of a Pressure Group." Master's thesis, University of Chicago, 1947.

Lewis, David Levering, ed. *The Portable Harlem Renaissance Reader.* New York: Penguin Books, 1984.

Lieberman, Joshua, ed. *New Trends in Group Work.* New York: Association Press, 1939.

Lincoln, C. Eric. *The Black Experience in Religion.* Garden City, N.Y.: Anchor Books, 1974.

Lindeman, Eduard. "Group Work and Democracy—A Philosophical Note." In *New Trends in Group Work,* ed. Joshua Lieberman, 47–53. New York: Association Press, 1939.

Locke, Alain. *The New Negro: An Interpretation.* New York: Albert and Charle/Boni, 1932.

Logan, Rayford W. *The Negro and the Post-War World Primer.* Washington, D.C.: Minorities Publishers, 1945.

———. "The Negro Wants First-Class Citizenship." In *What The Negro Wants,* ed. Rayford W. Logan, 1–30. Chapel Hill: University of North Carolina, 1944

———, ed. *What the Negro Wants.* Chapel Hill: University of North Carolina, 1944.

Long, Richard A. "Burroughs, Margaret Taylor Goss." In *The Oxford Companion to African American Literature,* ed. William L. Andrews, Frances Smith Foster, and Trudier Harris, 111–12. New York: Oxford University Press, 1997.

Lord, May Sweet. "Herrick, Mary Josephine." In *Women Building Chicago, 1790–1990,* ed. Rima Lunin Schultz and Adele Hast, 383–84. Bloomington: Indiana University Press, 2001.

Mathews, Jane De Hart. *The Federal Theatre, 1935–1939: Plays, Relief, and Politics.* Princeton, N.J.: Princeton University Press, 1967.

Mavigliano, George J., and Richard A. Lawson. *The Federal Art Project in Illinois, 1935–1943.* Carbondale: Southern Illinois University Press, 1990.

McKinzie, Richard D. *The New Deal for Artists.* Princeton, N.J.: Princeton University Press, 1973.

Meier, August, and Elliott Rudwick. *Along the Color Line: Explorations in the Black Experience.* Urbana: University of Illinois Press, 1976.

Meyerowitz, Lisa. "The Negro in Art Week: Defining the 'New Negro' through Art Exhibition." *African American Review* 31 (1996): 75–89.

Mikva, Zorita. "The Neighborhood Improvement Association: A Counter-Force to the Expansion of Chicago's Negro Population." Master's thesis, University of Chicago, 1951.

Mjagkij, Nina, ed. *Organizing Black America: An Encyclopedia of African American Associations.* New York: Garland Publishing, 2001.

Moore, Brenda. *To Serve My Country, To Serve My Race: The Story of the Only African American WACs Stationed Overseas during World War II.* New York: New York University Press, 1996.

Moreno, Paul D. "President's Committee on Government Employment Policy." In *Organizing Black America: An Encyclopedia of African American Associations,* ed. Nina Mjagkij, 590. New York: Garland Publishing, 2001.

Morgan, Madeline. "A Bank Project." *Chicago Schools Journal* 22 (September–October 1940): 83–84.

Morris, Harry Wesley. "The Chicago Negro and the Major Political Parties 1940–1948." Master's thesis, University of Chicago, 1950.

Moses, Earl R. *The Negro Delinquent in Chicago.* Washington, D.C.: Public School, 1936.

———. "Delinquency in the Negro Community." *Opportunity* 11 (October 1933): 304–7.

Mullen, Bill. *Popular Fronts: Chicago and African-American Cultural Politics, 1935–46.* Urbana: University of Illinois Press, 1999.

———. "Popular Fronts: *Negro Story Magazine* and the African American Literary Response to World War II." *African American Review* 30 (Spring 1996): 5–15.

Murray, Florence, ed. *The Negro Handbook 1949.* New York: MacMillan, 1949.

Myrdal, Gunnar. *An American Dilemma: The Negro Problem and Modern Democracy.* New York: Harper and Brothers, 1944.

Naples, Nancy. "Activist Mothering: Cross-Generational Continuity in the Community Work of Women from Low-Income Urban Neighborhoods." *Gender and Society* 6 (September 1992): 441–63.

———. "'Just What Needed to Be Done': The Political Practice of Women Community Women in Low-Income Neighborhoods." *Gender and Society* 5 (December 1991): 478–94.

Nemiroff, Robert. *To Be Young, Gifted and Black: Lorraine Hansberry in Her Own Words.* Englewood Cliffs, N.J.: Prentice-Hall, 1969.

Nichols, Charles H., ed. *Arna Bontemps-Langston Hughes Letters.* New York: Dodd, Mead, 1980.

O'Connor, Francis V., ed. *Art for the Millions: Essays from the 1930s by Artists and Administrators of the WPA Federal Art Project.* Greenwich, Conn.: New York Graphic Society, 1973.

"Opinion of W. E. B. Du Bois: In Black." *Crisis* (October 1920): 263–64.

Pardee, Ruth. "A Study of the Functions of Associations in a Small Negro Community in Chicago." Master's thesis, University of Chicago, 1937.

Park, Robert Ezra. *The Collected Papers of Robert Ezra Park.* Edited by Everett C. Hughes, Charles Johnson, Jitsuichi Masuoka, Robert Redfield, and Louis Wirth. Glencoe, Ill.: Free Press, 1950.

Pellow, David Naguib. *Garbage Wars: The Struggle for Environmental Justice in Chicago.* Cambridge, Mass.: MIT Press, 2002.

Penkower, Monty Noam. *The Federal Writers' Project: A Study in Government Patronage of the Arts.* Urbana: University of Illinois Press, 1977.

Perkins, Kathy A. *Black Female Playwrights: An Anthology of Plays before 1950.* Bloomington: Indiana University Press, 1989.

Pinderhughes, Diane M. *Race and Ethnicity in Chicago Politics.* Urbana: University of Illinois Press, 1987.

Placksin, Sally. *American Women in Jazz, 1900 to the Present: Their Words, Lives, and Music.* New York: Wideview Press, 1982.

Plotkin, Wendy. "Deeds of Mistrust: Race, Housing, and Restrictive Covenants in Chicago, 1900–1953." Ph.D. diss., University of Illinois at Chicago, 1999.

Porter, Dorothy B. "Negro Women in Our Wars." *Negro History Bulletin* 7 (June 1944): 195–96, 215.

Porter, James A. *Modern Negro Art.* New York: Dryden Press, 1943.

Powdermaker, Hortense. *After Freedom: A Cultural Study in the Deep South.* 1939. Reprint. Madison: University of Wisconsin Press, 1991.

———. *Probing Our Prejudices: A Unit for High School Students.* New York: Harper, 1944.

Ray, David, and Robert M. Farnsworth, eds. *Richard Wright: Impression and Perspectives.* Ann Arbor: University of Michigan Press, 1973.

Reckless, Walter C. *Vice in Chicago.* Chicago: University of Chicago Press, 1933.

Record, Wilson. *The Negro and the Communist Party.* Chapel Hill: University of North Carolina Press, 1951.

Reed, Christopher. *The Chicago NAACP and the Rise of Black Professional Leadership.* Bloomington: Indiana University Press, 1997.

Reiff, Janice L. "Rethinking Pullman: Urban Space and Working-Class Activism." *Social Science History* 24 (2000): 7–32.

Reuter, Edward B., ed. *Race and Culture Contacts.* New York: McGraw-Hill, 1934.

Reynolds, Gary A., and Beryl J. Wright. *Against the Odds: African-American Artists and the Harmon Foundation.* Newark, N.J.: Newark Museum, 1989.

Rice, Jon. "Prescott, Annabel Carey." In *Women Building Chicago, 1790–1990,* ed. Rima Lunin Schultz and Adele Hast, 713–15. Bloomington: Indiana University Press, 2001.

Riches, William T. Martin. *The Civil Rights Movement: Struggle and Resistance.* New York: St. Martin's Press, 1997.

Rieser, Lawrence. "An Analysis of the Reporting of Racial Incidents in Chicago, 1945 to 1950." Master's Thesis, University of Chicago, 1951.

Roberts, Janet M. "Thompson, Era Bell." In *The Oxford Companion to African American Literature,* ed. William L. Andrews, Frances Smith Foster, and Trudier Harris, 729. New York: Oxford University Press, 1997.

Robertson, Fay Lee. "A Study of Some Aspects of Racial Succession in the Woodlawn Community Area of Chicago." Master's thesis, University of Chicago, 1955.

Robeson, Paul. *Here I Stand.* Boston: Beacon Press, 1958.

Rogoff, Natalie. "Racial Attitudes in a White Community Bordering on the Negro District." Master's thesis, University of Chicago, 1947.

Rosenberg, Anna M. "Womanpower and the War." *Opportunity* 21 (April 1943): 35–36.

Savage, Barbara Diane. *Broadcasting Freedom: Radio, War, and the Politics of Race, 1938–1948.* Chapel Hill: University of North Carolina Press, 1999.

Sayre-Lewis, Lydia. "Caricature and Portrait in Children's Books." *Chicago Schools Journal* 12 (September-October 1940): 41.

Schietinger, Egbert. "Racial Succession and Values of Small Residential Properties." *American Sociological Review* (1961): 833–34.

Schechter, Patricia A. *Ida B. Wells-Barnett and American Reform, 1880–1930.* Chapel Hill: University of North Carolina Press, 2001.

Schultz, Rima Lunin, and Adele Hast, eds. *Women Building Chicago, 1790–1990.* Bloomington: Indiana University Press, 2001.

Shack, William A. "Social Change in an Isolated Negro Community." Master's thesis, University of Chicago, 1957.

Shaw, Spenella. "Charlemae Hill Rollins." In *Notable Black American Women,* ed. Jessie Carney Smith, 949–53. Detroit: Gale Research, 1992.

Sheppard, Harold Lloyd. "Conflicting Business Associations in Chicago's Black Belt." Master's thesis, University of Chicago, 1945.

Sitkoff, Harvard. *A New Deal for Blacks: The Emergence of Civil Rights as a National Issue: The Depression Decade.* Oxford: Oxford University Press, 1978.

———. "Racial Militancy and Interracial Violence in the Second World War." *Journal of American History* 5 (December 1971): 661–81.

Smith, Jessie Carney, ed. *Notable Black American Women.* Vols. 1 and 2. New York: Gale Research, 1996.

Smith, Joe. *Sin Corner and Joe Smith: A Story of Vice Corruption in Chicago.* New York: Exposition Press, 1963.

Smith, Michael G. *The Economy of Hausa Communities of Zaria.* London: H. M. Stationery Office for the Colonial Office, 1955.

Smith, Preston H., II. "The Quest for Racial Democracy: Black Civic Ideology and Housing Interest in Postwar Chicago." *Journal of Urban History* 26 (January 2000): 131–57.

"Social Group Work." *Opportunity* 16 (September 1938): 79–83.

Southern, David W. *Gunnar Myrdal and Black-White Relations: The Use and Abuse of an American Dilemma, 1944–1969.* Baton Rouge: Louisiana State University Press, 1987.

Spear, Allan H. *Black Chicago: The Making of a Negro Ghetto.* Chicago: University of Chicago Press, 1967.

Spillane, Joseph. "The Making of an Underground Market: Drug Selling in Chicago, 1900–1940." *Journal of Social History* 32 (Fall 1998): 27–47.

Strassman, M. Morton. "The Activities of Parent-Teacher Associations in Elementary Schools in Chicago." Master's thesis, University of Chicago, 1936.

Stratton, Madeline Robinson. *Negroes Who Helped Build America.* Boston: Ginn and Co., 1965.

Strickland, Arvarh E. *History of the Chicago Urban League.* Urbana: University of Illinois Press, 1966.

———. "The Schools Controversy and the Beginning of the Civil Rights Movement in Chicago." *Historian* 58 (Winter 1996): 717–29.

Sugrue, Thomas J. "Crabgrass-Roots Politics: Race, Rights, and the Reaction against Liberalism in the Urban North, 1940–1964." *Journal of American History* 82 (September 1995): 551–78.

Tarry, Ellen. *The Third Door: The Autobiography of an American Negro Woman.* Tuscaloosa: University of Alabama Press, 1966.

Thompson, Era Bell. *Africa, Land of My Fathers.* Garden City, N.Y.: Doubleday, 1954.

Thompson, Mildred L. *Ida B. Wells-Barnett: An Exploratory Study of an American Black Woman, 1893–1930.* Brooklyn: Carlson, 1990.

Thorpe, Earl E. *Negro Historians in the United States.* Baton Rouge, La.: Fraternal Press, 1958.

"Three Years of the Negro History Bulletin." *Negro History Bulletin* (November 1940): 44.

Travis, Dempsey. *An Autobiography of Black Chicago.* Chicago: Urban Research Institute, 1981.

———. *"Harold, The People's Mayor."* Chicago: Urban Research Press, 1989.

Treadway, Sandra Gioia. "Stokes, Ora Brown (1882–1957)." In *Black Women in America.* Vol. 2, ed. Darlene Clark Hine, Elsa Barkley Brown, and Rosalyn Terborg-Penn, 1118–19. Brooklyn: Carlson, 1993.

Turner, Lorenzo D. *Notes on the Sounds and Vocabulary of Gullah.* Greensboro, N.C.: American Dialect Society, 1945.

U.S. Work Projects Administration, Illinois. *Chicago Negro Community.* Chicago: W.P.A. District 3, 1939.

Vanterpool, Rudolph V. "Open-Textured Aesthetic Boundaries: Matters of Art, Race, and Culture." In *The Critical Pragmatism of Alain Locke,* ed. Leonard Harris. Lanham, Mass.: Rowman and Littlefield Publishers, 1999.

Venkatesh, Sudhir Alladi. *American Project: The Rise and Fall of a Modern Ghetto.* Cambridge, Mass.: Harvard University Press, 2000.

"Violette Neatley Anderson (1882–1937)." In *Notable Black American Women.* Vol. 2, ed. Jessie Carney Smith, 12–15. Detroit: Gale Research, 1996.

Walker, Margaret. *For My People.* New Haven, Conn.: Yale University Press, 1942.

———. *Richard Wright: Daemonic Genius. A Portrait of the Man, A Critical Look at His Work.* New York: Warren Books, 1988.

Walker, Sheila S., ed. *African Roots/American Cultures: Africa in the Creation of the Americas.* Lanham, Mass.: Rowman and Littlefield Publishers, 2001.

Ward, Jerry W., Jr. "Walker, Margaret." In *The Oxford Companion to African American Literature,* ed. William L. Andrews, Frances Smith Foster, and Trudier Harris, 752–53. New York: Oxford University Press, 1997.

Warner, W. Lloyd. *American Life: Dream and Reality.* Rev. ed. Chicago: University of Chicago Press, 1962.

Warner, William Lloyd, Buford H. Junker, and Walter A. Adams. *Color and Human Nature: Negro Personality Development in a Northern City.* Washington, D.C.: American Council on Education, 1941.

Weaver, Robert C. "Chicago: A City of Covenants." *Crisis* 53 (March 1946): 75–78, 93.

———. "Negro Labor since 1929." *Journal of Negro History* 35 (January 1950): 20–38.

———. "No." *Negro Digest* 9 (February 1946): 38–41.

Weems, Robert E., Jr. *Desegregating the Dollar: African American Consumerism in the Twentieth Century.* New York: New York University Press, 1998.

———. "Robert A. Cole and the Metropolitan Funeral Association: A Profile of a Civic-Minded African-American Business." *Journal of Negro History* 78 (Winter 1993): 1–15.

Werner, Craig Hansen. "Chicago Renaissance." In *The Oxford Companion to African American Literature,* ed. William L. Andrews, Frances Smith Foster, and Trudier Harris, 132–33. New York: Oxford University Press, 1997.

———. *Playing the Changes: From Afro-Modernism to the Jazz Impulse.* Urbana: University of Illinois Press, 1994.

Wesley, Charles. *The History of the National Association of Colored Women's Clubs: A Legacy of Service.* Washington, D.C.: National Association of Colored Women's Clubs, 1984.

———. "The Negro Has Always Wanted the Four Freedoms." In *What The Negro Wants,* ed. Rayford W. Logan. Chapel Hill: University of North Carolina, 1944.

White, Deborah Gray. *Too Heavy a Load: Black Women in Defense of Themselves, 1894–1994.* New York: W. W. Norton, 1999.

Wilkerson, Margaret B. "Hansberry, Lorraine." In *The Oxford Companion to African American Literature,* ed. William L. Andrews, Frances Smith Foster, and Trudier Harris, 338–39. New York: Oxford University Press, 1997.

Wilson, Sondra Kathryn, ed. *The Messenger Reader: Stories, Poetry, and Essays from The Messenger Magazine.* New York: Modern Reader, 2000.

Winget, John A. "Teacher Inter-School Mobility Aspirations Elementary Teachers, Chicago Public School System, 1947–48." Ph.D. diss., University of Chicago, 1952.

Wirth, Louis and Margaret Furez, eds. *Local Community Fact Book, 1938.* Chicago: Chicago Recreation Commission, 1938.

Wixson, Douglas. *Worker-Writer in America: Jack Conroy and the Tradition of Midwestern Literary Radicalism, 1898–1990.* Urbana: University of Illinois Press, 1994.

Wolcott, Victoria W. *Remaking Respectability: African American Women in Interwar Detroit.* Chapel Hill: University of North Carolina Press, 2001.

"Women at War." *Brown American* (Summer 1943): 4–5.

Woodson, Carter G. *The Mis-Education of the Negro.* 1933. Reprint. New York: AMS, 1977.

———. "Proceedings of the Annual Meeting of the Association for the Study of Negro Life and History Held in New York City, November 8–12, 1931." *Journal of Negro History* 17 (January 1932): 1–7.

Woolley, Lisa. *American Voices of the Chicago Renaissance.* Dekalb, Ill.: Northern Illinois University Press, 2000.

Workers of the Writers' Program of the WPA in the State of Illinois, comp. *Cavalcade of the American Negro.* Chicago: Diamond Jubilee Exposition Authority, 1940.

Wright, Richard. *American Hunger.* New York: Harper and Row, 1977.

———. "Early Days in Chicago." *Negro Digest* 8 (July 1950): 52–68.

———. *Native Son.* New York: Harper, 1940.

———.*Twelve Million Black Voices.* New York: Viking Press, 1941.

Yeyarwood, Ruby Bryant. "Women Volunteers Unite to Serve." *Opportunity* 21 (April 1943): 60–62.

Index

ANNE MEIS KNUPFER is a professor of educational studies at Purdue University, where she teaches history of education courses. Her books include *Toward a Tenderer Humanity and a Nobler Womanhood: African American Women's Clubs in Turn-of-the-Century Chicago* and *Reform and Resistance: Gender, Delinquency, and America's First Juvenile Court.*

The University of Illinois Press
is a founding member of the
Association of American University Presses.

Composed in 10.5/13 Minion
at the University of Illinois Press
Manufactured by Sheridan Books, Inc.

University of Illinois Press
1325 South Oak Street
Champaign, IL 61820-6903
www.press.uillinois.edu